MANAGEMENT IN GOVERNMENT

MANAGEMENT
IN GOVERNMENT

DESMOND KEELING

for the
ROYAL INSTITUTE OF PUBLIC ADMINISTRATION
LONDON

GEORGE ALLEN & UNWIN LTD
Ruskin House   Museum Street

First published in 1972

© George Allen & Unwin Ltd 1972

ISBN 0 04 350033 1 Cased
0 04 350034 X Paper

The royalties from the sale of this book are divided between the Royal Institute of Public Administration and the Civil Service Benevolent Fund.

Printed in Great Britain
in 10 point Plantin type
by
Alden & Mowbray Ltd
at the Alden Press, Oxford

For
Widmerpool, Short and Blackhead

ACKNOWLEDGEMENTS

My debts are many. Synonyms for gratitude are few. I hope my appreciation of the help that I have received will seem in no way devalued if I record it formally in the manner of the theatre.

ENCOURAGEMENT offered by the Royal Institute of Public Administration which has sponsored publication of the book.

SABBATICAL LEAVE granted by the Civil Service Department.

CENTRES OF STUDY Emmanuel College, Cambridge through the award by the Master and Fellows of a fellow-commonership for Michaelmas Term 1969.
London Graduate School of Business Studies for the period January to July 1970.

LIBRARIES AND THE ASSISTANCE OF LIBRARIANS Royal Institute of Public Administration; The Marshall Library, Cambridge; London Graduate School of Business Studies.

CRITICISM AND COMMENT Dr John Bourn of the Ministry of Defence and Centre for Administrative Studies read, and commented on, an early draft of the opening chapters. Professor Peter Self of the London School of Economics and Mr Jack Wood of the National Coal Board read the completed manuscript on behalf of the RIPA. Both offered valuable comments to the author—as did Mr Richard Bird of the Civil Service Department.

OPPORTUNITIES TO EXPOSE IDEAS TO INFORMED CRITICISM WERE PROVIDED BY a seminar of academic staff from the Departments of Economics and Politics at the University of York.
a seminar of academic staff at the London Business School.
the senior Executive Programme at the London Business School.

ACKNOWLEDGEMENTS

SOURCES: many are indicated in the notes attached to each chapter. But these may fail to recognize fully the extent to which the author's views were formed by listening to, and in discussion with, those who contributed to civil service courses in the period 1963–69, including, in the subject area covered by this book, economists such as Dr Ralph Turvey, Professors Michael Beesley, Maurice Peston and Alan Williams; operational research specialists like Professors Stafford Beer, Patrick Rivett and Mr W. T. Bane; from the behavioural sciences Professor Elliott Jaques (and, more recently, at the London Business School, Professor A. T. M. Wilson); from management consultants and business companies Mr John Humble (Urwick-Orr), Mr Allen Stewart (McKinsey) Mr Alan Sykes (RTZ Ltd).

If any of those mentioned should find an accurate reflection of their views in any part of this book, I hope they will accept this statement by way of acknowledgement.

RESPONSIBILITY FOR OPINIONS rests solely with the author. The views expressed should not be regarded as reflecting in any way those of the Royal Institute of Public Administration, of the Civil Service Department, with which the author was serving when he wrote the book, or of the Ministry of Agriculture, Fisheries and Food, in which he is employed at the time of publication.

PREFACE

In his book *Decision in Government*, Dr Jeremy Bray suggested that 'out of 600 officials at or above the level of Under Secretary one would certainly hope for two or three good books a year on government or at least something a little more substantial than the usual published lecture'. If this modest annual quota remains unfilled, the reasons are not hard to find. The civil servant accepts that there is an imbalance between published material worthy of study and the time available to him for reading. But few see the solution as lying in an increase in the former variable. Even fewer see themselves contributing to such an increase. The official, faced with a choice between writing a book or cultivating his garden (literally or in the Voltairean sense) adopts that characteristic approach in which realism, scepticism and coolness are combined in much the same proportions as those in which vodka, vermouth and ice create a martini in Washington. He observes that a badly written book results in the author being regarded as incompetent; that a book received critically is seen as evidence of imprudence; and that a well-reviewed book brings only a reputation for eccentricity. Weighing up these possible outcomes, the civil servant prefers composting to composition. Perhaps this will be regarded as evidence of conventional attitudes. But even if the official applies, as Dr Bray would encourage him to do, the more sophisticated analysis of decision theory he will find after constructing a matrix, assessing probabilities and attaching values to all outcomes, that under both the minimax and the minimax regret criteria he is directed firmly to the garden. And even that criterion which the civil servant would by temperament be least likely to apply—the maximax—gives the same result, unless the chances of selling the musical comedy or television serial rights in the book are given a higher probability than history suggests would be justified.

The reader might assume that the appearance of this book is evidence of an indifference on the part of the author to gardening, decision theory or martinis. This is not so: the book represents in fact a triumph of experience over hope. The experience was that which I acquired over a period of six years, following the establishment of the Treasury Centre for Administrative Studies in 1963, in which I was involved in the rapid growth in management training for the civil service. It was a decade in which management in the public service developed greatly in status, but not in definition; in application, but not in analysis; in assertions of realized or potential benefits but less frequently in their measurement or proof. As a result, a gap was revealed on courses between the general acceptance of management at the highest levels of the service as important and beneficial, and the application of new techniques, or, say, the installation of computers at the operational level. Within this gap apparently simple questions proved difficult to answer with authority—or even without it. Some civil servants remained unclear whether they were or were not managers. Others remained sceptical whether the application of even a whole battery of new techniques proved conclusively that a course of action adopted in the name of management was preferable to an alternative. There was a lack of published work to which questioners could be referred. I waited hopefully but in vain for someone better qualified than me to meet the need.

The area of management in government which I decided to study has an equivalent in business management. But here they are more fortunate. The initial Lewis and Clark exploration was made before the war by Berle and Means. It has since been studied intensively in this country by writers like Robin Marris. And in the U.S.A. the territory has been not only surveyed but annexed: it is now Galbraith country or Druckerland. Unfortunately these two distinguished men have applied their considerable gifts of analysis, prophecy and polemic only marginally to the problems of management in the public service—the former to argue that the public sector should have a higher proportion of the national resources to manage: the latter to argue that the use of resources by public bodies should be so reduced that the question whether management was good or bad would cease to be important. However, although the gap in the literature which I had identified in the mid-sixties remains, there are encouraging signs that it is recognized and is being closed. Although the principal field of their interest lay elsewhere, there was reconnaissance of the area in which I am interested in the second half of the decade by British writers like Andrew Shonfield (*Modern Capitalism*), Stafford Beer (*Decision and Control*) and by Jeremy Bray in the book to which I have already referred. In the U.S.A. the arrival of Programming—Planning—and Budgeting forced a valuable debate of some of the relevant issues, which is recorded in proceedings of conferences organized by the Brookings Institution and in *Public Administration Review*. Yehezkel Dror's *Public Policy Making Re-examined* is most relevant to the subject matter of this book. By 1970 a new international quarterly *Policy Sciences* was appearing with a field of interest similar to that of this study. And early in 1971 Sir Richard Clarke delivered in London, under the auspices of the Civil Service College, not one but six lectures which will be of general interest if published later as a book. Perhaps I should have waited patiently a little longer. . . .

I gave this book originally the title *Management in the Civil Service*, changed it to *Management in the Public Service* when the former seemed too restrictive and finally adopted the present title at the suggestion of the RIPA. I hope it will be clear that *Management in Government* is a title of the same species as *Crime and Punishment* or *Guys and Dolls*. It indicates the broad area of the author's interest rather than promises a comprehensive or definitive account of both, or even of one of, the subjects in the title. I trust also that no one will expect to find the single text-book on management in the public service for which he may have been waiting to enhance his reputation as a manager or, more probably, to qualify for some diploma in the subject. Equally disappointed will be those looking for a catalogue and detailed exposition of management techniques. There are already glossaries of techniques and excellent descriptions of every technique known to me—and, I do not doubt, of many unknown to me, for techniques multiply at a rate equalled only by religions in California. General books on management practice and leaflets on techniques can be as useful to the civil servant as works such as 'How to become a star at football' or 'How to kick goals with both feet' to the sportsman. But the latter would be likely to start with a clear understanding whether the football in which he is interested is soccer, rugby (of the Union or League variety) or even American football. And hopefully he would know the rules of the game, how points are scored and games won—and who provides the referee. It is the equivalent of questions of this kind in management to which the answers are lacking—at least in the public, if not in the business, version of the game.

Although I started with a clear view of the scope of the work, I was undecided whether to direct it primarily—in so far as I could be selecting an appropriate style and treatment—to an academic audience, to my colleagues in central and local government, or to those members of the general public who may be interested and in varying degrees informed on the subject. I received conflicting advice on this choice. One persuasive voice from the academic world assured me that there would be no interest in that area unless I made the fullest use of the concepts and specialized terminology of the underlying academic disciplines. But it appeared to me that there are at least six such disciplines. Is the academic specializing in one of these disciplines at home with the concept and language of all the remainder? Some may be, but my experience in training suggests that this is not to be taken for granted. And, even if I had been more confident than I was of my own familiarity, rather than passing acquaintance, with the full range, there seemed a risk that if I travelled down this road I might end by expressing every platitude as a mathematical equation with an acknowledgement of the kind conventional in the circumstances to a research assistant for some not too precisely defined help. A civil service voice urged me to take the opposite road and to seek to write the first book on management entirely free of jargon—a term which seemed to embrace the whole specialized terminology of academic disciplines and, I suspect, all mathematics. This too I found to be an objective which I was unable, or unwilling, to pursue.

On style I had also to weigh up advice before starting. A distinguished professor of government begged me 'not to write in the manner of a White Paper with an "it is hoped" in every sentence'. An American economist placed the emphasis of his advice elsewhere. 'If you must write a book, let it not be one of those goddam British books with a quotation from *Alice in Wonderland* at the head of every chapter.'

The book will show, it is hoped, that due weight has been given to all these views and that the advice has been accepted in principle and incorporated in the text as fully as circumstances and presentational considerations permitted. In short, I have followed my own inclinations.

CONTENTS

CHAPTER I

MANAGEMENT, ADMINISTRATION AND POLICY

'The question is' said Alice 'whether you
can make words mean so many different things.'
'The question is' said Humpty Dumpty 'which is
to be the master—that's all.'
    Lewis Carroll: *Alice through the Looking-Glass*

THE ARRIVAL OF MANAGEMENT IN THE PUBLIC SERVICE

The public service, since the first came into being, has exercised responsibilities which today would be described as management. In experience it has, therefore, an advantage of several thousand years over the business corporation with which management is now so closely associated. And those happy few whose interests embrace both history and management may amuse themselves by selecting distinguished men of the past who deserve to be awarded posthumously an Alfred Sloan Prize for their contribution to management in the public service. A British nomination of Samuel Pepys is already on the record.[1] Amusement might develop into instruction.[2] Lessons can be learned from studying success as well as failure.

When the business company appeared as a competitor it did not establish immediately any clear superiority. A century ago John Stuart Mill commented:[3]

'Whatever is left to spontaneous agency can only be done by joint stock associations will often be as well and sometimes better done, as far as the actual work is concerned, by the state . . . the defects of government management do not seem necessarily much greater, if necessarily greater at all, than those of management by joint stock.'

The use by Mill of the word management in relation to government activity was exceptional. It was not until well into the first half of the twentieth century in the U.S.A. and a generation later in Britain that management was to come into common use in the public service of these countries.

The start of what might be thought of as the era of management in the public service can be dated to 1937 in the U.S.A. when the Brownlow Committee reported to President Roosevelt on what it described as 'administrative management'.[4] According to this report:

17

'Good management will promote in the fullest measure the conservation and utilization of our national resources and spell this out plainly in social justice, security, order, liberty, prosperity, in material benefit and in higher values of life.

It will be seen from this quotation that management in the public service was associated from the start with what some regard as its characteristic feature—overstatement of what it will achieve. This is often combined with under-explanation of what it is and of precisely how it is to achieve the outcome expected.

The interval before management aroused in the public service in Britain the degree of interest which the Brownlow Committee report had achieved in the U.S.A. was to be of much the same length as that which elapsed between the publication in Britain by Keynes of his General Theory in 1936 and the adoption by the U.S.A. Administration, and acceptance in some measure by American public opinion, of actions based on this theory in the period 1962–64.[5] In Britain a civil servant writing in 1964[6] commented on the recent arrival of the word 'management' and said 'some fifteen years ago . . . nobody troubled about management'. Certainly few used the word in the public service before the late fifties. Management began to enter the vocabulary of the civil service through a Treasury circular issued in June 1957, by, as he then was, Sir Norman Brook, Head of the Civil Service which included the comment 'I am sure that members of the administrative class are not sufficiently alive to the great responsibility which they should carry in these management matters . . . . They alone can insist upon— and personally secure—maximum efficiency at every level, cost-consciousness all along the line, and effective communication within the organization and with those we serve.'

But a growing awareness of the relevance of management to the civil service owes much to the work of the Committee on the Control of Public Expenditure of which Lord Plowden was Chairman. It was appointed by the Chancellor of the Exchequer in 1959. The recommendations of this Committee started a series of reforms in public expenditure planning and control during the sixties, which are still being developed and which were a necessary, if not sufficient, condition of any significant improvement in management in the public service. The Committee claimed, in its final report published in 1961,[7] to have been impressed with the importance of management to the public service. In this report, the Plowden Committee used the word management in a way that attracted more attention later than at that time. It referred to the 'work which falls on Permanent Secretaries in carrying out their triple functions of policy advice, finance and management'. The civil servant, from whose article in 1964 I have quoted above, commented that 'there is something slightly confusing, however, about the Plowden Committee's separation of management, as if it was a self-contained element, a function wholly distinct from "policy advice" and "finance" '.[8] It was a perceptive remark but it did not lead, at that time, to any elucidation of the confusion.

Elsewhere in the Plowden Report management was given a wider meaning, not entirely divorced from finance: for example, in a passage in the report where management is said to include

'the preparation of material on which decisions are taken'
'the technical efficiency with which large operations of administration are carried out'
'the cost consciousness of staff at all levels'
'the provision of special skills and services (scientific, statistical, accounting, O. & M. etc.), for handling particular problems, and the awareness and effectiveness with which they are used'
'the training and selection of men and women for posts at each level of responsibility'

The civil service and some other parts of the public service came to think of management in the narrower rather than in the broader of the Plowden uses. This tendency was influenced by the establishment, as one of the changes arising from the Plowden Report, of a separate part of the Treasury known as 'the Pay and Management' side. This came to give management in the civil service a predominantly 'personnel management' meaning although with some interests beyond the responsibilities normal to personnel management in business. The implications of this did not pass unnoticed at the time. In 1962 a Third Secretary of the Treasury speaking[9] on 'The Management Functions of the Treasury' in one of a series of lectures on the Plowden Report, commented:

'Much, probably the major part, of the work that goes on in the Treasury could find a place, naturally and without strain, inside the scope of the title taken for this talk. Take government expenditure, and the central role of the Treasury in the management of the national economy. ... To control the purse strings, to give or withhold financial approval, to co-ordinate financially a variety of requirements, are characteristics of management everywhere. But as we are using the expression "management" in our recent reorganization of Treasury business, there is imparted a somewhat technical, almost a professional limitation.

'... we now talk of the Management side of the Treasury as distinguishable from the economic and financial side. Much is comprehended in this classification of Treasury business—the label attaches to a kind of hold-all containing within a variety of assorted subject matter. The content, in fact, bears, in a wide degree, a close family likeness to the work of Establishments with which we in the Civil Service are so familiar. I am not going to take you through the composition of this management aggregate, bit by bit, subject by subject. It would be difficult to give a clear picture of how the parts mesh together. . . . We include pay and pensions, complements and grading. The subjects of O. & M. and Training, which some would claim characterize the more constructive efforts of management as such, are there.'

The same view of management was taken by an inter-departmental committee, of which the Treasury official, whom I have just quoted, was Chairman. It reported[10] in 1962 on the training of assistant principals recommending a new course in which economics and statistics were to be allocated a substantial part of the time and in which the subjects studied in the remaining time were to include 'some understanding of how a business operates'. But the Committee concluded that 'although management seemed a prominent candidate at one stage it has been omitted from the syllabus'. However this comment did not prevent the courses which developed, following this report, at the Treasury Centre for Administrative Studies being listed by the Treasury within a year or two under the category 'management training'.

I have explained how what came to be the 'official', or an official, definition of management had its origins in the use of the word which fitted the internal organization of the Treasury. Certainly its use as a concept primarily relevant to organization and staffing problems was to spill over into other parts of the public service. For example the report[11] published in 1967, under the title *Management of Local Government*, of a Committee of which the then Sir John Maud was Chairman, would be regarded by many readers, particularly from business, as concerned with only one aspect of management in local government. This is not surprising since the terms of reference of the Committee were 'to review in the light of modern conditions, how local government might best continue to attract and retain people (both elected representatives and principal officers) of the calibre necessary to ensure its maximum effectiveness'. Within the civil service—and in local government—the development of management in the years from 1960 took place against a background of a variety of official uses of the word. We have at one extreme the breadth of the introductory statement by Brook and the recognition that the use of the word management as in business would bring the financial activities of the Treasury within management; we have the Plowden troika in which management is seen in more restricted terms as something different from either policy or finance: we have the use of management to coincide with the particular responsibilities assigned to the Pay and Management side of the Treasury—to mean management *of* rather than *in* the civil service.

Uncertainty about the role and scope of management would have been inevitable in the circumstances. But the variety of 'official' uses of the word are but the visible part of an iceberg. Within the service many quite different views, some of them incompatible with *any* of the official uses, continued to be held. At times it has been a case of *quot homines tot sententia* but I believe that most opinions fall, or can be forced into, one of four groups. The first comprises those who implicitly define management as an activity peculiar to business and who believe— often on the basis of their personal experience in the public service— that the view that management is relevant to the service is a fallacy. By far the best account of the civil service leading to this conclusion is that presented by C. H. Sisson, a civil servant, in his book *The Spirit of British Administration*.[12] I shall discuss later some of the views presented in this book. It is sufficient at this point to comment that Sisson's description of the work and qualities needed at the higher levels of the service could suggest to a manager from business that the tasks and the environment were entirely unsuited to his skill and experience.

The second group bears the same relation to the first as anti-matter to matter: at every point the sign is reversed. The group sees the work of the public service as predominantly managerial, exactly or almost exactly as in business. Implicitly this group's definition of management seems to be any corporate activity involving expenditure. The members seem to believe that at present efficient management is almost non-existent in the civil service and local government. Their remedy would be to bring businessmen into the Cabinet (The Board of Directors of Great Britain Limited) and to strengthen the higher civil service, to send civil servants to business firms for experience and to rely mainly on business schools for training, to make all government departments and local authorities value their assets and outputs and inputs to produce annual accounts as similar as possible to a business company. This point of view has but few spokesmen or even silent adherents within the civil service or local government: in the nationalized industries and in business support may be greater.

The third group resembles the first in believing that the public service has little to learn from management in business—but for different reasons. The members are not antipathetic to management but see it as no more than a new word to describe activities which the public service has performed efficiently for many years. The group's attitude to management is very much that of *le bourgeois gentilhomme* to prose. Discounted cash flow, management by objectives, information systems, network analysis—there is nothing that can be mentioned which the members of the group would not claim to have been doing 'in their own way', 'under another name' for a long time. In short, management in the public service is defined as what the public service does.

The fourth group tend to divide the public service laterally with management as a 'below the line' activity. Some members see it as a third 'implementation' layer of a decision making hierarchy below both 'policy' (the responsibility of Ministers, elected local government representatives, the Councils or Boards of public corporations) and 'administration' (advice on policy making, decisions on plans and other major financial and personnel decisions). Other members of this fourth group would see management as the lower of only two broad categories of responsibility, e.g. J. H. Robertson in his evidence to the Fulton Committee,[13] refers to '... the distinction between the secretarial functions and the managerial functions of Civil Servants. The implication is that these functions should be split'. Similarly, if not identically, Dr Drucker's dichotomy[14] between 'government' ('to focus the political energies of society. It is to dramatize issues. It is to present fundamental choices') and 'doing' which Drucker appears to identify with management: he asserts that 'Government is a poor manager'. He favours 're-privatization' or hiving off of management functions to private firms. Robertson's prescription is the hiving off of management responsibilities to public corporations and agencies free of detailed political control. This kind of tripartite or bipartite division of decision making has its parallels in business where some writers see a significant distinction between 'strategic planning', 'management control' and 'operational control'[15] and others between 'doing (operations) activities' and 'pre-doing (non-operations) activities'.[16] But the difference is that whereas in business all these divisions are seen as part of management, the tendency has been that where similar divisions are applied in the public service the word 'management' is normally used to define only the lower 'doing', 'operational' or 'implementation' kind of activity.

Towards the end of the decade the Fulton Report on the Civil Service was to provide in 1968 a further description[17] (if not a definition) of management which was to be wider than any of those previously described and which was consistent with the use of the word in business:

'Management, as we understand it, consists of the formulation and operation of the policy of the enterprise. This can be seen as a continuum ranging from first line supervision through a hierarchy of the managers to the board of directors. At each level assets—whether human, financial or material—have to be deployed in the manner best calculated to achieve particular objectives which contribute to the overall policy objectives formulated by the Board.'

But a little later this part of the Fulton Report seems to extend the frontiers of management even farther.

'Four aspects ... make up the total management task of the Civil Service:
  (a) formulation of policy under political direction
  (b) creating the "machinery" for implementation of policy
  (c) operation of the administrative machine
  (d) accountability to Parliament and the Public.'

Management here seems almost synonymous with the work of the civil service. By the late sixties those parts of the public service most in touch with the world of business, such as management services and training units, tended to give 'management' a broad meaning as in the first section of the above quotation from the Fulton Report (but not all of these would have accepted that all the 'four aspects' were accurately described as management). Elsewhere management was used at times officially in the narrower Plowden troika or Pay and Management sense to mean the management of the civil service or the personnel management of public servants. Frequently the use implied that management was involved in the implementation, not in the taking, of decisions on resource use. Within the public service these 'official', and various unofficial, views and implicit definitions of management, have co-existed throughout the past decade and survive today. But confusion is compounded by the fact that any discussion of management in the public service will sooner or later, within the same paragraph or page, lead on to references to 'policy' and 'administration'. We shall soon discover that these other members of this semantic *menage-à-trois* also display the ambiguity appropriate to such situations.

POLICY

It might seem sacrilege to seek to define precisely a word of such survival power as policy, for it has remained for more than 2,000 years an activity in which any man could announce his involvement with pride. But Sir Geoffrey Vickers has already explored the subject thoroughly in his book *The Art of Judgment*.[18] Before considering his views, it may be illuminating to notice how the word is used in practice by officials. The following examples are selected at random from memoranda submitted to a single Sub-Committee of the Select Committee on Estimates 1967–68:[19]

'The export promotion policy of the Board (of Trade) can be briefly summarized as the stimulation of industry to export and the provision of services designed to increase exports. . . .

'The Board [of Trade's] policy is to encourage and assist British firms to take part in suitable trade fairs overseas as a means of exploring markets abroad and establishing and maintaining a position in these markets.

'It is accepted policy that . . . commercial work should be a first charge on the resources of the Diplomatic Service.

'It is accepted policy that several members of the Diplomatic Service should attend courses in management each year.

'The basic policy of the Ministry of Technology and the British Standards Institution is to support international harmonization of standards to the greatest possible extent.'

Even from these five examples it will be seen that the word policy may describe several different concepts:

objective defining
priority setting (assuming that to be *a* first charge has this implication)
a description of a plan

But there is another use of the word common in the public service and that is as a decision rule, e.g. a policy that a civil servant may be granted sabbatical leave on only one occasion in his career. This is neither objective nor plan. It is a decision, possibly taken initially on an individual case, which now acts as a precedent or as case law in predetermining all future cases of the kind until the 'policy' is changed, or an isolated exception to the policy approved. The example is of a minor decision rule but they can be of major importance, e.g. that all contracts must be let by open competitive tender.

There seems to be four distinct elements—objectives, plans, priorities and decision rules—any one or more of which may be intended by the current use in practice of the word policy (even if I ignore the tendency to use the word for what is no more than a brief description of the activities of the organization, e.g. the policy of the Department of Adult Education is to educate adults. However, plans, priorities and decision rules all might be related in some way to objectives. The meanings could belong to the same family. A word which would describe a set of interrelated and mutually consistent decisions in all these areas would certainly be valuable. And policy has this meaning in a proportion of the cases in which the word is used (about 5 per cent would be my approximate assessment of that proportion).

But Sir Geoffrey Vickers in his most thorough and illuminating analysis of policy defines the concept in a way which does not coincide with any of the practical uses of the word which I have described. He defines[20] policy as a set of standards or norms.

'Below the level of these ideal norms is the set of standards which the Council (local authority) has decided to accept as the best realistic governors of their efforts within the time-span for which they plan having regard to the total expected resources and the total expected claims upon them. This set of standards constitutes the Council's current policy.

'. . . this is the standard which operates as a norm in the regulation of current action yielding, when compared with actual performance and estimated trends, those signals of match and mismatch on which regulation depends.'

We can be certain that Vickers does not see policy as embracing objective setting for he emphasizes the point:

'I have described policy making as the setting of governing relations or norms, rather than in the more usual terms as the setting of goals, objectives or ends. The difference is not merely verbal; I regard it as fundamental. I believe that great confusion results from the common assumption that all course holding can be reduced to the pursuit of an endless succession of goals.'

Nor are we to be allowed to adopt what would at first sight seem the obvious solution of assuming that the setting of an objective would normally embrace the setting of standards of performance or norms:

'Those who recognize the difference should not . . . be content to mask it by giving to goal setting and goal seeking a meaning wide enough to include norm setting and norm holding; for goal-setting is a distinct form of regulation with its own specific mechanisms; a form less important, in my view, than norm setting.'

I believe it was most useful for Vickers to call attention to the importance in the public service (and elsewhere) of the setting of standards of performance which, because they cannot always be quantified precisely, are often not seen as a variable which explicitly or implicitly is subject to a decision. Thus the 'quality' of much of the output of the public service is determined by convention; the established conventions are defined by Vickers as 'policy'. But whether policy is likely to be understood to mean primarily, if at all, such standards or norms, rather than given one of the several other meanings I have described, seems doubtful. And on the dichotomy between objectives and standards, and on the greater importance of the latter, I shall not say that I am unconvinced by Vickers' logic, for conflicting conclusions are seldom to be attributed to differences over logic but to unstated assumptions or semantic problems. Probably misunderstanding arises here over words such as aims, objectives and goals since Vickers' implicit definition of an objective seems to require it to differ from the situation currently in being and if it is realized, needing to be replaced immediately by a new objective.[21] It is true that in setting short-term targets some management consultants emphasize that these should 'stretch' those seeking to reach them. But I know of no inherent quality in objectives and objective setting, that may involve longer term considerations, which rules out the adoption where appropriate of the objective of maintaining the present situation: indeed when circumstances are unfavourable this may itself 'stretch' the ability of all concerned more than an expansionist objective in a more favourable environment. In military operations, where the need for clarity of definition of objectives was first recognized, the objective of simply maintaining a position in defence has never been regarded as unacceptable as an objective.

Policy has not only various meanings but a variety of myths have in the past been associated with it:

(a) that policy is exclusively an activity conducted at the highest levels—perhaps only by politicians in central and local government with senior officials allowed to participate as policy advisers;

(b) that it can be sharply differentiated from the work of implementing policy decisions;

(c) that the making of policy always precedes in time the taking of decisions on individual cases.

All these myths have come to be suspect both within and outside the public service.[22] Policy, of the decision rule kind, may be made at any but the lowest levels of the public service depending on the importance (which embraces the political sensitivity) of the issue. Nor in practice can any sharp distinction between policy and implementation be maintained. Most policies need to be implemented through, say, legislation and the subsequent enforcement of the law or through the carrying out of plans for establishing and staffing organizations, schemes of physical construction, etc. Feedback information on the practicability of implementation is needed by the policy makers and may in some cases constrain the choice of, and occasionally even determine absolutely, the policy. Finally it would be within the experience of most public servants that frequently policy does not precede individual decisions. On the contrary, policy is often only defined at the point at which the need to do so becomes pressing—enquiries by select committees or royal commissions have great policy-creating effects—and the terms in which policy is defined are such as to be consistent with a series of decisions already taken *ad hoc* on their merits or with future decisions which can be foreseen as necessary to be taken on this basis. Perhaps this degree of pragmatism is more characteristic of British administration than in

other countries: but there is no evidence that the quality of the decisions—or of the policy when it emerges eventually—is any the worse for
it.

ADMINISTRATION

If we clear away some of the myths surrounding policy, it remains a
word used to describe fundamentally different activities. What of
'administration'? Here the varieties of meaning are no less great. First
there is a habit, particularly among writers on business, of using
administration and management as synonyms. Others in business give
administration a more limited role as no more than a part of, and the
inferior part of, management, e.g. Brech's definition[23] of administration
as 'that part of management which is concerned with the installation
and carrying out of the procedures by which the programme is laid
down and the progress of activities is regulated and checked against
plans'. But in the public service when administration has been differentiated from management it has tended to be regarded as the higher
of the two activities—administration meaning policy advice and the
making of important decision rules, management meaning the implementation of the policy in accordance with decision rules. Theoretical
writers who at one time saw a sharp dichotomy between policy and
administration have more recently come to see both activities inter-
relating at every level of the hierarchy with decisions taken at one level
serving as the 'policy' for the decisions to be taken at the next lower
level.

We have found in current use a series of views on the relationship
between management (M) administration (A) and policy (P) which can
be expressed.

$$M > A$$
$$M < A$$
$$P > A > M$$
$$A \equiv P$$
$$P > M$$
$$M > P$$
$$M \equiv A$$

If I had employed a research assistant to introduce mathematics into
my presentation, he would have resigned at this point!

It is clear that any scene in which the leading roles are played by
management, administration and policy will today have a Pinteresque
quality. And there is a supporting cast in the wings well equipped for
the minor roles in such a performance, or even to take over the leading
parts if needed. I have in mind words of such promising and developing ambiguity as 'efficiency', 'information', and 'planning'. Nor should

we overlook the claims of 'research'—versatile enough to cover activities ranging in scale and purpose from exploring the fundamental nature of matter through a linear accelerator costing millions of pounds to allocating the time of a secretary to discover whether there are direct flights between Manchester and Milan.

I might have opened this book with the statement that 'the public service is today developing *management* to the level of *efficiency* achieved in *administration*: knowledge from *research*, the review of *policy* and the impact of the business schools on the role of *information* are all contributing to this *planning*'. I doubt whether it would have seemed any less plausible or profound than many such statements. But almost any permutation and combination of the words italicized will produce a statement of which much the same claim could be made. Those combinations which seem to lack something in plausibility will be found to acquire on this account a compensating gain in originality.

I should emphasize that the public service has no monopoly rights to a debased semantic coinage in this area of communication. Other writers have made similar criticisms of much of the general terminology of business management. Certainly Gresham's Law applies throughout this area. Perhaps I may recall the words written by J. B. S. Haldane[24] more than forty years ago:

'Mechanics became a science when physicists said what they meant by such words as weight, velocity and force, but not till then.'

The sentence was quoted in a recent article[25] entitled a 'Plea for Semantic Sanity' calling for clarity of definition in business management.

Whether 'semantic sanity' would raise management to the scientific level of mechanics is not a proposition which I should care to argue at this stage. But it is a toll-gate through which I must pass for the sake of readers of this book.

NOTES ON CHAPTER 1

1. P. D. Nairne in 'Management and the Administrative Class' (*Public Administration*, Summer 1964) suggested that Samuel Pepys showed in the Admiralty a thorough understanding of management by the standards of his time. He quotes from Pepys diary: 'to my office where I fell upon boring holes for me to see from my closet into the great office without going forth. . . .' Perhaps Pepys may have been the first of Whitehall's Theory X Managers!

2. I believe that the study of past achievements, as well as failures, might be instructive, for it may be doubted whether the public service has learned as much from its long experience in the use of resources as it might have done. In Britain it is probable that failures are more fully recorded and the lessons learned incorporated into current practice (through the work of the Public Accounts Committee) than are achievements. For example, consider the slow response to the success of the development group set up by the Architects and Building Branch of the Ministry of Education in 1949.

3. John Stuart Mill, *Principles of Political Economy*, Book V.

4. Report of the Committee on Administrative Management to the President of the U.S.A., U.S. Government Printing Office, 1937.

5. This 'generation gap' may or may not be significant but I am not implying that the normative value of the Brownlow Report corresponded to that of the General Theory.

6. Nairne, op. cit.

7. *Control of Public Expenditure* (Cmnd. 1432), HMSO, 1961.

8. Nairne, op. cit.

9. W. W. (now Sir Wilfred) Morton, 'The Management Functions of the Treasury', *Public Administration*, Summer 1963.

10. For a fuller summary of the report of the Morton Committee see: C. D. E. Keeling, 'The Development of Central Training in the Civil Service 1963–70', *Public Administration*, Spring 1971. It is perhaps of interest that the secretary of the Morton Committee was Mr Peter Jay who as Economic Editor of *The Times* stated in an article 'The Tools of the Treasury' (Feb. 19, 1971) that 'efficient management is just another phrase for efficient use of resources.' Just so. . . .

11. *Management of Local Government*. Report of the Committee under the Chairmanship of Sir John Maud (now Lord Redcliffe-Maud), HMSO, 1967.

12. C. H. Sisson, *The Spirit of British Administration*, Faber and Faber, 2nd ed., 1966.

13. J. H. Robertson, Memorandum No. 143 published in Volume 5 (2) of the report on the Civil Service by the Committee under the Chairmanship of Lord Fulton (HMSO, 1968). This detailed memorandum of evidence is of particular interest as one of the first applications in

Britain to the civil service of a broad analysis based on management sciences. Earlier Sir Geoffrey Vickers had in *The Art of Judgment* deployed a comparable although not identical breadth of view.

14. Peter Drucker in Chapter 10, 'The Sickness of Government' in *The Age of Discontinuity*, Heinemann, 1969. Public servants who find this depressing reading may revive their spirits on the vigorous note of rebuttal by an anonymous U.S.A. official published under the title 'Dr Drucker: The Great Healer' in *Public Administration Review*, July/August 1969.

15. This tripartite classification of management functions originated in the work of Professor Robert Anthony. See also John Dearden, 'Can Management Information be Automated', *Harvard Business Review*, March/April 1964.

16. John A. Beckett, 'The Total-Systems Concept: Its Implications for Management' in *The Impact of Computers on Management* (ed. Charles A. Myers), MIT Press, 1967.

17. See the section 'Management and Organization' in the Report of a Management Consultancy Group published as Volume 2 of the Fulton Report on the Civil Service.

18. Sir Geoffrey Vickers, *The Art of Judgment: A Study of Policy Making*, Chapman and Hall, 1965. Earlier Professor H. A. Simon had explored the meaning of policy in *Administrative Behaviour*, The Macmillan Company, 1947.

19. Report of Sub-Committee F of the Estimates Committee Session 1967–68.

20. Vickers, op. cit., p. 98.

21. This restless, 'Flying Dutchman' quality in those pursuing goals seems to be attributed by Sir Geoffrey Vickers to Parsons and Shils, who in *Towards a General Theory of Action* use an example of a man driving a car to go fishing in which the driving is described as an action directed to the end 'to be fishing'. Vickers comments that a man may like fishing rather than catching fish and 'maybe he likes driving'. This seems to be precisely what defining objectives is intended to make clear. Is fishing or catching fish more important? If driving is itself a cause of satisfaction, is fast driving down a motorway or slow driving down country lanes more enjoyable and how does the satisfaction expected from either form of activity compare with that expected from fishing (or catching fish)? If in the end a long journey down country lanes, and a short time spent relaxing in a part of the lake where fish are seldom found, seems the best use of time, this constitutes an objective—and one which is rational however undesirable it may seem to fast motorists and competitive fishermen. Similarly a maximum rate of increase in national income, a stable conflict-free society and increased leisure are all equally objectives, even if not equally acceptable as objectives to different people.

22. See for example, Sir Oliver (now Lord) Franks, *The Experience of a University Teacher in the Civil Service*, Oxford University Press, 1947. 'Who are the Policy Makers', particularly the articles by Sir

Edward Playfair, Professor Keith Lucas and Nevil Johnson (*Public Administration*, Autumn 1965). Paragraph 109 of the Maud Report *Management of Local Government* 1967, referring to evidence by D. N. Chester and by Professor Griffith to that Committee.

23. E. P. L. Brech (ed.), *The Principles and Practices of Management*, Longman, 1963.
24. J. S. Haldane, 'Science and Politics', in *Possible Worlds*, Chatto and Windus, 1928.
25. Lyndall F. Urwick, 'Are the Classics Really Out of Date—a Plea for Semantic Sanity, *S.A.M. Advanced Management Journal*, July 1969.

CHAPTER 2

DEFINITIONS, BOUNDARIES AND ASSUMPTIONS

Out, idle words, servants to shallow fools,
Unprofitable sounds, weak arbitrators!
Shakespeare: *The Rape of Lucrece*

THE PUBLIC SERVICE AND GOVERNMENT

I shall use 'the public service' to mean those organizations which are non-profit-making and for which government (central, regional and local) accepts either full or a degree of responsibility for their performance, and over which it exercises some measure of control. In Britain the nationalized industries would fall within this definition of the public service and in common usage are often so regarded. But recent developments have resulted in management in these nationalized industries approaching more closely that of large private corporations and having less in common with that in other parts of the public service. It will therefore be convenient in this book to use the term 'government' to describe the public service excluding the nationalized industries. The principal sections of 'government', as I shall use the term, include government departments, local authorities, all parts of the health service, the armed forces and police, and many public corporations or autonomous bodies to which responsibilities have been 'hived off' but which, because of the nature of their task, find inappropriate the approach to management of the more commercial nationalized industries.

MANAGEMENT

My approach to the definition of management is that, since clarity of communication between the public service and industry can only be helpful, the use of the word management in the public service should be broadly consistent, and if possible identical, with its use in business. To seek consistency in the use of the word management in the public service and in business is at this stage neither to assert nor to refute claims that there is much in common between the public service and business. When I refer to management in this book I shall mean

THE SEARCH FOR THE BEST USE OF RESOURCES IN
PURSUIT OF OBJECTIVES SUBJECT TO CHANGE.

The key words in this definition are 'objectives' and 'resources'. In both the public sector and in business this is where management is relevant. Definitions of management in business are legion but mine does not, I believe, conflict with the spirit of most of them. For example business management 'describes the behaviour of those responsible for the decisions that determine the allocation of the physical and human resources within an organization'[1] or 'management is responsible for organizing the elements of productive enterprise—money, materials, equipment, people, in the interest of economic ends'.[2] My use of 'resources' also embraces money, materials, equipment and people. Nevertheless this statement does not settle all difficulties arising from the concept of resources. To decide in any given situation what resources are relevant to the decision and how to value them, remains one of the main problems of public service management. I shall return to it from time to time.

What do I mean by 'objectives' which is another word which may contribute to semantic confusion? At different levels of any decision-making hierarchy there will be found different, but mutually consistent, objectives by which I mean the achievement which is sought and against which performance (outcome) will be measured. Characteristically objectives at the highest level will be broad and long-term: at the lowest levels they will be detailed and short-term.[3] Desirably the various words used in this area would each be associated with a different level of the objective hierarchy. I shall try to use them in this book in descending order of generality and time-span—aims, goals, targets. I shall retain objectives as a generic term to embrace all three.

I have associated with objectives and resources three words: 'search', 'pursuit' and 'change' which are intentionally emotive. They emphasize the essentially dynamic nature of management. We are not concerned with a static situation of the kind on which most traditional economic theory was based in which in a state of equilibrium a small change is made in one variable, while everything else remains unchanged, and a new state of equilibrium is reached. Management is concerned with movement from one state of disequilibrium to a new state of disequilibrium by way of changes in a number of variables: on occasions objectives will not remain constant throughout this process of change.[4] I shall reject throughout this book the concept of an 'optimal use of resources in the public service' as an aim which might, if all tried hard enough, be achieved. Management in the public service is not like that at all. The most we can hope to achieve in management is to move as frequently and quickly as possible to better positions from worse. Management in the public service is for those who can travel hopefully not for those who expect to arrive. I hope my definition makes at least this clear. My choice of the word 'best' rather than the word 'optimal',[5] which has come to suggest a precise mathematical solution, was made with this fact in mind. If I refer to 'sub-optimal' decisions or changes I shall mean those affecting the part rather than the whole of a structure or process.[6]

But my decision to use words like 'best' or 'better' rather than optimal still leaves obscure issues of crucial importance to management. If we refer to the better use of resources for whom is the new situation to be better? By what criteria is it to be adjudged better? And by what process, in accordance with what theory of social choice, is the decision to be made? The development of management in the public service would seem to require these questions to be capable of being answered clearly and unambiguously. Unfortunately so, for it is an area of dispute and of many unreconciled theories. The need to debate and define the concept of a better or best use of resources has become evident in recent years in the U.S.A. but did not come to the forefront in the early stages of development of management in the British public service. This was due mainly to the extent to which management was defined, or regarded implicitly, as concerned with the implementation, rather than with the taking, of decisions on resource use, or with improvements in organization or staff management which also tend to take the objectives and strategies of resource use as given. I shall return in the next chapter to this point. In the public service there are some problems of management which are serious, but not desperate, and others which are desperate, but not serious. To have criteria to determine what is better is for management both serious and desperate. Without these, the management consultant, the businessman, the civil servant trained in management will be of little effect. I shall explore this problem in some detail in the following chapter.

ADMINISTRATION

If management is an activity concerned with objectives and resources what is *administration* about? I could use it as a synonym for management like writers who believe that the use of the words alternately, in the way in which others misguidedly use 'training' and 'education', improves their style.[7] But I am not inclined to sacrifice a good word for literary cosmetic surgery. Since we have already too many meanings chasing too few words, we can use administration more profitably than as a synonym: I suggest it can best be used for an activity peculiar to the public service and consistent with the traditional use of the term 'public administration'. I shall use 'administration' to mean:

THE REVIEW, IN AN AREA OF PUBLIC LIFE, OF LAW, ITS ENFORCEMENT AND REVISION; AND DECISION MAKING ON CASES IN THAT AREA SUBMITTED TO THE PUBLIC SERVICE.

This is no more than to try to preserve the use of the word administration to describe the traditional 'control' or 'regulatory' functions of government. There should be objectives in this work: it must, like all activity, involve some use of resources even if in the extreme case they consist of the time or part of the time of one person. But administration as defined is distinct conceptually from management as I am using the word: it is an activity in which the best use of resources does not lie at the centre of the task. Here too my use of the word does not conflict with other definitions, e.g. 'the administrative process is, in essence, the making of rules, the adjudicating of cases, and the issuing of orders affecting the rights and obligations of private citizens and parties by public officials other than judges or legislatures'.[8]

Nor does it conflict in any fundamental way with a definition of administration within a business organization such as that by Brech quoted in the previous chapter. This definition makes the point, to which I shall wish to return later, that within any organization, private or public, there may develop activities which by their emphasis on procedure, regulation, control, resemble closely the external public service/society relationship which I have described as 'administration'.

POLICY

To find a definition of policy which I could use consistently throughout this book proved far more difficult than in the case of management and administration. To confine 'policy' to the sense in which Vickers uses it as the prevailing conventional norms has attractions, for these norms are important to management and a term to describe them is lacking. But it is one of the less frequent meanings attached to the word in discussion. I was thus more inclined to adopt an alternative valid, and more conventional, use of policy as a term to describe a set of inter-related and consistent objectives, plans and decision rules. But I was still undecided whether I had any hope of persuading the reader to concentrate his mind on this—or even on any single—definition of policy, when I first obtained a copy of Professor Yehezkel Dror's *Public Policy Making Re-examined* which gave promise of solving the problem for me. As I had found Dror's views sympathetic in some of his earlier published work, I hoped to follow his example on the use of the word 'policy', and on 'public policy making' which seemed likely to prove an activity to which I should have frequent occasion to refer. I studied therefore with some care Dror's statements[9] on the subject matter of his book such as 'The direct output of public policy-making is "public policy" which can be thought of as a continuous flow of more or less inter-dependent policies dealing with many different activities. The indirect output of public policy making is how it affects real situations which range from behaviours involved in secondary decision making and policy execution to society as a whole.'

I found that this statement had the effect, which Dr Johnson had observed in execution of a different kind, of concentrating the mind wonderfully. I decided to exclude the word policy from this point onwards and survive as best I could without the aid of the benevolent distinction which the word seldom fails to impart. I shall, however, use the word 'strategy'[10] in the sense of an objective/plan relationship. By plan I mean a series of related actions or proposed actions over time.

BOUNDARIES AND ASSUMPTIONS

I shall discuss management, or the use of resources, in the public service within certain defined bounds and on the basis of certain assumptions. I shall do so in the knowledge that some of the subjects excluded by my terms of reference are closely related to the quality of resource allocation and use in the public service and that change in one or more of these excluded areas may in some countries on some occasions be a necessary condition for any but the most marginal improvement in management. But every analysis must be conducted within some limits and on some assumptions, in the interest of the author and hopefully of the reader too. The subject which remains is by no means narrow. The problems which arise within it are both many and complex. And in all the excluded areas there is already a substantial theoretical and descriptive literature which is absent from that which I wish to explore.

The areas which I shall exclude and in which I shall be making assumptions either of constancy or of change not directly initiated by, or decided in the sole interest of, management are as follows.

(i) *The Machinery of Government*
This comprises such elements relevant to management as the constitutional framework; the executive/legislative relationship; the division of responsibility between central, regional and local authorities; and between such bodies and other public corporations responsible on broad issues but not in detail to elected authorities; within central and local government the number and size of central departments and local authorities. The relevance of such issues to the allocation and use of resources is great—in some countries decisive. But in Britain while change favourable to management can easily be envisaged, and in some cases has taken or is about to take place, it is not my personal view that in any but a few limited areas the constraints set by present structures or processes are so severe that improvement in management need await change in the machinery of government. Innovation in both areas can, I believe, proceed on parallel lines (which does not of course mean in

total isolation from each other). And since both the form and timing of change in the machinery of government will never, and should never, be determined solely by the criterion whether the use of resources will be improved, it would be unwise for those interested in management to rely too heavily on machinery of government changes. Management in the public service needs to be robust enough to survive and improve without the help of such changes while taking any opportunities that arise to benefit from them.

(ii) *Division of Responsibility between Ministers or Councillors and Officials*

This relationship can be of critical importance to the quality of management. In Britain it has been claimed to be particularly so in local government. But it has been analysed intensively elsewhere. And in central government I have no general theory or even helpful generalization to offer the reader in this area. I am encouraged not to take my failure too much to heart by academic research into the behaviour of organizations which suggests that the concept of an individual 'taking' a decision as opposed to influencing, delaying, ratifying or exploiting a decision is an over-simplification.[11]

(iii) *Macro-economic Planning or the Management of the Economy*

At an even more general level of decision making than that at which resources are allocated in the public service between broad heterogeneous ends we find the activities sometimes described as 'the steering of the economy' in pursuit of an objective comprising such ends as economic growth, a favourable balance of payments, full employment, a degree of price stability and perhaps others. From the decision making progress at this level emerges for most public authorities the total level of resources in the coming year and, hopefully, a measure of provisional approval for a planned total use of resources over several future years. Incorporated in such decisions may be a number of constraints on the distribution of such resources for at this level the distinction is more sharply relevant between the direct use of goods and services by public authorities and transfer payments or purchases of assets. And certain uses of resources by public authorities, e.g. expenditure overseas may directly affect macro-economic objective variables such as the balance of payments. The whole of this area has been the subject of a vast literature, both theoretical and descriptive, particularly since 1936 when Keynes' General Theory was published and British performance in the post-war period has been analysed in several excellent studies.[12] I shall exclude it entirely from this study but the fact that there is a continuous interrelationship between the macro-economic model and those determining the use of resources in many parts of the public

C 37

service needs to be kept in mind throughout this book or an over-simplified picture of the problem of using resources in the best way may be created.

(iv) *Fiscal Policy*

This is a subject which at times is incorporated in books in, say, public finance, with a discussion on public expenditure. But it belongs in my view more logically under macro-economic planning for those, like me, who take the Keynesian view that neither the quantity nor the form of taxation can be regarded primarily as the method by which funds are provided to pay for government expenditure. Again it is a subject which is anything but neglected and its exclusion from this book will be no loss.

(v) *The Role of the State*

In most countries there exists, in a way which is I believe real and important even if ill-defined, a concept of the scope of activity appropriate to public bodies rather than to the individual citizen, the business firm or the private charity. It has its origins in history in the degree of acceptance won in particular countries by such divergent approaches as the various forms of *Étatist* philosophy[13] found in continental European countries, *laissez-faire* philosophy more dominant in Britain and in the U.S.A. in Marxian theory or pragmatic advocacy of the nationalization of industry. It is an important determinant of the climate of opinion in any country within which public authorities use resources. And it affects the degree of self-confidence shown in resource use in the public service, being highest in some continental European countries, lower in Britain (although it has increased since the war) and lowest in the U.S.A., where at times the attitude seems defeatist and justification is found for it—'the logic of American government required the public service to be ineffective, to be increasingly unsatisfactory in the performance'.[14] I shall assume the role of the state to be given rather than debate whether it should expand or contract. The quality of management which is capable of achievement in the public service may be relevant to any such debate.

Having defined some important terms and the main boundaries within which I shall seek to analyse management in the public service, I shall look first at the areas where the foundations of management are located. If the ground proves firm a major development is possible. If shifting sands are found, a massive investment in management is likely to be unrewarding.

NOTES ON CHAPTER 2

1. Article on 'Business Management' by Richard M. Cyert in *International Encyclopaedia of the Social Sciences*, Macmillan and Free Press, 1968.
2. *The Human Side of Enterprise in Leadership and Motivation: Essays of Douglas McGregor*, MIT Press, 1966.
3. This time variation in the hierarchy of objectives seems to be related to the time span of discretion theory of organizational levels and salary differentials developed by Professor Elliott Jaques, e.g. in *Equitable Payment*, Penguin, 1967.
4. Peter Drucker, in 'Making the Effective Decision', *Management Today*, May 1967, comments: 'The most common cause of failure in a decision lies not in its being wrong initially. Rather, it is a subsequent shift in the goals—the specifications—which makes the prior right decisions suddenly inappropriate. And unless the decision-maker has kept the boundary conditions clear . . . he may not even notice that things have changed.'
5. E.g. 'Optimum has become a technical term connoting quantitative measurement and mathematical analysis whereas "best" remains a less precise word more suitable for everyday affairs.' Wilde and Beightler, *Foundations of Optimization* (Chapter 1), Prentice-Hall International, 1967.
6. See, for example, Professor Douglas Hague, 'The Economist in a Business School', *The Journal of Management Studies*, October 1965, pp. 316 and 317. In management this is the conventional use of 'sub-optimal', which since it implies that the *scale* of the decision will be less than ideal, is often used as a term of disparagement. Economists, however, may use 'sub-optimal' or 'second-best' (since a theoretical welfare optimum is incapable of achievement) to mean the best real-life situation capable of being reached—a term of commendation. See the section headed 'Second-best Matters' in 'Cost–Benefit Analysis: A Survey' by A. R. Prest and R. Turvey, *The Economic Journal*, December 1965.
7. This comment should not be taken as applying to Bertram Gross who makes explicit in a section on terminology which is a model of its kind that his use of management and administration as synonyms is made *faute de mieux*. See Chapter 2, 'Organizations and their Managing', Collier-Macmillan, Canada Ltd, 1965.
8. Article on 'Administrative Process' by Norton Long in *International Encyclopaedia of the Social Sciences*, op. cit.
9. Yehezkel Dror, *Public Policy Making Re-examined*, Chandler Publishing Company, 1968.
10. Dr Jeremy Bray, *Decision in Government* (Chapter XI), Gollancz, 1969. '"Strategy" is the name I have given to that complex of activities

39

embracing the choice of an objective in the area of concern, devising a model which will link the actions available through the behaviour of the system to the objective, the choice and implementation of action and the watching of performance.'

11. Herbert A. Simon, *Administrative Behaviour*, op. cit., writes in the Introduction to the second edition: 'Who really makes the decisions? Such a question is meaningless—a complex decision is like a great river, drawing from its many tributaries the innumerable component premises of which it is constituted.'

See also James C. March and H. A. Simon, *Organizations* (Chapter 3: 'Motivational Constraints: Intra-organizational Decisions'), John Wiley, 1967.

12. E.g. Samuel Brittan, *Steering the Economy*, Secker and Warburg, 1969; J. C. R. Dow, *The Management of the British Economy 1943–60*, Cambridge University Press, 1965.

13. For any British readers unfamiliar with the *Étatist* approach it is well described and discussed in Andrew Shonfield, *Modern Capitalism*, Oxford University Press, 1965, p. 71. See also the essay in this book on some political implications of active government, p. 385.

14. *Nation's Business*, November 1928 quoted in John D. Millett, *Management in the Public Service*, McGraw Hill, 1954. It is difficult not to detect the same attitude in the views of Peter Drucker, op. cit. (note 14 to Chapter 1).

CHAPTER 3

CRITERIA FOR MANAGEMENT DECISIONS

The characteristic feature of the state in respect of the development of its wants consists in the superior rationality of the state as compared with the private economy of the individual . . . it is inherent in the nature of the state that its demands, taken as a whole, go through a clarifying process or are the outcome of intelligent deliberation.

Gustav Cohn: *The Science of Finance*

RATIONALITY AND THE BEST USE OF RESOURCES

If Cohn's claim is as true today as he believed it to be when he made it 100 years ago, we might expect to find that such apparently simple questions as those I have posed, about the criteria and processes by which one use of resources was to be adjudged better than another, would soon be answered by the application of 'intelligent deliberation' and 'the superior rationality of the state'. But the application of many minds over many years has in this area, as in nuclear physics, uncovered increasing layers of complexity rather than a profound underlying simplicity.

But Cohn's introduction of the word 'rationality' requires me to make explicit my assumption that any significant development of management in the public service, any intensive and sustained search for a better use of resources, must be founded on a rational basis of decision making. The same assumption must underlie the development of management in business—indeed some would define its purpose as to increase the proportion that rational decisions bear to irrational. To some readers, this assumption may seem self-evident, its meaning clear and unambiguous. I wish I could persuade myself that all would be of this view for the question 'what is meant by rationality?' is one to which whole books and large parts of other works have been devoted to trying to answer. I do not find it central to my argument to seek to define or explain rationality. It is sufficient at this stage that irrationality can take many forms, all of which, including corruption and nepotism, are likely in varying degrees to be antipathetic to management.

CRITERIA FOR ASSESSING DECISIONS ON RESOURCES

Starting from an explicit if undefined assumption of rationality we must now return to the problem I left unsolved in the previous chapter—that of determining which of alternative uses of resources is 'better': which of several strategies is 'best'; and why has this somewhat obvious and apparently simple question not been answered long since? The reason is that there are three clearly defined levels of decision on resource use. At the simplest level progress in management can be made without a great debate on criteria: what is 'better' is obvious. At the highest level decisions on the allocations of resources can be seen to be but little affected by that form of rationality that underlies management, or by any criteria other than 'political'. It is at the middle level that this problem of criteria is intense: the development of management in the public service has only recently begun to make progress at this level.

THE FIRST LEVEL OF IMPROVEMENT IN MANAGEMENT

The characteristic of this level of decision making on resources is the 'implementation of decisions' approach. In the public service resources used can be regarded as inputs which produce 'outputs' expected to achieve or contribute to the fulfilment of the objective (the 'outcome' measures the extent of the achievement). In education, for example, resources devoted to construction produce an output of school buildings to contribute to an objective of more and/or better education. In a hospital resources are translated into outputs which include operations for the removal of tonsils. But the objective is the reduction in throat infection and the outcome is the extent to which this is achieved. It will be seen that in the use of resources there are two key relationships—that of input to output and that of output to outcome. In the public service output will in some cases be difficult, even impossible, to quantify in any meaningful way but over a wide area some quantification (which may require an assumption of constant quality) can be made and a relationship with input established. It may not be a linear relationship—there may, for example be economies or dis-economies of scale. But the possibility of measuring this relationship and of improving it is that on which the first level of improvement in management tends to concentrate by:

(i) achieving a given (quantity/quality) output by less input of resources
(ii) improving the quality and/or quantity of output for the same input of resources.

The techniques used in the first level of improvement of management may be simple (e.g. organization and methods, work study, clerical work measurement, network analysis) or may extend into some complex forms of operational research.

The limited terms of reference of the first level of management by-passes the complexity associated with the concept of a best use of resources for, within the limited terms of reference, success in achieving either (i) or (ii) in the previous paragraph would be agreed generally to constitute a better use of resources and thus to have improved management. But these approaches tend to be based on a number of assumptions in which the true choices, the real problem, may be assumed away. Not only is the objective taken as given—a frequent but not always wise assumption[1]—but the main elements of the plan also. A given strategy is assumed. This implies that the effect of output on outcome is that expected and that improvement is not to be sought by exploring this area. Frequently other constraints, such as assuming the main features of organization and process to be given, limit the scope of improvement in management at this level.

The activities I have described as the first level of improvement in management are necessary, have some outstanding achievements on the record and seem likely to expand. But it is important to keep in mind that however poor the strategy being pursued—indeed however worthless or even socially harmful the activity may be—it is still possible for first level improvement to make it 'better'. If management in the public service were to be confined exclusively within those limits many of the most promising opportunities would be lost—in the phrase of the American economist Arthur Okun:[2] 'Locating the least soggy spot in a swamp is not optimizing if high ground is accessible outside the swamp.'

But before moving on to consider the second stage of management, which is certainly orientated towards the higher ground, it may be appropriate to refer to certain other activities which are often to be found at the first level and which give management in government some of its most characteristic features. They also provide some evidence for those who claim that the public service provides a basically irrational environment for management.

The first of these activities that should be mentioned is the practice of claiming an increase in efficiency when costs have been reduced, while output is unchanged, although on examination it is found that from the point of view of national resources no saving in resources has resulted. All that has happened is that some 'cost' has been transferred from the organization claiming the improvement to some other organization or to the public. The wages of some clerks are, for example, now met by another organization while continuing to provide some service for the first organization. Or the public may be required to address an envelope for their reply whereas previously an addressed envelope had been provided. But more common than *cost transfer* is *cost transformation* in which a use of real resources, on ceasing to be a charge against an organization, takes on a new form, but without any reduction in extent, on transfer elsewhere. For example an organization with responsibility for the capital cost, but not for the running costs of buildings or equipment, claims improved efficiency by achieving a reduction in capital costs, although this may involve higher future maintenance or other continuing costs falling on some other body, even to such an extent that, if the future flow of extra cost is discounted, its present value may equal or even exceed the claimed saving in capital cost. All these forms of 'improvement' in management can best be described as *cost shunting*—for they frequently consist of to-and-fro movement accompanied by loud and discordant noise. In business, this practice also forms part of efficiency in management and some firms have developed a model of near optimal quality within parameters set by law, ethics and convention. But whereas the rationality of the activity in relation to management in business is clear, it is by no means so obviously an improvement in government merely to shunt costs around various parts of the public service or between government organizations and the public. Of course, much cost transfer and cost transformation will stand up to critical examination. At the end it can be established that the new situation is a preferred position to that existing earlier: there is some net reduction in cost or some other change for the better. But this should not be taken for granted and whether costs have been saved or shunted is a question to be asked of many changes at the first level of improvement.

One version of cost shunting, which is far more commonly found in the public service than in business, arises from the extreme, and some would say extra-ordinary, preoccupation in government with the total number of directly employed staff carried on the pay-roll rather than with, say, budgetary control over the total use of resources or even total monetary cost of pay. This frequently provides an additional constraint in management in government and may lead to a situation where services are bought in by the payment of fees at a higher cost than if the same service had been provided by directly employed staff. The contribution to efficiency in management of 'this economy in the use of staff' is hardly obvious. This fact of life is of course a reflection of public opinion and concern. But, while a concern with the total demands on manpower made by the state is rational, the information relevant to this concern would be statistics showing the total manpower employed in any part of the economy on meeting the demands of government—including the total manpower employed in companies on activities like completing returns on various forms of taxation. It is, of course, arguable that except in times of war when manpower allocation may be needed to supplement financial allocation of the national resources, the information as provided in the form of numbers employed, directly or indirectly, on behalf of government would not add very much to the picture that emerges from comparing the total annual expenditure of government on goods and services, making a direct claim on economic resources, with the total gross national product.

I have suggested that economy in manpower may not be synonymous with efficiency in management. Indeed all claims made in the name of economy and which are so common at this first level of improvement in management need to be scrutinized. Many will survive such claims: some will not. For although economy is consistent with and essential for efficiency, it can be applied irrationally—and in some countries has been —with the result that the road to a highly, and almost irretrievably, inefficient public service can in retrospect be seen to have been paved with worth-while economies. The most common form in which this outcome has occurred is due to the widespread belief that it is economical, and therefore efficient, to seek to recruit and retain staff at the lowest of the range of reward (this incorporates a number of variables of which pay is but one although an important one) which a broad level of skill can command on the market. In some cases it may be. But in others there is a cumulative effect on output and outcome over time. Owing to the stock-flow situation, the short-term effects are masked. In the end—and the end may be a generation ahead—the outcome may be more staff employed at a higher total cost to produce a smaller output. It may be doubted whether there is any country in the world which is entirely free of this problem. In some, it so dominates the level of efficiency attainable in management as to make many forms of investment in improving decision making a waste of resources. This disease is hard to eradicate once it has seized hold. The patient, the doctors and the public share a reluctance to recognize the symptoms.

I have emphasized the dangers of a naive acceptance that all improvements in management at this first level of seeking change within restricting assumptions, and that all economies, necessarily contribute to management and efficiency. But many can be proved consistent with efficiency. The purpose of management is to seek this proof.

When management is competent to analyse rationally the payments side of the account, the skill can then be applied to the receipts side where *charges* and increases are as complex as costs and economies. Is it better at an ancient monument to have a charge of 10p and 10,000 visitors or a charge of 20p and 5,500 visitors—assuming costs are unchanged which would imply that the marginal cost of one additional visitor was nil. If so, is the use as far as possible of the season ticket method of charging preferable? Can the cost of such a ticket be determined solely by the maximization of receipts? Should foreign visitors pay the same, more, or less, than citizens of the country? Is an average cost basis of charging for some services on the grounds that it is commercial, and therefore efficient, in fact neither commercial nor efficient?

If I do not answer these questions here, it is not only because they are difficult. They can only have an answer in terms of a very precise understanding of the objective of the use of resources. By 1970, in Britain, progress towards a rational theory of charging in government had made less, some would say even less, advance than had been achieved in the field of costing. All these complexities on what is better can arise (but may be overlooked or disregarded) even at the first level of improvement in management when the strategy is assumed to be given. But as I have emphasized, this assumption is too limiting for efficient management.

THE SECOND LEVEL OF IMPROVEMENT IN MANAGEMENT

A public service interested in management cannot concentrate exclusively on the first level of improvement but must constantly seek the higher ground by adopting approaches which bring under review, within a given sector of public expenditure (by which I mean the type of broad category of end-use such as defence, transport, arts, education, health and welfare on which the British planning of public expenditure[3] is based), the mix of strategies being pursued, of possible alternative plans to those being pursued within a given objective and in particular, seeks to establish what is the reality, rather than the assumption, of the output to outcome relationship. Experience suggests that output may have little or no effect on achieving the outcome intended or may even have a negative relationship, i.e. create the opposite effect to that intended.[4] It is in these areas that what is 'better' is seldom self-evident as in first level improvement and where problems of complexity arise which need to be recognized and if possible resolved, if management in the public service is to have the scope needed for its development. It is the area of programming–planning–budgeting (PPB), of programme analyses reviews (PAR), of statistical decision theory and of much operational research.

THE THIRD LEVEL OF IMPROVEMENT IN RESOURCE ALLOCATION

I have defined the second level of improvement in management as lying within a single broadly homogeneous sector such as defence or education. But to seek the best use of resources must also imply that the allocation of resources between such broad heterogeneous sectors is also in some sense 'best'. In scale and complexity this kind of choice is primarily found in central government, although in a limited form it can be seen to exist also in local government. It does not arise in more specialized public corporations nor, in comparable magnitude or complexity, in even the largest and most diversified business conglomerate. It can be thought of as third, highest, level of management improvement in the public service. That there is scope for improvement in this area of decision making few would deny. But techniques do not lie readily to hand. One possibility is the provision of information on the implications of the choices available to the decision makers at the margin—for this is the area of choice where incrementalism prevails and will continue to do so. But not all would use the word 'management' to describe such 'improvement' seeing the decision making process as fundamentally different from that appropriate to the first and second levels of management improvement.[5] I have no doubt that 'management' must embrace both the first and second levels, but it is a matter of personal choice whether we wish to assert a relationship of all 'resource' decisions by attaching the word management to this highest level of allocation—in much the way in which some describe economic steering as the management of the economy while others do not. What is important is to recognize this macro-allocation stage as one which needs to be considered separately from other kinds of decision making on resources.

CRITERIA RELEVANT TO DECISIONS ON RESOURCES AT THE SECOND LEVEL OF MANAGEMENT

When management in the public service is seen to be concerned, as it is in business, with achieving the best mix of strategies and with attaining the right level of efficiency (outcome:input ratio) it becomes necessary to know both the criterion, or criteria, by which one resource use or one claim to efficiency can be assessed as better than another and the process by which choice is to be made. Those concerned with decisions on resources find they are exposed to criticism from five groups each with a distinct approach to what is 'better' and to the criteria and process which should determine the superiority of a course of action over any alternative. I must emphasize that I am describing the present situation rather than seeking to describe some theoretically optimal form of classification. Of the five distinct conceptual approaches to this criteria/process issue, two are 'economic' the others 'political'. The economic approaches are as follows.

Commercial (Business) Criterion
This approach would apply to uses of resources by public authorities much the same criteria as those by which private business operates. All inputs would be purchased, whether obtained externally or received from other parts of the public service, at market rates and

charges made for output. No use of resources would be justified where receipts did not at least equal expenditure and varying degrees of commercial rigour could be applied as appropriate to require a minimum level of return on capital employed or even the maximization of this return. In many cases where this criterion has sought to be applied in practice it emerges that public authorities cannot act precisely as commercial undertakings. Concepts of 'equity' and 'service' lead to the provision of some output at a loss. It is argued that there are 'social costs or benefits' present which justify this. This approach merges therefore at the margin with the next one.

Cost–benefit Criterion[6]
Under this approach a use of resources is justified if the benefits, measured usually but not necessarily in money, to those who gain (less the dis-benefits to those who lose, i.e. are affected adversely) exceed the costs: of two substitute resource uses the 'better' is that which has the highest difference between benefits and costs (not, as is sometimes suggested, the higher ratio). The approach embraces a range of degrees of application, from that in which the directly incurred monetary expenses and receipts to the resource using organization are regarded as representing costs and benefits through that in which these transactions are adjusted in value better to reflect social costs and benefits to 'true' or 'comprehensive' cost–benefit analysis in which a far more extensive range of transactions are brought into the account on both benefit and cost sides to allow the 'full' net social benefit to be assessed. It will be seen that this approach is both selective and weighted, i.e. the decision is determined by those citizens who are directly affected and they influence the decision to the extent that their interests are affected and are measured either in a monetary value, or by having the effects described or quantified in some unit other than money, and brought into the balance sheet. The cost–benefit approach provides a criterion but not a process for decision making—it can be associated with a variety of processes.

The 'political approaches' comprise:

Voting Criterion[7]
Under this approach a use of resources on behalf of the public is justified if a majority of the citizens (electors) decide by voting that it is justified: of substitutes both of which can command a majority the 'better' is that which enjoys the greater majority. Within this conceptual framework voting can take a variety of forms—a referendum, voting by surrogate through elected representatives, sample surveys of public opinion—and can incorporate methods designed to allow some weight to be given to differences in hostility to as well as to

support for certain proposals. It will be seen that this approach is basically a process but it can at the same time provide a criterion for deciding what is a 'better' use of resources, i.e. what the majority regards as a better use. It is unselective and unweighted (each citizen has one vote).

The Achievement of a Consensus through Bargaining. (The Pluralist Approach)[8]

This is basically a process approach which sees decisions on resources as emerging from bargaining between groups representing interests involved (some of whom might not be interested parties under a cost–benefit analysis) in which the greatest measure of consensus is sought. But it can also be regarded as providing a criterion if the decision on resource use which produces the highest degree of consensus is regarded by definition as the 'best' decision. It has been so regarded by some who see the decision which results from this process as an 'optimum', in the way in which classical economic theory suggested that the 'right' price for a commodity would emerge from bargaining in a free market between sellers and buyers. It is an approach which embraces a variety of applications from the ideal envisaged in the free market concept, through less idealistic horse trading processes to the kind of situation in which Professor Galbraith claims[9] that large business corporations exert pressure or persuasion on state agencies.

The National Interest

Under this approach a decision on the use of resources by the state may be justified, and an alternative regarded as better than another, simply on the grounds that it is regarded by those with responsibility for such decisions as in the best interests of the nation, even if it conflicts with what would emerge from an analysis of costs and benefits to those directly affected or would fail to win the support of a majority of citizens. It is both a process and a criterion. References to the 'nation' or 'state' should not obscure the obvious existence of this approach in regional and municipal decision making.

Those responsible for the use of resources in the public service must be prepared to find decisions monitored against any one, any combination and even all, of the criteria I have mentioned. And the public servant will often find a criterion personified: an individual or group will be clearly identifiable as believing that one criterion should be decisive. This is so evident that I do not doubt that if Thomas Love Peacock were alive today we should have new novels with titles like *Ditchley Park* or *Sunningdale*, to place on the shelf alongside *Headlong Hall* and *Crotchet Castle*. At the weekend there would be assembled, to enjoy the hospitality of institutional hosts no less generous than Squire Headlong and

49

Ebenezer Mac Crotchet, such experts on the use of resources by the public service as Mr P. E. Ratio, the distinguished businessman; Dr Shadow Price, the cost–benefit analyst; Frank Debate M.P. and Sir Con Census from the political world, with Lord Toptable to protect the national interest in which he has apparently acquired the copyright. With Whitehall sending Sir David Draftaway and his young colleague Ned Nodeworthy there would be no reason to suppose that the cut and thrust of debate would fall below Peacock's normal level. Alas, my readers will find what follows less entertaining without being more illuminating.

It would perhaps be the view of some academic authorities that the situation confronting the public service is not as I have described, or that if it is, then it should not be. And that those concerned with the use of resources should not waste that valuable resource, their own time, by taking account of criteria in the form in which I have described to them. There would be two grounds for this claim. The first would be that the list of criteria meets none of the normal scientific requirements for an acceptable classification. The second is that the criteria overlap and some can be argued to be identical rather than distinct. In this way a much shorter and more logical classification can emerge, for example that involving majoritarian pluralist and individualist frames of political decision.

The other ground on which academic opposition to my initial list of criteria might be based is that some which I mention lack the basic pre-requisite of rationality. Some academic writers appear to view some of the criteria in much the same spirit as that in which Keynes made his well-known observation: 'madmen in authority, who hear voices in the air, are usually the slave of some defunct economist'. It is true that most of the criteria I mention can trace back their origin to writers of the past. But not all were economists: not all may be defunct. Nor would I be inclined to denounce as madmen those who believe in the relevance of any of the criteria, which I have mentioned, without more study and evidence.

I believe that explicit agreement on criteria is by far the most important problem facing the public service in seeking to improve management. I shall, therefore, need to explore more fully each of those I have mentioned to see whether the list can be shortened and whether surviving criteria can be reconciled or integrated. And whether those who support criteria which survive are 'rational' or 'madmen' (whether in or out of authority).

But before doing so, I must refer also to certain other factors relevant to assessing what is a 'better' decision on resources in government. The first of these is that one or all of the five approaches I have mentioned can be applied from different geographical points of view, nation, region or locality and are capable of producing different decisions on what is 'better', e.g. cost–benefit analysis conducted in terms of a town or county may show a net benefit: from a national point of view a net dis-benefit or vice versa. Or a town may apply the criteria of municipal *Étatism* while nationally cost–benefit analysis criteria may reach different conclusions on what is 'better'. Which is relevant to the particular decision on the use of resources?

The second factor is that a decision on resources can from some point of view be regarded as 'better' than another if, other things being equal, it generates less social conflict or provides a higher degree of open democratic participation in the decision making process. The former may be related to the pluralist approach but must be distinguished from it since a consensus derived from bargaining between groups will not necessarily minimize social conflict unless an assumption is made, which fails to correspond with reality in any country, that every interest, every minority, has a group to represent it with a weight which corresponds to the intensity of involvement. The latter is related to voting, the most democratic process, but again needs to be distinguished from it. Questions in Parliament or to a local council are relevant to this factor as is the search for minor revisions important to the individual, which is possible at say a public inquiry. These may represent a higher order of participation than a simple right to vote on a yes:no or make an either : or choice. Some writers see efficient management in the public service as needing to exclude both these minimizing of social conflict and participative considerations and regard them as constraints on the best use of resources. This leads to the search for organizational or process changes which would allow these constraints to be circumvented in the interests of 'better' management. 'Hiving off', to free organizations of detailed control of elected bodies, is one method. The alternative approach is to see minimization of conflict and open participation in decisions as part of the objective function which the best use of resources is seeking to maximize, and to be as willing to trade-off at the margin gains to other objectives in the interests of these ends in the way in which such trade-offs are necessary and rational between objectives where there is more than a single aim.

In both these further areas of imprecision management in the public service needs a set of ground rules, on how alternatives are to be evaluated, which we must seek in a more detailed analysis of these five criteria and of their interrelationship.

ECONOMIC CRITERIA: COMMERCIAL AND COST-BENEFIT

In practice these criteria, if applied in turn to a given set of circumstances, will frequently lead to different conclusions on what is the better use of resources. But, underlying both, there is a foundation of conceptual belief in the sovereignty of the consumer and in the role of the price mechanism in a market economy to allocate resources in an optimal manner if, under the commercial criterion, the market values attached to inputs and outputs are left to operate without interference or, under the criterion of cost–benefit, values are adjusted to correct 'distortions' in free market prices and extended to allow monetary values to be assigned to certain goods and services for which no commercial market or prices exist. Although in the more extreme and intensive examples of adjustment and extension of pricing in the name of cost–benefit, the activity may seem totally remote from a commercial or business approach, it remains true, as Roland McKean has commented,[10] that cost–benefit starts from an initial assumption that '. . . government is a huge industry catering to consumers, accepting consumers' valuations, and trying to attain economic efficiency in the usual sense'.

To find relevance in these economic criteria, it is, therefore, necessary to accept that when public authorities use resources, the price mechanism—in the raw or suitably tarted-up—should be decisive. This requires an act of faith. Over the past fifty years most of the theoretical foundations of classical economics, on which rested the claims of the price mechanism to be an optimal system of allocation of resources, have been demolished one by one, e.g. in the analysis of the distinction between revenue or expenses to the firm and benefits or costs to society (Pigou); by the exposure of the distorting consequences of monopoly and imperfect competition (Joan Robinson and Chamberlin), by the evidence that many business corporations do not see their primary task as the maximization of profits (Galbraith, Marris and others); on the limitation of consumer sovereignty (Galbraith); and by doubts on the validity of the concepts of the rate of profit and marginal productivity of capital (Piero Sraffa).

It may seem surprising that the market price mechanism survives at all, let alone that anyone should wish to use or develop an equivalent tool for use in the public sector. But, just as a performance of the Indian rope trick in which the rope not the boy disappears, would attract more, not less, admiration, market prices are now seen not as a means of ensuring an optimal allocation of resources but, more realistically if less idealistically, as the least unsatisfactory system of allocation available. It is a position of strength: the reputation of the sinner being more secure than that of the saint. A new literature has developed in economics from the work of Pigou and Lerner providing the theoretical basis for government intervention to correct the distortions which arise in practice in a completely uncontrolled market price system. It is a massive task and no government has yet applied more than a small proportion of the legislative controls, taxes, subsidies and other measures suggested by certain economists: most governments have applied some, with varying degrees of enthusiasm and of pleasure or disillusionment with the outcome. But before considering in more detail that adaptation of the price mechanism incorporated in cost–benefit analysis, let us consider further the more basic use of market prices through applying the commercial criterion to management in government.

The Commercial (Business) Criterion

This criterion may seem to need less elaboration or explanations than others since the main elements of business management are well known, and a number of public service organizations already operate commercial accounts although this is no more than an approximate indicator that the commercial criterion is being applied fully. But, as I shall wish to discuss more fully in a later chapter in which I shall compare management in business and in government, the criteria which determine the use of resources in business are far from as clear-cut or explicit as is sometimes assumed. Certainly any public authority given no more information than that it was to operate on a system of commercial accounts would lack precise criteria on which decisions could be based. Should it aim to maximize profits and, if so, in the short-term or longer-term? Or should it operate on more modest goals of the kind described as 'satisficing' such as seeking to cover costs from revenue or, more ambitiously, to earn a constant and stated return on capital employed each year? If these questions are answered unequivocally, it may be ready to take decisions on the use of resources once it has found a valid method of valuing the capital it is employing without resort to circular reasoning— a problem which tends to be of a different order of magnitude, rather than of kind, for the public authority by comparison with the business corporation.

Even with all these points of uncertainty resolved, the public authority is likely to embark on management under the commercial criterion subject to a number of constraints of which it may be hoped that at least some will be made explicit in advance. It may, for example, be instructed to follow a practice of equating all the prices it charges for goods and services with long-run marginal costs save in exceptional circumstances. And, if it can understand what this constraint means, it may even act consistently with it, until it learns the hard lesson that all circumstances tend to be exceptional. Other constraints will, whether stated explicitly or not, soon begin to influence decisions. Concepts which developed originally in 'administration', i.e. in the regulatory tasks of the public service such as 'equity' and 'service' spill over into 'management' areas to an extent which even the explicit adoption of the commercial criterion and commercial accounting can only eliminate gradually if at all. Differential charges between customers, the refusal of service on the grounds that the cost of provision would be too high, and the use of the price mechanism as a means of rationing output if there is a shortage in the short-term, may arouse in various commercial or near-commercial areas of public authority management hostility to a far greater extent than when pursued by business firms.

This usually results in even 'commercially' managed public bodies undertaking activities which they would prefer not to or pursuing price strategies which are clearly uncommercial. It is said that social benefits justify this. But if these benefits are not reflected in cash payments, the accounts will fail to reflect performance. Thus the commercial criterion tends at the margin to merge into the next which sets out from the start to evaluate social costs and benefits.

Cost–Benefit Analysis

The approach of cost–benefit analysis is to track down the beneficiaries (i.e. consumers) of the output (of goods or services) of public authorities. If it is impracticable—or thought undesirable for some reason—actually to charge prices, or if the prices charged do not coincide with the 'correct' economic prices (i.e. those equal to long-term marginal costs), the benefits to these consumers are assessed in terms of what they might reasonably be expected to pay for the benefits if an appropriate price system existed. From this sum can be deducted the 'negative benefits' of those adversely affected by the activity—the amount required to 'compensate' them—and total net benefits calculated in monetary terms for comparison with costs—also calculated on a 'social' rather than narrow 'expenditure incurred' basis. It will be seen that the basis of this form of rationality in decision making is that it is those *directly* affected—either as beneficiaries or 'losers' or as 'inputs', i.e. of labour to provide the goods or services—who determine the outcome of the analysis and the *strength* or weight of their involvement can be measured through this form of analysis.

The uses of resources by public authorities can be seen to fall into one of several different categories within each of which the attempt to measure costs and benefits encounters different problems:

   (i) Resources used for purposes where all members of the community are to benefit and where the benefits can neither be quantified nor valued. Defence, law and order and improvement in health (as distinguished from a reduction in illness) all fall within this category.

   (ii) Resources used for purposes where beneficiaries (and those incurring costs and dis-benefits) can be identified but where the extent of benefits or losses are difficult to quantify and/or to value in monetary terms. Education and saving of life in various ways fall in this category.

(iii) Resource use for purposes where the beneficiaries can be identified and where the benefits (or losses) can be quantified and valued in monetary terms with varying degrees of precision but where it is impracticable or thought undesirable actually to charge beneficiaries, e.g. use of roads or bridges; entrance to some art galleries or museums.

The evaluation of costs and benefits will be particularly relevant to decisions on resource use in category (iii). In category (ii), analysis can also throw a helpful light on choice between uses of the same broad kind, e.g. within say education or the hospital service by devising methods of quantifying outcome and of valuing it by imputing prices to benefits. In certain cases, substantial improvements in resource use can be obtained in mathematical terms or in terms of physical units through certain operational research approaches without the need to express the outcome in monetary terms. It should therefore be noted that this approach to decisions is not the exclusive preserve of the economist—although there are some issues, e.g. assessing the relevance, if any, of changes in property values where the economist's knowledge will be essential, however valuable the contribution which the mathematician, operational research specialist and, in some cases, behavioural scientist may make to this kind of analysis. It is, therefore, an inter-disciplinary area of work in which the economist has a leading but not an exclusive role. But neither the economist nor his colleagues from other disciplines is likely in category (ii) uses of resource to contribute any significant insight into choices between outcomes of a totally different kind. The structures of quantification/imputed values are based on too many assumptions to stand the strain of being brought into direct comparison with one another. In much the same way models have been constructed which with the aid of computers have allowed in one area changes in share prices to be forecast and in another the prediction of the finalists in the 1970 World Cup in football. Within each of these areas such forecasts may in varying degree improve the quality of decision making. But on whether a bet at 3 to 1 against Brazil or the investment of the same sum of money in a share expected to rise would produce the better expected return, such models can throw no light.

In category (i) decisions, where beneficiaries are assumed to be the whole population and the extent and value of benefits unquantifiable, such as those in defence expenditure, this kind of analysis has to operate within the more limited bounds of cost–effectiveness. Different plans or mix of plans are analysed to find the 'best' way of fulfilling a particular defence requirement or of reducing air pollution in the interest of health to a low level. But the breadth and scale of such studies will often be close to those of full cost–benefit analysis.

Certain aspects of this cost–benefit criterion for the use of resources by public authorities should be noted by the decision maker. The first is that commonly some citizens will receive benefits: others incur dis-benefits or costs. If benefits exceed costs is it clear that the use of resources is justified? Only if some assumption is made that the distribution of income is 'satisfactory' in some social sense before, and after, the resources are used. Otherwise a use in which the benefits were enjoyed by millionaires, and the dis-benefits suffered by poor widows, might not seem to be identical in value with one with the same net benefit but where the poor widows were the beneficiaries and the millionaires incurred the costs. But subject to this assumption most economists argue that the use would be justified wherever potential 'Pareto optimality' exists, i.e. the benefits are sufficient to allow the losers to be compensated. However economists are divided on whether the compensation need actually be paid, with some arguing that it need not be but can be taken into account in decisions on, say, taxation when distribution of income considerations arise. The latter approach is persuasive bearing in mind that the losers may not be easy to identify, the extent of the payments needed to compensate them may not be easy to assess and the funds to compensate them may not be readily available, particularly since charges to direct beneficiaries may not always be capable of being levied, and that it is normally the case that the charging of secondary, indirect, beneficiaries is totally impracticable. Nevertheless the view that while compensation must be capable of being paid out of benefits it need not actually be paid seems to rest on the assumption that the 'loss' suffered by someone who is entitled to compensation of $£x$ but does not get it is $£x$. It could be argued, from a study of legal actions, that there is a 'grievance multiplier' and that the uncompensated 'loss' acquires a value of $£x^2$ or x^3. If this is so, it is possible that large amounts of social conflict may be generated by a reluctance to incur quite minor costs in compensation payments.

The second is that, while cost–benefit analysis is often seen as a way of reducing distortion in the use of resources by allowing projects or programmes to proceed where social benefits exceed social costs, even if on narrower financial criteria they might not seem to be justified, it can in itself become a source of distortion if used infrequently and at the instigation of the proponents of particular proposals. This will mean that uses where social benefits exceed social costs are likely to come to light: cases where social costs exceed social benefits will not. Logically, therefore, this form of analysis should be applied throughout the public service for resource use wherever social benefits or costs seemed *prima facie* to diverge from directly incurred financial payments and receipts.

But even this could be distorting for it is likely that within 'the private sector' where resources are being used by business there are instances where an increase in output would be justified if social benefits were brought into the reckoning or a reduction in output if social costs counted. And increasingly, although still very unsystematically, government action in many countries has sought to translate such social benefits into receipts and such costs into payments incurred.

It would furthermore be distorting if any general use of cost–benefit analysis in the public service were to embrace the practice of calculating benefits on a basis which included consumer's surplus, i.e. the receipts which a discriminating monopolist could extract for the goods or service. There is a logic in this approach within the severely limiting assumptions made by the economists who advanced it—that the resource use is small and of marginal significance to incomes. But applied simultaneously to a succession of major schemes it would surely result in the total claims on resources within the public service, and the demands on taxation, reaching unacceptable levels and to a distortion in the division of resources between the public and private sectors.

In considering the contribution which cost–benefit criteria can make to decisions on resources and on analysis as a process in decision making I have emphasized some conceptual problems. There are others such as the lack of agreement on the choice of a discount rate—or on how to attach a precise value to the variety of rate preferred; I shall return to this issue later in the chapter. Here as elsewhere the decision maker must make up his mind and tell the analyst. The whole approach depends on a dialogue between decision makers and analysts. And cost–benefit analysis must be both competent and unbiased. It lends itself easily to debasement, and here too Gresham's Law applies.

I have called attention to areas of dispute, risks of distortion, imprecisions and limitations in the cost-benefit approach. But it remains an important and valid criterion for decisions on the use of resources. And in practice the issue is not whether the cost–benefit approach is ideal, problem-free or foolproof, but only whether decisions will be better or worse if made with the help of it than if made without it. The question whether cost–benefit analysis through the Roskill Commission helped at all to establish the right site for the Third London Airport is, in my view, irrelevant to a discussion on whether cost–benefit has a role in management decisions in the public service. While it is certainly useful to establish the conceptual and practical limitations of any criterion, it is equally important to keep in mind what it can contribute in suitable cases. Provided some of the main risks of distortion are avoided, provided that it is accepted that in some cases analysis may yield little of value and provided that the decision makers are sufficiently informed and interested to have a meaningful dialogue with the analysts, I believe that the approach can lead to better decisions, although not to uniquely correct decisions or to an optimal use of resources. But as I have said, management in the public service must set its sights realistically on a better use of resources, and, within the limitations and degree of humility which this implies, the cost–benefit approach has an important contribution to make.

POLITICAL CRITERIA

The two economic criteria which I have discussed are both analytical: the right management decisions will emerge if the analytical approach of the businessman or of the cost–benefit expert is applied to the choice. They imply nothing about the process by which the decision should be reached. 'Leave decisions to the manager and judge him only on his total achievement' is often implicit in the commercial criterion. Cost-benefit is neutral on process. Such well-known examples of cost-benefit analysis as the Victoria Line Tube, the earliest studies of water resource investment for the Tennessee Valley Authority, and the Third London Airport study have been associated with quite distinct processes of decision making which involved very different degrees of public participation. I shall now discuss two political criteria—voting and pluralism—which are solely process based. The better use of resources in management decisions in government is that which is regarded as better under the process. No analysis, or many different forms of analysis, may be involved.

Voting as a Basis for Social Choice
The next decision criterion is not a derivant of the sovereignty of the consumer but of the sovereignty of the elector. Under this version of the theory of social choice, the preferred and rational decision between alternatives is that selected by a majority of 'voters'. Voters in this approach would normally be a broader group than those directly affected by a project. This kind of approach does not rule out the use of the kind of cost–benefit analysis previously described. It could be used as a source of information to voters or as a means of eliminating clearly undesirable proposals and concentrating choice on those which seemed to yield positive returns. This approach can be seen either as a theoretical basis for evaluating proposals or as a method of decision making which can be applied in practice, e.g. in the requirement in the U.S.A. that proposals for new bond issues to finance investment projects for the development of services in local communities must be supported by a majority of the voters (or electors). Occasionally a 'town meeting' in Britain may serve a similar function but voting in the form of a referendum on resource choices is rare in this country. The problems of operat-

ing this sytem are in practice not less than under cost–benefit analysis. And the theoretical difficulties are formidable. It is by no means obvious whether the outcome of any system of voting can in some absolute sense claim to be 'the social choice'. Even in the election of representatives, rather than the choice of projects, a variety of voting systems operate in different parts of the world, each claiming to display the choice of the community in a way superior to the others. In general this approach does not distinguish between those directly affected, those concerned (feeling strongly for or against, although not directly affected) and the relatively indifferent: all have a vote. In theory, all should vote as 'citizens' representing the interests of society and not in accordance with their private interests if they are directly concerned. This can hardly be guaranteed in practice.

Nor does the approach enable the voting to be weighted in proportion to *strength* of opinion (or of direct involvement). Various forms of ranking order voting between proposals or devices (like the alternative vote) may give some weight to differences in hostility felt to competing proposals but it will be indirect and imprecise. Nor is it clear how society should react to strength of hostility. Is a proposal supported by 60 per cent and opposed (mildly) by 40 per cent a better (and more rational) social choice than one which is supported by 90 per cent but opposed so strongly by 10 per cent that they are prepared to demonstrate on the streets (or take even more extreme action) to prevent it? And theoretically this method is as incapable as the first of producing a clear social choice on an allocation of resources between say defence/hospitals/opera. In the absence of a social welfare function the fact that one mix of resources between objectives in those three categories might achieve 'A' votes and another 'B' votes has little validity. Indeed it is possible if the choice put to voters is limited to a succession of alternatives for 'X' to be preferred to 'Y', 'Y' to 'Z' and 'Z' to 'X'.

But despite these difficulties, it remains a basis for rational decisions on the use of resources to claim that the 'best' use is that which is regarded as best by the majority of voters. In so far as the approach is actually applied, it is not inconsistent with effective management but is discouraging to it. As we shall see later, change is an important aspect of management. Majority voting systems of any kind are inimical to change. No particular proposal for change may be able to command a majority. Yet if the *status quo* was itself put to the vote it might command fewer votes than any of the proposals to change it. Anyone who has been involved in changing the rules of a club is familiar with this dilemma.

The Pluralist Approach

The fourth approach to public decisions on resources seems to some more realistic and even desirable than any so far described. They would deny that decision making in the public service, even on the use of resources, is primarily an economic activity assisted by quantitative analysis but see it as concerned basically with pressure or conflict as part of a constant interaction between those with power and other groups representing a variety of interests. In this model the variables are conflicts, some interrelated, measured in terms of pressures. The best decision is not one which uses resources in the best way but which obtains the best consensus between incompatible views or which minimizes conflict and grievance.

This 'pluralist' view of society and of public decisions would seem to many with experience of the public service to conform more closely to reality than suggestions that the decision making process is involved with models, variables and quantitative methods of analysis. Consultations with, and representations from, interested groups conducted through meetings, deputations, questions in the House of Commons, letters to newspapers, White Papers etc., seem more characteristic of public life than analytical studies in depth. But it should be kept in mind that much of this activity arises on problems which under my definition would be described as 'administration' rather than 'management'. They are normal and appropriate to debates on changes in say abortion or gambling. But it cannot be denied that the processes are at times found also in issues of resource use. The question is whether they dominate such decisions or influence them significantly.

There are some who see the work of most public bodies, certainly of government departments, in the way described in the previous paragraph and who believe in consequence that the public service has no more than an insignificant role for ways of thought, approaches, techniques and skills relevant to management in business. It leads some to suggest that those who will be most successful in a world of conflicting pressures will be those who have no commitment to any course of action or even to any precise objective. C. H. Sisson, for example, suggested:[11]

'The essential character of government, and so of the administration by which alone it is effective, is a process of maintaining the unity of a political group. . . . The administrator steers what may appear to be a craven course among the various pressures of public and still more of semi-public opinion and the opinion of groups, and his concern is to come off with victory not in the sense that his opinion prevails, for he has no right to one, but in the sense that at the end he is still upright and the forces around him have achieved a momentary balance. . . .

'There is no need for the administrator to be a man of ideas. His distinguishing quality shall be rather a certain freedom from ideas. The idealisms and the most vicarious appetites of the populace are equal before him. He should be prepared to bow before any wisdom whose mouth is loud enough.'

Sisson, in the passages quoted, may have been thinking of the activities which I have described as administration, rather than the resource using activities I have defined as management. But he denied significance to the distinction which another writer has drawn between regulation and the provision of a service:

'For if a government provides a service, it does so for precisely the same reason as it applies to a regulation. It does so because it thinks that that is the best way of governing.'

Sisson's views seem to be based on a wish to describe reality rather than to advance a normative theory. But in the U.S.A. a similar view of the decision making process has been developed into the pluralist process theory by writers like Lindblom and Wildavsky and argued to possess a much greater degree of rationality and even aspirations to optimality than my extracts from Sisson might suggest. The process by which pressure groups contribute to decisions on resources is seen as not merely democratic (responsive to the views of the electorate) but a form of market mechanism in which all those affected by decisions have their interests (and weight of involvement) represented by a pressure group. These groups thus act as surrogates for consumers in the market in bargaining over public goods. 'Log-rolling' fulfils a similar role in this theory to that of 'compensation' in cost–benefit analysis. A consensus which is an optimum or at least a sub-optimum is bound to result.

To assume that all those affected by public decisions on resources are likely to be represented by pressure groups, or that the relative weight and influence of such groups will reflect even approximately the relevant considerations which might emerge from cost–benefit analysis, requires an act of faith. But discounting the normative value of this description of the decision making process does not dispose of its claims to realism. And few who have served in the public service would not find in their experience decisions which were made much in the manner Sisson describes. But I do not believe it to be generally true today. The passive, adjusting to competing pressures, process is likely to be found mainly in decisions where the use of resources is small and where ethical or aesthetic considerations are dominant. Most proposals to erect statues have been, and may well continue to be, decided as regards timing, site and design by this kind of process. In management decisions, those concerned primarily or significantly with the use of resources, my experience suggests the public service has never been as passive as this process assumes and increasingly in recent years analytical methods have come to be used to limit the effects of pressure except when it is itself supported by research or analysis. But whatever the limitations of bargaining as a method of reflecting economic (in which I include social costs and benefits) considerations, it serves to call attention to the conflict-creating implications of proposals for the use of resources and to call attention at least crudely (which is probably the one way in which they can be measured) to the weights of these conflicts. It was an able economist, A. Radomysler, not a political scientist or a civil servant, who wrote just after the war:[12]

'In many countries, the central economic problem is no longer poverty but conflict. Everyone wants more; no one wants less. Many want more leisure, more income, and less work. Some want no interference, others want control. Some want control of others, but not of themselves. Some want to keep private enterprise, others want nationalization. Some want to see justice but what justice is, is not agreed. Some want stability, others want change. It is a problem of conflict, for all wants of all cannot be satisfied. What we need, both for each individual and for society as a whole is some sort of balance between many conflicting desires. Once this is seen, the search for the maximum, whatever Bentham may have thought, will be at an end. We would be content to see all happy; and if not happy at least happier than now. The difficulty is not only that the means to do this conflict, but conflict itself is its greatest foe. And this perhaps is the welfare economist's chief task; to show how conflict arises and how it can be reduced.'

With the pluralist philosophy of decisions we can detect variants ranging from the idealistic to the cynical. We have at one extreme the Radomysler point of view in which the weight given in decision making to the minimizing of conflict is for the highest motives—that it is of benefit to society to sacrifice at the margin some economic wealth for some reduction in conflict. And we have the American pluralists who see the process as a broadly satisfactory one. We have the neutral Sisson point of view in which a passive public service responds to pressures, and to loud demands or complaints more than to quiet, for neither good nor bad motives but because that is the reality of public life. At the other extreme we have the belief that the attention paid to pressures is usually for motives related to power and authority rather than to any form of economic or social welfare. A number of writers have taken this pessimistic view from Adam Smith, who saw the government and legislature as likely to be 'diverted by the clamorous importunity of partial interests' to Peter Drucker who considers[13] that 'politics is focused on crises, and problems and issues. It is not focused on doing a job. Politics, whatever the form of government, is not congenial to managerial organization and makes government slight managerial performance. . . . By excelling as a manager no one in politics will ever get to the top. . . .'

In the allocation of resources, the pluralist approach is likely to be closely associated with incrementalism for in this, rather than in deeper more far-reaching reviews of alternatives, lies the best hope of consensus. Indeed some suggest that in the incremental approach to budgeting the outcome is usually clear to both parties before the negotiations start and that these must be seen as a form of ritual conducted in accordance with rules and conventions rather than as a decision making process. For these reasons pluralism is not only unlikely to lead to a vigorous search for a best use of resources even in a homogeneous area of use but will move towards a better use of resources only slowly, if at all.

In the generality of decisions on resources, pluralism seems difficult to justify as a general criterion which determines the best use of resources, although in some areas of choice it may remain the best criterion which we have. It remains a valuable process by which information relevant to decisions is obtained, attitudes to alternative plans or projects assessed and modifications made, information about decisions communicated. And if the minimizing of social conflict is seen as a valid criterion (although one distinct from obtaining a consensus among whatever pressure groups may exist and intervene), pluralist processes may provide a measure of such conflict—although not inevitably so, as a group or social unit concerned may lack effective representation. If this conclusion is relevant to Britain but not to the U.S.A., it may be because our machinery of government facilitates decision making outside of pluralist processes whereas the American system, e.g. the division of responsibility between agencies and Congress, forces decisions on resources into such processes.

THE INFLUENCE OF PRODUCERS ON PUBLIC RESOURCE DECISIONS

Whereas the pluralist school is concerned with all pressure groups, Professor Galbraith sees the public service as largely subject to the influence, almost to the control, of one group—business corporations. Extending to the public service his theory that in the private market the sovereignty of the consumer is being supplanted by the sovereignty of the producer, he claims[14] that 'The state . . . comes close to being the executive committee of the large producing organization—of the technostructure. It stabilizes aggregate demand . . . reflects the will of large organizations in the mix of military and non-military goods, provides such needed public artifacts as highways for the management of specific consumer demand. . . .' He believes that the effect is both to reduce the size of the public sector below what is desirable and to misallocate resources within it. This theory if true would have serious implications for management in the public service. But it seems difficult to see the demands for roads and university education in Britain as explained by '. . . the automobile companies can get the highways that are essential for a consumer preference for automobile transportation' and 'in the universities large numbers of students are brought together by the unprecedented demands of the industrial system for qualified manpower'. Nor are some recent decisions within the defence procurement programme in Britain, or the change over the past five years in the balance between the allocation of resources to defence and education, consistent with 'decisions [on weapon systems] are taken by the producers, i.e. the armed services and the supplying firms, in pursuit of their own goals. The Congress and the public are then accommodated or commanded thereto.'[14]

If pressures of this kind cannot in Britain seem decisive they should not be assumed to be non-existent. Potentially they could, as Galbraith points out, have serious distorting consequences in the use of resources in the public service. But not always or necessarily so: there may be times when appeals by manufacturers to the public service to take standard lines of products, or to order in bulk certain specially standardized articles for the public service, may represent a better use of resources and better public management than a multitude of small public orders, each with detailed specifications for the need of a particular body, which might result in the needs being met 5 per cent better than from standard products but at 25 per cent higher costs. There may even be times when appeals to support advanced technology in the long-term national interest may be in the long-term national interest. But if, as I have suggested, pluralism seems inadequate as a criterion for management decisions, it can be rejected on grounds other than the circumstances which Galbraith describes.

THE NATIONAL INTEREST

Many decisions in government are taken by those who claim to have a special responsibility for the national interest. Some of these decisions are primarily concerned with resources: they are management decisions. They are justified by no analytical criteria but by an assertion, which may or may not be accompanied by supporting argument, that the decision is in the national interest. In many countries, particularly in Europe, this has long been accepted as a valid and rational approach to decision making which is as relevant to decisions on the use of resources, and thus to management, as to other areas of public affairs. In France for example, Mr Andrew Shonfield observes[15] the acceptance of the view that:

'... the effective conduct of a nation's economic life must depend on the concentration of power in the hands of a small number of exceptionally able people, exercising foresight and judgement of a kind not possessed by the average successful man of business. The long view and the wide experience, systematically analysed by persons of authority, are the intellectual foundation of the system.'

Shonfield comments that, in accepting this approach, France demonstrated a 'sustained polarity' from the attitude of Britain and saw between the two countries a 'sharp contrast in national style and practice ... not noticeably modified over the centuries'.

But if in Britain there was a far greater conviction that the national interest would emerge—and might even be defined as what did emerge—from the interplay on decisions of individuals and groups pursuing their own interests, history is by no means lacking in references to the national interest when particular decisions were made: such references have increased rather than decreased over time. Some see this as no more than a 'presentational' device and would deny the right of the national interest to be regarded as a separate criterion in its own right.

This latter point of view has had much academic support in the U.S.A. where it has been argued that group interests are not necessarily narrow or selfish but will frequently be modified or extended to take account of broad national considerations. This too leads to the denial of the national interest as a distinct criterion: pluralist processes will take account of it as fully as is necessary. In an interesting study of 'Agriculture and the Public Interest'[16] Professor Peter Self and Herbert Storing confirmed that group interests may take account of, and incorporate, broader considerations of the national interest but concluded:

'In a democracy the wishes of a majority may be accepted as providing a prima facie indication of the public interest, but they do not provide a final or unqualified verdict. Nor is the public interest adequately defined as an accommodation of special interests.

'Since the strength of special interests has developed *pari passu* with a growth in the range and importance of public interests, the defence of the latter against the former becomes much more important and more difficult. ... These developments throw an increasing burden of responsibility upon the guardians of the public interest, the Ministers of the Crown and the senior civil servants who advise them.'

If, as this passage suggests, the national or public interest exists as something distinct from the substance of majoritarian votes or pluralist negotiations, it is equally probable that it is not fully or adequately represented by the economic criteria of the commercial approach or through cost–benefit analysis. If the national interest can be regarded as a rational decision criterion in its own right, the spheres of influence where this claim would seem to have most validity are those where the 'horizon' of the problem is a significant factor. It may be a spatial horizon—in international affairs and defence the bounds of interest of individuals and groups are often more limited than those of decision makers or advisers concerned with the national interest. The development of a remote region of the country may also concern such decision makers more than it does the majority of voters or the preponderance of groups.

But it is the temporal horizon which gives the national interest its best claim to provide a distinct point of view. 'Is the individual naturally led to consider the needs of succeeding centuries as is the nation?' was the question asked by Friedrich List and soon answered in a way not in conflict with the point of view expressed recently by a writer, of very different convictions, Professor Joan Robinson:[17]

> 'There is a choice between jam today and more jam the day after tomorrow. This problem cannot be resolved by any kind of calculation based on "discounting the future" for the individuals concerned in the loss or gain are different. The choice must be taken somehow or other but the principles of Welfare Economics do not help to settle it.'

But, while List and Mrs Robinson were referring to generations yet unborn, the growing practice of public bodies of discounting the estimated cash flow on future investment projects, at rates equivalent to those adopted by private business corporations, can produce situations which are not self-evidently in accordance with the national interest. It is for example possible to envisage a major investment project in, say, town planning, or the reduction in some dangerous form of pollution, or even some technological development with an assured export potential when complete, under which in each of the first ten years expenditure is expected to exceed receipts to a total extent over the decade of £100m. but where from the eleventh to the twentieth year income would exceed expenditure each year to a total over the decade of £220m. At a discount rate of 10 per cent a series constructed to illustrate this example has a present value which is negative. Now it is clear why a business corporation would be wise to reject this scheme for, with given conventions on the rate of return expected on equity capital and with given assumptions about the cost of loan capital, the project may represent a road to insolvency. But some may assert that, particularly in the use of resources to enhance or preserve the environment, an outlay of £100m. in this decade to acquire a return valued at £200m. in the next decade is worthwhile. If so, I do not find this so irrational an attitude that I should be inclined to describe those who advance it as madmen in authority or to write off their views as no more than the reflection of the theory of a defunct economist—or of Friedrich List.

Two other claims have been made to justify the national interest being regarded as a distinct criterion. The first is that 'risk' has a different significance and would require to be given a different numerical value if a project is assessed from the point of view of the nation rather than from that of an individual or group. This is valid but can be met under the cost–benefit criterion or even under the commercial approach. The last claim is one for which least sympathy is likely to be felt by the reader. It is the view that those concerned with the national interest may know better what is in the interests of individuals and groups than they themselves may do. Adolph Wagner for example wrote:

'Universal military training may yield indiscriminate benefits in the form of national health and character building which may be conducive to economic progress.'

Fortunately those who feel inclined to reject this final claim for 'national interest' can do so, without destroying the case for regarding this criterion as rational and valid in some circumstances.

A DECISION FUNCTION

I have described various criteria by which a decision on resources may be adjudged better than another. These criteria may conflict conceptually and in practice. Each of the criteria applied in isolation to the same circumstances could produce a different solution of what was 'best'. And as the criteria can also be applied collectively in a large number of permutations, each incorporating varying rates of 'weighting' of the different criteria, it would almost be possible to claim that there is no use of resources which cannot be argued to be 'best' by the application of some mix of criteria at some rates of weighting. This would be a pessimistic conclusion. A book on management in the public service could end at this point. But this would in my view be too extreme a view of the problem facing those concerned with decisions on management in government. Our requirements fall far short of a normative theory of decision in government, or of social choice. We require no more than that the relevant criterion or criteria should be predictable and consistent—consistent in the sense that decisions on the use of resources are evaluated *ex post* by the same criteria as those on which they are taken *ex ante*. Whether these are the criteria on which decisions *should* be taken, is not an issue to be settled as a by-product of management.

The criteria which we must accept, reject or relate are:

B (commercial — the payments/receipts balance
and
business)
E (economic) — the social benefit/social cost balance
V (voting) — the support of a majority of electors
A (agreement) — the achievement of the greatest measure of con-
sensus through the negotiation
N (national) — the national interest
C (conflict) — the minimizing of social conflict
D (democratic) — public information and participation in decision
making

And there is the geographical factor G—to be kept in mind. We shall
also note that public authorities like business corporations need to in-
form and consult their own employees—and in Britain the Whitley
machinery exists for this purpose in many public authorities, and similar
consultation machinery in others. Some, although not all, decisions on
resources, may require such consultation and the agreement of staff
associations on a matter like, say 'saving resources by decentralizing
work from London' makes it a 'better' decision generating less social
conflict internally than one made without consultation or agreement. C
and D, which are 'external' criteria, have therefore 'internal' counter-
parts 'c' and 'd'. Similarly there is an internal counterpart of A—a
negotiation or bargaining between the parts of government organizations.

We can at this stage pause to express a heartfelt agreement with Professor Walter Heller[18] who wrote 'to get all of these considerations into
the decision making equation . . . requires a wisdom which goes well
beyond the field of economics. This may be the reason why so few
economists enter politics. . . .' It might also be a fair comment to say
that it also goes well beyond the field of business management. But we
can take courage from the fact that since in Britain neither the decision
making processes nor the criteria are completely or even substantially
unpredictable, there must be a structure to be discovered even if some
may be sceptical whether it rests on more than convention or even
inertia.

When these issues have been debated it has often been on a high
level of generality—analysis versus pluralism or pluralism versus *Étatism*, as if a single criterion would emerge triumphant if the debate were
pursued to a logical conclusion. In practice each kind of choice on resource use acquires through decision, convention or experience, an
appropriate criterion, or a mix of criteria between which the relative
weights are seldom explicitly defined but emerge perhaps through trial
and error. They are not always stable. They may vary with, say,
changes in decision makers (different governments may apply different

criteria or vary weights between criteria) changes in public opinion, changes in the environment and in knowledge, e.g. if analysis has become more influential recently it owes as much to the fact that better analysis is available as to any change in political philosophy. Each unit of the public service using resources operates within known criteria or criterion which it applies to choice on the use of resources. Most possible combinations may be found subject to such considerations as:

(i) V is almost non-existent in Britain as a criterion.

(ii) B and E are alternatives which at the boundary become indistinguishable.

(iii) N will tend to be associated with scale and long time horizon, international or defence considerations, or major choices in the distribution of resources within a country. It will often be the sole criterion, but as the scope of analysis improves E will increasingly be associated with it—to 'price' the decision to be made in the national interest.

(iv) E and A will often be alternatives. As the scope of analysis increases, as the quality improves, as possibilities of getting 'neutral' analysis grow, E will in some areas drive out A, the concensus achieved through bargaining, leaving pluralism as a process rather than a criterion. But in some important areas, e.g. the division of subsidies between different forms of art or the allocation of a total sum for basic scientific research between competitive proposals from many disciplines or even the allocation of resources between faculties in a university, the role of analysis is and seems likely to remain small: decision by consensus will survive.

Sometimes public authorities will clearly apply the wrong criteria or criterion. Plans for a Third London Airport seem to have been based originally on a vaguely B criterion. But public opinion has forced reconsideration on E, C and D criteria. The weights between them may be deduced from the report of the Roskill Commission. And historians can assess the criterion or criteria on which a final decision is made.

The establishment of the weights between criteria is complex. It can be argued that a road scheme decided by criteria E, C, D, by which the start has been delayed two years to allow public inquiries to be held into the route or compulsory acquisition orders for the land required and the cost increased by 10 per cent by a diversion to minimize conflict, is 'better' than one decided by E alone. But is it 'better' than if C and D had been given greater weight and delays of three years and extra cost of 15 per cent accepted. Or if the delay had been reduced to twelve months if extra cost of 20 per cent to reduce conflict had been acceptable, would this have been 'better'. It seems improbable that

E

trade-offs between such different criteria can ever be measured precisely. Nevertheless there is perhaps scope for research here to establish how the C and D criteria can best be given appropriate weight at least cost to the E criterion. There seems no reason to assume that what exists is best.

The complexities described are in total formidable but others, less peculiar to this area of decision making, must also be taken into account. All the difficulties which I have described so far would arise even if there were 'perfect knowledge' in certain respects. Reality differs from that happy state:

  (i) As I have pointed out in Chapter 2 the relationship (in some cases even the sign) between output and outcome is unknown, or has to be assumed on a low-confidence basis, in certain areas of resource use.

 (ii) Some relevant information is missing and some which is available, even in statistics of apparently impressive precision, will be found on examination to be subject to such a range of error that it may even be a form of irrationality to use them at all[19]— certainly if the sensitivity of alternative plans is not tested over the range of confidence limits of the information.

(iii) no organization manned by human beings has yet been devised which can guarantee that from a vast possible range of alternative strategies the short list of those selected for detailed analysis will contain all the most promising.[20]

It must also be kept in mind that, within a single criterion, different objectives may co-exist and these too must be related and some rate of trade-off between them assessed before one decision can be said to be better than another. Within the N criterion for example a particular choice may affect, in different directions and to a varying extent, relations with EFTA, EEC and the Commonwealth, with all of which good relations are regarded as in the national interest. Within the E criterion the road scheme will have objectives associated with traffic movement, safety, and the preservation of the environment. Typically therefore the 'best' use of resources in the public service is a multi-criterion, multi-objective decision.

CONCLUSIONS

We find in government complexity, but not I believe irrationality, in assessing whether one use of resources is 'better' than another. It is one of the most significant aspects of management in government. This complexity has serious consequences when it comes to the evaluation of decisions on resources by those who have not been parties to the decision. What was a 'good' management decision by the criteria and objectives against which it was assessed may, and indeed probably will, appear a 'bad' choice if evaluated against different criteria, objectives or even if the same are applied with different weights. And as we have seen earlier all the criteria/objectives can produce different 'best' decisions if applied from the point of view of different areas—nation, region or locality. What is certain, therefore, is that however competent the public service becomes in management, all decisions on resources will continue to be subject to criticism which, within its own terms of reference, will be fair and valid. In this sense one must agree with Roland McKean's view:[21] 'Choices about government expenditures then are "group choices" for which . . . there is no ultimately correct preference function—choices whose preferredness cannot be subjected to any ultimate test. A corollary . . . is that there is no uniquely correct set of prices or trade-off ratios.'

Management in government can be seen to have much in common with the general problem of pay settlements. Most people would subscribe to the proposition that it would be preferable if public authorities used resources more efficiently: as many to the proposition that it would be desirable that all pay claims should be settled on a fair and rational basis. In both areas we find some whose criterion of what is better or fair is one of process, e.g. the view that a fair wage settlement is by definition that which emerges from, say, arbitration or a court of inquiry. We find in pay the equivalent of the two economic criteria, i.e. the 'leave it to supply and demand' school of thought and the 'yes provided that you correct the distortions due to monopoly or monopsony and you must accept the indeterminacy when monopoly negotiates with monopsony' point of view. There is the 'social' attitude to wage claims which sees fairness as ensuring that the nurse earns more than the pop singer. There is the national interest criterion which leads to complaints if, during times of difficulty in the balance of payments, a survey of earnings shows that sales managers responsible for exports earn on average less than those in charge of the home market. Relativities are important in both areas. And in both there is found the condition to which I shall refer on occasions throughout this book, in so far as it affects management, but which applies also to pay—the privileged position enjoyed by the *status quo*, i.e. the implicit view that what exists at any time does not need to be justified by argument as any change proposed must be. Finally there is the tendency in both areas for any explicit debate on criteria to be avoided. The attitude would seem to be 'give us efficient management or fair pay settlements and it will be time enough then to worry about criteria'.

I started this chapter in the hope of finding firm foundations on which management in government could be built. We can hardly claim to have found rock. Some critics may suggest that our trial borings have rather revealed a filled-in rubbish tip of discarded theories. I would not see the site as quite so unstable. A few underground streams and springs underlie it and the occasional earthquake may occur. But buildings of lasting quality have been erected on such sites by architects following the example of Frank Lloyd Wright in designing a hotel in Tokyo and concentrating on the foundations and structure, in a clear appreciation of the ground and of the risks, before designing the decorations of the reception rooms. In management in government we need the services of the structural engineer before we call in the interior decorators.

But if the manager in government faces problems in deciding what is a better use of resources, or an improvement in efficiency in management, we have yet to answer the question 'who are these managers?' To this simple question, I shall devote the next chapter.

NOTES ON CHAPTER 3

1. Aaron Wildavsky, 'The Political Economy of Efficiency: Cost-Benefit Analysis, Systems Analysis and Program Budgeting', *Public Administration Review*, December 1966. 'The good systems analyst ... looks down upon those who say they take their objectives as given, knowing full well that the apparent solidity of the objective will dissipate during analysis and that, in any case, most people do not know what they want because they do not know what they can get.'

2. Arthur M. Okun, *The Political Economy of Prosperity* (Chapter 1), The Brookings Institution, 1970.

3. See for example *Public Expenditure 1968–69 to 1973–74* (Cmnd. 4234), HMSO, 1969.

4. To take a hypothetical example a public authority pursuing the objective of reducing loss of young trees by damage from squirrels might use resources to shoot them. Output: dead squirrels. Outcome: no improvement, as killing squirrels within bounds of practicality proves to have no significant effect on size of surviving squirrel population which is determined by other factors in nature. Those who wish to study this kind of output/outcome problem in depth can do so in the case of the renewal of slum areas of towns where Professor Jay Forrester's *Urban Dynamics* (MIT Press 1969) suggests both the complexity and counter-intuitive nature of some of the output/outcome relationships, e.g. 'This model of an urban system suggests that many past and present urban programs may actually worsen the conditions they are intended to improve' (Chapter 1).

5. 'Perhaps the study of budgeting is just another expression for the study of politics' is the view of Aaron Wildavsky, 'Political Implications of Budgeting Reform', 1961, Reprinted in *Public Budgeting and Finance*, F. E. Peacock Publishers Inc., 1968.

6. Since this book will not provide an introduction to approaches and techniques mentioned, I shall assume either that the reader is already familiar with the basis of the approach/technique or will refer to other published sources which in the case of cost–benefit analysis might include in increasing order of complexity: Martin S. Feldstein, 'Cost-Benefit Analysis and Investment in the Public Service', *Public Administration*, Winter 1964. H. G. Walsh and Alan Williams, *Current Issues in Cost–Benefit Analysis*, CAS Occasional Paper No. 11, HMSO, 1969. A. R. Prest and R. Turvey, 'Cost–Benefit Analysis: A Survey'. *The Economic Journal*, December 1965 (reprinted in Volume III— *Resource Allocation Surveys of Economic Theory*, MacMillan, London, 1966). Samuel B. Chase Jr (ed.), *Problems in Public Expenditure Analysis*—particularly the contributions of Samuel B. Chase and Roland N. McKean. The Brookings Institution, 1968.

7. For a much fuller discussion of voting as a process of social choice

see: Professor Kenneth J. Arrow, *Social Choice and Individual Values.* 2nd ed. John Wiley, New York, 1963.

8. For a full statement of the pluralist approach see Charles E. Lindblom, *The Intelligence of Democracy*, The Free Press, Glencoe, 1965. Aaron Wildavsky, *The Politics of the Budgetary Process*, Little, Brown and Co., Boston, 1964, and for a critical commentary: Allen Schick, 'Systems Politics and Systems Budgeting', *Public Administration Review*, March/April 1969.

9. Professor John Kenneth Galbraith, 'Economics as a System of Belief'. Paper delivered at the American Economic Association meeting, New York. December 1969.

10. Roland N. McKean, 'Use of Shadow Prices', in *Problems in Public Expenditure Analysis*, op. cit.

11. C. H. Sisson, op. cit. (Chapter 1).

12. A. Radomysler, 'Welfare economics and economic policy', in Part I of *Readings in Welfare Economics* (edited Arrow and Scitowsky), George Allen and Unwin, 1969.

13. Peter Drucker, 'The Sickness of Government' in *The Age of Discontinuity* op. cit. (Chapter 1).

14. Galbraith, op. cit.

15. Andrew Shonfield, *Modern Capitalism*, op. cit. (Chapter 2).

16. Professor Peter Self and Herbert Storing, *The State and the Farmer*, George Allen and Unwin, 1962.

17. Professor Joan Robinson, *Economic Philosophy*, C. A. Watts and Co., 1967.

18. Professor Walter Heller, 'Economics and the Applied Theory of Public Expenditure' in *Public Budgeting and Finance*, op. cit. The 'all these considerations' of Heller's statement are not identical with my set of criteria.

19. Although his book is not confined to decision on resources, almost all the points made by Oskar Morgenstern in *On the Accuracy of Economic Observation*, Princeton University Press, 1963 are relevant. It should be required reading for all public servants *after* they have acquired an interest and skill in numeracy!

20. This important constraint which even in isolation would make 'best' decisions unattainable and even 'better' decisions hard to achieve has been explored fully in the writings of Professor Herbert A. Simon, e.g. *Administrative Behaviour*, op. cit. (notes to Chapter 1).

21. McKean op. cit. I do not find it inconsistent to agree with McKean's point of view on *proof* while at the same time sympathizing with the views in the same book of, say, Samuel B. Chase and Julius Margolis, who are more optimistic that analysis can contribute *something* to decisions on resources.

CHAPTER 4

A SYSTEMS APPROACH TO THE PUBLIC SERVICE

Observe how system into system runs
What other planets circle other suns.
Alexander Pope: *An Essay on Man*

THE COMPLEXITY OF THE PUBLIC SERVICE

The first apparently simple question which I set out to answer, 'what do we mean by a better use of resources?', exposed the complexity of the problems arising in making and evaluating decisions on resources in the public service. A second, and also apparently simple question, 'who, in the public service are managers?' will involve an analysis of the heterogeneity of the public service. It is, of course, well known that the public service in general, and sections of it like the civil service and local government, are far from homogeneous. But while the point is often made, generalizations, which seem to assume a high degree of homogeneity, abound. To establish the role of management and identify the managers it is necessary to concentrate on the diversity of the public service. And since our concern is with the use of inputs to produce outputs to achieve defined objectives, we shall not find the normal classification into government departments, local authorities and public corporations or, within any of these organizations, into organizational units like divisions or branches to be the most useful for our purpose. While the composition of groups responsible for using resources in pursuit of a particular objective may coincide with some organizational unit, this coincidence is far from general.

I believe that the most useful concept for this analysis is that of the 'system'. I have decided to use it despite the fact that it is regarded by some as one of the semantic carpet-baggers following in the path of the advancing army of management, which produces in those who see it in this light much the same reaction as the word culture aroused forty years ago in a certain German. In fact the academic pedigree of the system is beyond reproach. More important, for my purpose, it is essential for any analysis of management in government.

SYSTEMS

In analysing the role of management in the public service, the twin concepts of the system and the model will prove of value. Both are concerned with relationships. The system is a concept which has developed in several different quarters—in physical science, in engineering (initially in mechanical, but in recent years particularly in electronic and automatic data processing) and in the behavioural sciences to which we owe the concept of a social system. There is now an attempt to develop a general systems theory, but at its present stage of development it does not provide an analytical tool applicable to my present task. The word system will have somewhat different connotations to, say, the biologist, the engineer, the computer specialist, the social anthropologist. But unlike the confusion surrounding words such as management, administration and policy, the word system still conveys generally the essential elements associated with the concept and illustrated by such definitions as

'an orderly grouping of separate but interdependent components for the purpose of attaining some predetermined objectives'[1]

or

'an array of components designed to achieve an objective according to plan'[2]

The definition in the *Oxford English Dictionary* is not very different:

'a set or assemblage of things connected, associated or interdependent, so as to form a complex unity'

The system is often associated with another concept; that of *the model*. Both have boundaries based on logic for the purpose they are fulfilling rather than on convention, accident or inertia which explain so many organizational boundaries. By a model I shall mean 'a structured statement of how the relevant factors interact with one another. These interactions are made explicit and are quantified. It is a simplification of the real system for a specific set of purposes.'[3]

I shall use the word system to describe a series of relationships designed to achieve an objective in a way which embraces both the system of the engineer and the system of the social scientist. In this way the public service can be seen as a vast number—a galaxy indeed—of systems, some consisting predominantly of machine–machine relationships, others of man–man relationships, but the majority will incorporate both these features and man–machine relationships ('socio-technical systems'). Between components there will typically be 'flows', which may consist mainly of physical goods in, say, a purchasing/storage system or, in different systems of information, flows which may take a physical form—letters, minutes, etc., or intangible form, e.g. telephone conversations or at the point at which communication becomes most informal, although not least important, of canteen gossip or 'the grapevine'. Typically there will be points in this system in which whatever constitutes the flow between components—physical goods and information or information only—is 'processed' and in this way 'inputs' to the system become transferred into 'outputs'. Processing may consist in changing physically goods passing through the system or in analysing information and reaching decisions: most systems will incorporate both kinds of processing.

It will be seen that there is no direct relationship between systems and computers, a point of some confusion due to the use of 'systems analysis' in Britain to describe the operations preceding the installation of a computer, although in the U.S.A. it means what the British describe as 'operational research'.[4] However one of the main spin-off benefits of computers is that they compel those ordering them (or, if they mistakenly opt out, those installing them) to think logically about the task to be performed. This logic is represented by the system.

A point on which all who use the concept of the system are agreed is that there is a hierarchy of systems. Typically a system exists as a sub-system of a larger system which is likely to be responsible for defining the objective for which the sub-system exists, controlling to a greater or lesser degree the inputs of the sub-system and perhaps receiving or at least monitoring the output of the sub-system. It is by no means uncommon for a sub-system to form part of two separate systems with different parts of its activities being based on a different series of relationships. Often one of these relationships will have primacy over the other. But sometimes they may be of equal importance. This is a point to which I shall return later.

PRIMARY TASK

In the use of the concept of the system, the relationship between the system and its objective should be emphasized (this important aspect of the system is missing from the definition in the Oxford dictionary). Here it is useful to incorporate the concept from the behavioural sciences of 'the primary task'[5] in thinking about the objectives of systems and sub-systems. As we move up the hierarchy of systems multi-objective situations become more common until, when we reach the macro-system level of government as a whole—the list of objectives is inevitably long. If they are condensed into a few statements these tend to be of such a broad order of generality as to cease to be meaningful for operational use within sub-systems. But at lower level sub-systems, if there are several objectives, one should be seen as 'the primary task' or—if the coefficients relating the several objectives can be quantified—the group of objectives can be regarded as constituting a single 'primary task' or objective function. Exceptionally neither a single primary task nor an objective function may be capable of definition. In such cases difficulty is inevitable.

The primary task has been defined as 'that which the organization must fulfil to survive'.[6] Within the public service the word 'survive' may create the wrong emphasis for on the whole the power of survival of organizations is remarkable, despite the evidence to the contrary provided by the demise of certain government departments and the possible forthcoming disappearance of certain local authorities. It may be preferable for the public service to think of the primary task in more positive terms as 'that in which performance determines success'. If we consider systems in this light, we can also note the possibility that a formal primary task (set by the higher order system of which the systems under study forms part) may conflict with a 'shadow primary task'—that on which the members of the system believe explicitly or implicitly that their own performance and advancement will depend. Such shadow primary tasks may for example arise within professional sub-systems. This tendency has been noted in business in the U.S.A. where the risk of professionalism conflicting with corporation loyalty and the concept of 'the corporation man', worries some (but not all) observers. But any sub-system can generate shadow primary tasks whether staffed by professionals or not. And apart from official and (possibly) shadow primary tasks, each individual is likely to have his own personal goals which may be different. In Michel Crozier's[7] words 'members of an organization . . . operate as autonomous actors each one with his own personal strategy'. It is an important issue which has been much developed and extended in the work of Professor Chris Argyris.

A SPECTRUM OF SYSTEMS

Let us now try to bring together a definition of management as concerned with seeking the best use of resources in pursuit of an objective, with the concept of a hierarchy of systems each with an objective or primary task. If we consider the public service in this light the feature which emerges most clearly is that only a minority of the many systems which make up the service have a primary task involving the best use of resources in pursuit of an objective—and even some of those which might reasonably be expected to have 'managerial' primary tasks of this kind have explicitly or implicitly adopted primary tasks of a different kind. Within a system the nature of the primary task largely determines the 'style' of operation, the kind of person who enters and prospers within the system—what some writers have described as 'the work culture'. What distinguishes the public service from business is that, whereas the latter genus is made up of different kinds and sizes of system, all of these have primary tasks involving *some* form of resource use/objective optimization and are to this extent all varieties of the same species, i.e. management. But the genus 'public service' is made up of a spectrum of major systems in which several distinct species are to be found. Systems with primary tasks concerned with the best use of resources comprise but one of these species. And, as I shall show, varieties and hybrids of all these species can be identified.

If we look at the spectrum of the public service we might begin by placing 'management systems' at one extreme where, with the nationalized industries, the spectrum merges with private industry. At the other extreme we might start by placing *the judicial system*. Without concerning ourselves over-much with the contentious issue whether this system should be regarded as just within the public service as broadly defined, or, on grounds of constitutional propriety, as existing outside the public service, we can I hope agree that within the judicial service the primary task would not be seen in any terms involving resource optimization. Whether the primary task would be defined as concerned with the administration of justice or, as the processes of the system might suggest, with 'the avoidance of injustice' is another matter which need not be debated here. It is sufficient to establish that the judicial system is not a management system and that even those most enthusiastic for a wider entry to the business schools have not suggested that such training should be given to all judges or barristers, as a necessary requirement for appointment. In Britain the commissioning of Lord Beeching to report on aspects of what might be called court management and the new appointments advertised in 1970 for Circuit Administrators (or as the job specification suggests they might have been described— Circuit Managers) is a recognition that to seek the best use of resources, specialists, not personally involved in legal processes, may be needed.

If we move clearly within the spectrum of the public service we find, as the nearest neighbours of the judicial system, a form of *quasi-judicial system* administering a growing volume of administrative law. These too form a species of system quite distinct from a management system. Moving further across the system we can identify '*administration systems*' using the word administration as I defined it in Chapter 2. Such systems will also see their primary tasks as concerned with issues distinct from resource-optimization. They are clearly not management systems. Nor are they judicial or quasi-judicial systems, although I shall argue in the next chapter their style and success criteria may have more in common with judicial than with management systems.

If we have at one extreme of the spectrum judicial, quasi-judicial and administration systems and at the other extreme central and local government management systems and nationalized industries, what lies between them? Or do administration and management systems merge imperceptibly together? In part, I believe they do and at the centre of the public service spectrum there are systems in which the primary task embodies both administration and management criteria and attitudes in such equal weight as to create hybrid systems in which success is particularly difficult to achieve. We may perhaps consider the system responsible for the siting of new airports as a possible example of such a hybrid. We have observed the siting of the Third Airport for London being studied by a Commission, headed by a Judge, supported by members possessed of a wide variety of analytical and administrative qualifications, using processes which include analysis by sophisticated cost–benefit and other mathematical models[8] through procedures for the hearing of evidence and objections which in form at least assume a quasi-judicial character. In local government the planning sub-system is one where the primary task is hard to specify.

But the spectrum cannot be completed merely by hybrid administration–management systems in the centre. There are clearly several other species of systems which have primary tasks which are neither those of administration nor of management systems. One which can be identified in central government, where it is of the highest importance, I shall describe as a *diplomatic system* (not to be regarded as synonymous with the Diplomatic Service which however is in effect a 'diplomatic system.)' The diplomatic systems would include the Cabinet Office and the Private Offices of the various departments. These particular varieties of 'diplomatic' system have the characteristic of operating without long-term objectives or primary tasks other than to keep the central machinery of government operating effectively. McLuhan might say that 'the system is the objective'. But the range of diplomatic systems in central government is much wider than that described. In most departments there will be found-sub-systems which neither administer any body of regulations nor deploy any resources other than their own staff time and the accommodation and supporting services required. The primary task might be to keep under review, in a general or co-ordinating role, some broad issue like pollution. Or more commonly to act as a point of focus and co-ordination for relations between central government and a particular industry. Information is gathered and circulated. Some attempt is made to forecast future developments which might concern government. Good relations are as far as possible cultivated, as in all diplomatic systems, between those concerned. Such a system assumes a passive role but, when intervention by government is thought desirable, it may take the form of legal and regulatory constraints or of the use of resources. At this stage these diplomatic systems hive off tasks to administrative or management systems—either of which may in time exceed greatly in scale, although not necessarily in authority, the diplomatic system from which they originated.

A management solution to a need might be in the use of resources by way of grants or subsidies or in the direct provision of goods or services by the public authority. Sometimes management and administration approaches are used in conjunction. They are all, as Sisson pointed out, methods of governing. But once such decisions are made either administration or management systems come into being. Different approaches, skills and success criteria become relevant which those who formerly were operating a diplomatic system may or may not be able to provide. For many of the skills needed in the diplomatic system are distinct from those needed in either management or administration systems. Traditionally the diplomatic skills have been most highly valued in British central government and opportunities to develop and display them keenly sought.

An interesting hybrid system which lies between and incorporates some of the attitudes, and skills of, the diplomatic system and the management system is the *integrative–allocative management system*. It arises from a feature of the public service which is the limited extent to which higher level systems have direct organizational control over sub-systems. Indeed in what seems to be a single system, from the point of view of primary task, information flows and decision making, many independent or quasi-independent organizations may comprise the hierarchy of sub-systems. The education system illustrates this feature. Probably most major systems in education, in the health service and in the armed forces are not management systems, i.e. they do not see their primary task as lying in the allocation and use of resources, and we may not find that those at the highest levels have been appointed primarily for their skills in management. It may nevertheless be found that the highest level systems responsible for education, health and defence become over a time a special variety of management system with the primary task of achieving the best allocation of resources in pursuit of defined national objectives rather than seeing their primary task in implementing, at the national decision making level, those objectives which, in the specialized educational, medical and military sub-systems, have primacy over the use of resources. It does not seem inevitable that central departments responsible for services of this kind will become primarily managerial in outlook. Structure may be relevant, i.e. whether the central organization is or is not staffed mainly from the sub-systems. And the extent to which resources are a constraint may also be significant. If the supply of resources is open-ended—'they must have what is needed to do the job'—it is less likely that at the highest levels these central co-ordinating systems will adopt a managerial approach.

It is indeed a general law that the importance of management in any system increases as resources become an increasingly severe constraint and this may at times lead to management becoming the primary task (if not explicitly then by the test of finding 'managers' appointed to the highest posts), where previously it had been a secondary or teritiary task. Developments in one British public corporation recently may illustrate this law at work. On the other hand, it is generally agreed to be favourable to a better use of resources, by re-allocation between objectives or strategies, if resources are increasing over time since to give all claimants more, with some receiving proportionately greater increases than others, is far easier than to allocate more resources to some ends when it implies that others must have less. Expansion and contraction can thus both favour management but in different ways. Some writers have identified as the feature of governmental organizations, which distinguishes them most markedly from business or other private organizations, their 'integrative and allocative functions'.[9] I do not personally find persuasive the argument that the primary task of administration systems as I have defined them is either integration or allocation. Nor are certain management systems in the public service solely concerned with these functions. But the managerial functions of some systems which I have mentioned and of bodies like, say, the Arts Council, are well described as 'integrative/allocative'. We can identify this as a variety of the species of management systems to be found in the public service.

But other larger species of system with more positive primary tasks can be identified. Medical systems constitute a clearly differentiated species. Although these need not necessarily form part of the public service, in Britain most of them are. Varieties of this system include the hospital whose special characteristics as a work culture and unique organizational forms have attracted the attention of a number of writers in management and administration. The general practitioner service and dental service are other varieties. In none of these would the 'best use of resources' be seen as the primary task of many of those at the highest levels of the system, although in each hospital a sub-system may be allocated to this role. Nor might the public—or the consumers of these services—find a more management orientated approach welcome. Experience of a really managerial dentist, optimizing the difference between his receipts and expenditure within National Health Service regulations, would soon establish this point.

The education system can also be seen as a separate species with the universities as a particularly interesting example of a system with equal primary tasks—researching and teaching. But management sub-systems, administration sub-systems and even some quasi-judicial sub-systems are also to be found in the university. Except for the absence (if indeed it is totally absent) of the diplomatic system, the university represents in microcosm the complexity and diversity of the public service as a whole, although with different species of system having in the university very different levels of status from those found in government.

MANAGEMENT AS A SECONDARY OR TERTIARY TASK

When we identify systems in which those at the highest levels regard one or more tasks as primary rather than that of management, it should not be assumed that those at the head of such systems attach little or no importance to the use of resources or that management must sink to very low levels wherever it is not the primary task. But if those at the head of such systems do not think of themselves primarily as managers, and do not expect success or failure in their careers to be determined mainly by the success or lack of success with which they use resources, it is essential that some person or some sub-system should be given the clearly defined task of seeking the best use of resources. And that when management criteria conflict with those arising from the primary task(s) of the main system, the trade-offs should not always or generally be such as to attach to the former nil or very low values and to the latter values of infinity or very high levels—although exceptionally this relationship might be justified. The ratio of such trade-offs will inevitably limit the scope for management in say a hospital or university, as indeed it will in an administration system within a government department or in a judicial system. In other words the best use of resources in such systems will never be identical with that appropriate to a management system. I have heard businessmen argue that both universities and hospitals could and should be run exactly as if they were businesses, i.e. management regarded as the primary task. They are certainly right to assume that in such circumstances resources would be used differently. But not that this would result in universities and hospitals much as we find them today only 'better managed'. They would be totally different institutions and whether 'better' involves a value judgement raising issues far beyond the scope of a study of management.

Other species of system found within the public service include the police and armed forces, varieties of social welfare system like probation or child care services. Research establishment in the public sector can probably be regarded as belonging to a distinct species of *research system* unlike R. & D. establishments in business firms. However it is not perhaps unknown in business for research establishments to generate 'shadow' primary tasks of their own not dissimilar from those of their official or even university colleagues and remote from management tasks. But despite the claim that classification is the first step towards knowledge, it is not my purpose here to produce a comprehensive list of species of systems to be found in the public service and of their varieties and of known hybrids. It is sufficient to call attention to the great differences in work culture which these many kinds of system will inevitably—and usually sensibly—develop and to suggest that any study of management in the public service, which fails to recognize at the outset that the best use of resources has a different significance in these different species of system will have no prospect of influencing the quality of management.

One outcome of a systems analysis of the public service is the recognition that, if only a minority of systems in the public service have primary
X tasks concerned with the best use of resources, the proposition, that all employed in the public service are managers, should think of themselves as managers or should be trained to act as managers, is invalid. This does not mean that all those using resources should not acquire, by training or other means, an 'appreciation' of management and of the attitudes and approaches justified in sub-systems which have been given the primary task of seeking the best use of resources. But to have this level of understanding of management, to be able to co-operate with and have a meaningful dialogue with managers, is not the same thing as to be a manager.

APPOINTMENTS AND PRIMARY TASK RECOGNITION

It is the characteristic of any system that the success criteria are related to the primary task of the system and that these determine selection for the highest posts in the system. Indeed it has been argued that in cases where the primary task of a system has not been stated explicitly or where the behaviour of the system seems to conflict with the formally defined primary task, the study of career development within the system may be the best way of deducing the primary task, e.g. Antony Jay in *Management and Machiavelli*:[10]

'I sometimes suspect that the tremendous significance of promotions and appointments is not fully realized in the corporations: you can issue directions and policy statements and messages to staff until the waste-paper baskets burst but they are nothing compared with promotions. Promotions are the one visible, unmistakable sign of the corporation's standard of values, an irrevocable declaration of the qualities it prizes in its staff, a simultaneous warning and example to everyone who knows the nature of the job and the qualities of its new incumbent.'

A similar point is made by J. K. Galbraith in *The New Industrial State*:[11]

'On coming on any form of organized activity—a church, platoon, government bureau, congressional committee, a house of casual pleasure, our first instinct is to enquire who is in charge. Then we enquire as to the qualifications or credentials which accord such command. Organization almost invariably invites two questions: Who is the head? How did he get there?'

And also by Peter Drucker:[12]

'In sharp contrast is the recent failure of a brilliant chairman and chief executive to make effective a new organization structure and new objectives in an old, large and proud U.S. company. Everyone agreed that the changes were needed. . . . But contrary to the action required to gain acceptance for the new ideas, the chairman—in order to placate the opposition—promoted prominent spokesmen of the old school into the most visible and highest salaried positions, in particular into three new executive vice presidencies. This meant only one thing to the people in the company "They don't really mean it." If the greatest rewards are given for behaviour contrary to that which the new course of action requires then everyone will conclude that this is what the people at the top really want and will reward.'

I do not believe that the application of this test to central and local government, to hospitals or public corporations (other than the nationalized industries) disproves my hypothesis that only a small proportion of the systems of the public service have management, as I have defined it, as their primary task. It cannot however prove that the proportion of management systems revealed by this test is in some sense right and that an analysis of public authorities would not find scope for more management systems.

So far we have been looking very generally at the public service and have identified various species of system across a horizontal band. But the complications increase when we explore each of these systems vertically and see each as comprising a hierarchy of sub-systems. What now becomes clear is that within a major system of which we can say that the primary task, the style, the success criteria, the higher appointments belong to a certain species, there may be found sub-systems of a different species. And I believe that it will normally be the case that as all systems use resources they must by definition all have management problems, and that in systems which considered as a whole are not management systems there will normally be found a sub-system, which may be powerful or weak, with management as a primary task. The hospital and the university illustrate this general rule. But it can also be seen in operation in government departments, particularly those which, taken as a whole, can be regarded as administration systems. Here the Finance and Establishment Divisions have traditionally provided not only a source of expertise in expenditure, and in the use of human resources, but have influenced decisively decisions on resources. Much use is also made of organization and methods studies, often not commissioned by those responsible for the work under study,

F

but undertaken on behalf of Finance or Establishment Divisions. It is implicit in these forms of organization and procedure, although seldom made explicit, that those in decision making posts within such systems may not use resources (financial or human) as well as those outside the system can do—however great their ability and experience in directions relevant to the primary task. The tendency has been, therefore, to limit the discretion of those operating the systems, in matters of expenditure and personnel management, by the heavy involvement of Finance and/or Establishment Divisions in such decisions, and by having the Treasury in reserve to approve or veto major decisions on resources (including staff)—and relatively minor decisions also until recent years when, as one outcome of the Plowden Report, delegations have in general been much increased.

This method of operation has always seemed bureaucratic and inefficient to businessmen on first taking up an appointment in a government department—and many of them do not see matters in any more favourable light on leaving it. But if we accept that many public service systems are not management systems and are not run by those who regard their primary task as management, there is logic in the way these matters have developed. Drucker has observed that as management is an economic process there is no presumption that those who are good at it will be good at other non-economic activities: the public service has operated traditionally on the basis that the converse is also true.

SYSTEMS AND ORGANIZATIONS

I referred at the beginning of this chapter to the fact that systems may bear little relationship to conventional boundaries between organizations. A single government department may incorporate several systems each of a different species and between which there is no greater interrelationship than that involved in having the same Minister and Permanent Secretary and sharing the same Establishments and Finance Divisions and management services unit. But each system may require different information flows and each may be affected by and influencing different parts of the environment. Elsewhere we may find the converse: what, from the point of view of information flows and decision making, would seem to be a single system can at times consist of several sub-systems controlled by several different government departments. The trend in Britain in the past decade towards larger departments can in part be seen as an attempt to reconcile organizations and systems.

RELATIONSHIP BETWEEN SYSTEMS

Finally an aspect of the public service on which the systems approach throws light is the complexity of relationships between systems. Thus a system comprising a hierarchy of sub-systems may typically be associated with:

a larger organizational and control system, e.g. a government department, a local authority or a public corporation;

a broader and more general system which may influence aspects of personnel management, e.g. 'the civil service' or 'local government'. The former is a more structured system than the latter: it will exercise more influence, impose more constraint on all sub-systems comprising it. For public corporations, no equivalent exists nor in general for private corporations, although in some cases employers' associations in an industry may exercise influence or constraints similar in character although normally less in extent;

the macro-economic planning system of government. Information flows generated in individual systems may therefore need to meet the requirements not only of those responsible for the management of the system, but what are quite likely to be the very different requirements of those responsible for managing the economy.

But perhaps the most important problem which arises for the sub-system is the relative weight to be given to vertical and horizontal relationships. Is a sub-system such as the education authority in a town, for example, to regard itself primarily as part of the national education system or as part of the local authority which is an employer/employee relationship. It is in a meaningful way part of both systems.[13] But conflict may arise in this dual relationship which would not normally arise in the case say of a Home Office official in the Prison Department (a clearly defined system) also forming part of another system 'the civil service'. The system to which the education authority sub-system will be most closely associated may be dependent on the answer given to the question, which arose in the previous chapter, whether the best use of resources is to be determined from a national, regional or local standpoint.

As Stafford Beer has observed[14] 'A system is not something given in nature but something defined by intelligence . . . to draw the conclusions that the collection is coherent, forming a system, it will be necessary to begin by inspecting the relationships of the entities comprising the collection to each other.'

THE CONTRIBUTION OF THE SYSTEMS APPROACH

The proposition I am advancing is that a classification of the public service into systems and sub-systems has a contribution to make to the development of management. It may well be that the scheme of classification which I have proposed will be found to fail the test of scientific rigour—that its terms should be both exhaustive and exclusive. I have sufficient awareness of the heterogeneity of the public service and confidence in the ingenuity of my colleagues to expect sub-systems to come to light which are truly indescribable under my—or perhaps any—scheme of classification. My claim for it is, therefore, the more modest one that it is both usable and useful. While I should not wish to claim the somewhat dubious distinction of being a random sample, I have on examination of my career confirmed that the ten posts I have held in the past can each be placed clearly as being a management, a diplomatic or an administration sub-system—and that in my present post I am responsible for two diplomatic, one management and two administration sub-systems. In this situation the official must remember, to use a Whitehall expression, 'to wear the right hat'—an indication that the proposition that different systems need different attitudes has long been recognized implicitly if not explicitly. I believe that a system classification is not in practice difficult to apply. Its value is not destroyed if a few indeterminate areas are found. The value of being able to distinguish ships from aircraft is not lost by the appearance of the hovercraft.

Different schemes of classification may each be of particular value for different purposes. I would claim no more for the systems classification than that it is more relevant to management than a division between economic/financial administration and social administration as proposed by the Fulton Committee, than categorization of posts based on specialization like financial control or personnel management, than classification by organizational form. All these approaches may for some purpose be superior to a systems classification. There may even exist some purpose which justifies categorization by activities, e.g. committee work or drafting papers. But management is not such a purpose. The role of the committee, the importance and form of drafting needed will vary significantly between management, administration and diplomatic or research systems—or should do in the interests of efficiency and effectiveness. The apparent similarity of activity may be misleading.

The basic contribution which the systems classification can make to management is that systems and sub-systems are—unlike organizations —related to an objective (or to two or more closely related objectives) and management is itself based on objectives and resource flows. It has been said that 'the systems concept is primarily a way of thinking about the job of managing'[15]: management is largely a way of thinking. The identification of the sub-system allows the different nature of its work culture and success criteria to be recognized. This is an essential pre-condition for efficiency.

SYSTEMS AND DECISION CRITERIA

The role of management in any sub-system can be identified if we bring together both the systems classification and the criteria relevant to the decisions being made within the system.

Primary task of major system
Species of sub-system
Variety of sub-system
Decision criterion (or criteria in decreasing order of importance) for analysis and process.

A coding of system and criteria in this way might provide a basis for beginning to understand the attitudes, skills and the experience or training relevant to work in particular parts of the public service. I shall therefore explore further in the next chapter some of the contrasts in attitude and skill found in three species of system (management, administration and diplomatic) and consider why the relationship between them is what it is, and whether more efficient management implies a change in this relationship.

NOTES ON CHAPTER 4

1. Robert J. Mockler, 'The Systems Approach to Business Organization and Decision Making', *California Management Review*, Winter 1968.
2. R. A. Johnson, F. E. Kast, J. E. Rosenzweig, *The Theory and Management of Systems*, McGraw-Hill, 1963.
3. W. T. Bane, *Operational Research, Models and Government*, CAS Occasional Paper No. 8, HMSO, 1968. The account of systems and models and their relationships in Professor Stafford Beer's *Decision and Control* is relevant, John Wiley and Sons, 1966.
4. 'Systems analysis is a new discipline, or, rather, a combination of disciplines. It is less than 30 years old, having originated as operational research with the British during World War II.' Joseph H. Engel, President Operations Research Society of America in letter published in *Public Administration Review*, July/August 1969, p. 433.
5. Dr A. K. Rice, *The Enterprise and its Environment*, Tavistock Publications, 1963, Chapters 2 and 21.
6. Rice, op. cit.
7. Michael Crozier, *The Bureaucratic Phenomenon*, Tavistock Publications, 1964, p. 183.
8. Roskill Commission on the Third London Airport. Papers and Proceedings. Vol. VII. *Proposed Research Methodology*. HMSO, 1970.
9. R. S. Parker and V. Subramaniam, ' "Public" and "Private" Administration'. *International Review of Administration Sciences*, 1964.
10. A. Jay, *Management and Machiavelli*, Hodder & Stoughton, 1967.
11. J. K. Galbraith, *The New Industrial State*, Hamish Hamilton, 1967.
12. Peter Drucker, 'Making the Effective Decision', *Management Today*, May 1967.
13. J. C. Swaffield in his address to the Royal Institute of Public Administration 1970 (published in *Public Administration*, autumn 1970), comments on the effect of analysis in throwing a clearer light on this central/local conflict which traditionally has been more emotive than analytical.
14. Stafford Beer, op. cit., p. 242.
15. Johnson, Kast and Rosenzweig, op. cit.

CHAPTER 5

ADMINISTRATION, MANAGEMENT AND DIPLOMATIC SYSTEMS

The person who sets out to study buildings on Manhattan on the assumption that all are alike will have difficulty in passing from the surviving brownstones to the skyscrapers. And he will handicap himself even more if he imagines that all buildings should be like brownstones and have load carrying walls and that others are abnormal. So with corporations.

J. K. Galbraith: *The New Industrial State*

Galbraith's comment is as true of public authorities as of corporations. The public service comprises a spectrum of systems, each comprising a hierarchy of sub-systems. We shall indeed handicap ourselves if we imagine that they are all, or should be, identical. Different species of system must be identified and in some cases varieties and hybrids distinguished. I have suggested in the previous chapter that this identification of systems throws light on the role of management in government. And since management is so largely an attitude of mind, a continuing concern with, interest and persistence in seeking to use resources more efficiently, I need next to explore the attitudes appropriate to certain species of systems.

A CONTRAST BETWEEN EXTREMES

I believe that a more detailed examination of the objectives, structures and processes of the two kinds of system—administration and 'pure' management—lying at the opposite ends of the spectrum can throw further light on some of the most characteristic features of the public service and of its attitude to the use of resources. The many points of contrast between an administration system and a management system include:

	Administration	*Management*
OBJECTIVES	In general terms, infrequently reviewed or changed.	Broad strategic aims supported by more detailed short-term goals and targets reviewed frequently.
SUCCESS CRITERIA	Mistake avoiding.	Success seeking.
RESOURCE USE	Secondary task.	Primary task.

	Administration	*Management*
STRUCTURE	Roles defined in term of areas of responsibility.	Roles defined in terms of tasks.
	Long Hierarchies: limited delegation.	Shorter Hierarchies: maximum delegation.
ROLES	Arbitrator.	Protagonist.
ATTITUDES	Passive: work-load determined outside system. Best people used to solve problems.	Active: seeking to influence environment. Best people used to find and exploit opportunities.
	Time insensitive.	Time sensitive.
	Risk avoiding.	Risk accepting but minimizing.
	Emphasis on procedure.	Emphasis on results.
	Conformity: national standards.	Local experiments: need for conformity to be proved.
SKILLS	Legal or quasi-legal	Economic or socio-economic.
	Literacy.	Numeracy.

I have explained in the previous chapter why the use of resources will have a different significance in an administration system than in a management system. But we should explore further some of the other points of contrast summarized above.

JUDICIAL ATTITUDES IN ADMINISTRATION

I have suggested that administration systems lie at the end of the spectrum closest to judicial systems and linked by a variety of quasi-judicial or administrative-judicial systems within the public service. It is, I believe, from the criteria and attitudes of mind appropriate to a judicial system that public service administration systems have derived many of their characteristic features:[1] it is a fact which can most readily be observed by studying the processes of government in European countries where there is no pretence that any rigid boundary separates legal from administrative processes. The greater informality of British processes of government may obscure those similarities but does not eliminate them. Both judicial and administrative systems are basically mistake-avoiding. In both, the reputations of those involved is determined by their worst mistakes not by their greatest successes. Timothy Evans; Crichel Down: who can name successes of equal weight ? There is also in both judicial and administrative systems a very clear and precise concept of a 'mistake' or 'error'. It may concern the outcome, e.g. Timothy Evans, but more frequently the incorrect use of procedure—the type of error often described as 'a miscarriage of justice' or 'maladministration'. In the latter case, a decision can while 'sensible' be 'wrong': if so, the latter takes precedence over the former. As we shall see later the concept of the 'mistake' in management is different, more complex and imprecise. Since mistakes in law and administration must be avoided, as much time can justifiably be spent in reaching decisions as is needed to reach the right decision through the correct procedure. We have, therefore, the expression in judicial and administrative circles 'no undue delay' which implies that some delay is both likely and appropriate, and that 'instant administration' like 'instant justice' is not assumed to be a desirable goal of either system. The resources used may be proportionate to time but in these areas there is no rate of trade-off at which risks of miscarriage of justice or maladministration can consciously be accepted in exchange for savings in time and thus in costs incurred.

Like the judicial system, an administrative system will tend to be both passive and defensive. Passive in the sense that the work-load (measured in both systems in terms of 'cases'), and most of the problems needing decision, tend to be determined outside the system and are neither under the control nor frequently subject to the influence of those within the system. Those employed in judicial systems do not themselves affect either the total or the variety of the cases entering the system: nor in cases requiring decision in administration systems is the total or distribution capable of control in the short-term. Only in the long-term the law or regulations can be amended, and the work-load on both judicial and administration systems changed. This passivity combined with the need to avoid mistakes has helped to produce in administration a characteristic form of organization which has been given the name bureaucratic. Long hierarchies, limited delegation, formal procedures are among the characteristics of such organizations and they provide a structure well-suited to the passive/defensive task of the administrative system.

THE DEFENSIVE STRENGTH OF ADMINISTRATION SYSTEMS

Indeed if the typical hierarchical organization chart of such a system is compared with the layout of a defensive position in depth fashionable during the Second World War—with the wide end of the organization pyramid where the clerks are communicating across the counter or by post with applicants regarded as the equivalent of the front line—the resemblance will be found to be close. Both systems operate on the basis that the front line deals with what it has the resources to handle (decision rules will define this). It is inherent in the mistake-avoiding culture of an administration system that decision rules on delegation are designed to allow the *least* competent member of the staff at that level to operate without risk of error. Except therefore in the rare situation (which requires a buyer's market for labour) of parity of competence in a given grade, frustration among the more able is often a characteristic of the lower and middle levels of an administration system. Cases regarded as too difficult for the front line are allowed to penetrate the system to be dealt with by the bigger guns in the second or third line and even farther back. Similarly the drafting of letters or statements will tend to start near the lower levels of such systems: the drafts will work their way through a variety of levels in which errors ranging from those of typing to those of law or an expression of heretical principles stand the maximum chance of detection and elimination. Such an administration system has great defensive qualities but like its military counterpart it is vulnerable in two respects. The first is that its strength is least at the boundary between two organizations particularly if they have separate communication networks. The best liaison arrangements seldom eliminate entirely this potential weakness. The second and more serious weakness is that since action originates outside the system the resources are deployed on the basis of forecasts and assumptions of where the weight of activity is likely to fall. Parts of the line will be held very lightly—with no more than an occasional patrol involved in reconnaissance, and some frontiers may not be defended at all. If a major action develops at such points the whole defensive administration system may be by-passed. With the benefit of hindsight we can now see that pollution of the environment has broken through in this way and now needs to be counter-attacked. And whereas in attack the military dictum 'always reinforce success' applies (the equivalent in management to Drucker's saying 'resources, to produce results, must be allocated to opportunities rather than to problems'), in defence and in administration it is the points of failure to which the reinforcements are rushed.

To pursue this military simile one further step we can also see a similarity between the characteristic of public service organizations to define roles in terms of 'areas of responsibility' rather than in terms of tasks to be achieved. It is similar to the concept of a military unit's defensive responsibility for a defined area of ground. With it goes an attachment to the concept of 'equal work-loads'—the idea that units of the same strength should be capable of holding a given length of front unless an exceptionally great or a negligible level of activity is forecast for that sector. And an administration system like a defensive system has always to be operational: its organization must have built in to it sufficient margin to allow it to operate without breakdown while some men are on leave or away sick. Here too the long hierarchies of the administration system can be seen to meet a need. There may be need to build other 'fail/safe' processes into administration systems, particularly when computerized.

THE REQUIREMENTS OF AN ADMINISTRATOR

It is, I believe, implicit in what I have said that to operate successfully in an administration system as in a judicial system requires men of a certain attitude of mind. Means must be seen to be as important and at times more important than ends. There is a 'right' or 'correct' decision to be found if time is taken and the correct processes of analysis applied to the case. Risks are by definition to be avoided. Legal concepts like equity, embracing such principles as the equality of all individuals before the law, natural justice and the right of the applicant to express his views before a decision is reached, must always be in the forefront of the minds of those working in administration systems. They will be reluctant to become too interested in a concept like opportunity cost if it causes them to think less of equity: they will be inclined to regard any sub-optimal resource allocation as by far the lesser evil to maladministration. While manipulation of figures will seem a skill which can be delegated and sub-delegated as far, or until, numeracy is found, the use and interpretation of the written word will seem an occupation justifying the time of even those at the highest levels. But the style is peculiar to the administration system. The aim is to achieve the unambiguous meaning in a legal sense. Brevity and clarity, in some cases all immediate communication of any kind, may be, and often are, sacrificed to this end.

If we regard the nature of decisions in an administration system as sharing many of the qualities of judicial systems it is of interest to note certain departures. Within a judicial system cases may go on appeal to several levels of the judicial hierarchy and a point of law decided at one level may be over-ruled at a higher, or even a summing up by a judge at one level found unsatisfactory at a higher, without the judicial system as a whole being regarded as having failed or adjudged guilty of error.

In quasi-judicial systems within the public service or in an administration system, like the tax system with defined appeals procedures, a similar situation arises. But in administration systems where there is no formal system of appeal other than by raising the matter with the

Minister or in the House of Commons, a peculiar feature is that the whole system tends to be, or to feel, 'committed' to the original decision however low the level at which it was decided.

MISTAKE AVOIDANCE

There are other features of administration systems which should be noted. Around the concept of the 'correct' or 'right' decision in each case the consequences of mistakes are asymmetrical. In the legal system it is an error of the utmost gravity if an innocent man is found guilty but one of much less gravity if a 'guilty' man (e.g. a man who has perhaps confessed in a statement which on legal grounds has been ruled to be inadmissible) has to be found innocent through some procedural error during the trial, and if his 'innocence' is based on a verdict of a jury there can by definition be no error in law. Within administration systems a similar asymmetry may exist. To deny a widow a pension to which she is in law entitled would rightly be regarded as a bad case of maladministration. But is it equally serious to pay a pension to a widow in a marginal and perhaps complex case if it were in the end found that legally she was not entitled to it? From one point of view the mistake could also be regarded as serious. If it creates a precedent—and not all decisions in marginal cases constitute precedents for in some the circumstances create a unique situation—the consequences could be costly. But from a wide social welfare point of view the 'mistake' may be seen as having a net social benefit. Public opinion is unlikely therefore to see such a case in the same light as the denial of a pension to a widow entitled to one. Taxation cases are handled by administration systems as I have defined them. Here too the mistake in one direction—the extraction of tax in excess of that which the tax-payer is legally liable (or the failure to refund any excess paid within a reasonable time, for in Britain the PAYE system not infrequently collects tax in excess of liability)—is regarded as a serious matter even if the amount involved is small. But is it a 'mistake' or form of 'maladministration' to fail to collect the last £5 of tax due from every taxpayer even if this means spending £50 of resources to obtain the amount due? Considerations of equity between taxpayers and arguments of the 'thin end of the wedge' kind may suggest that the system should operate on a 100 per cent collection basis. It seems unlikely that public opinion—well informed by the Press on the bankruptcy proceedings of film stars—is under any illusion that the system achieves this ideal. Public opinion may be ambivalent on whether the system should have such an objective: there might be widespread support for a greater writing off of marginal sums even if this were inequitable in favour of releasing resources to concentrate on larger cases of tax evasion which seem far more inequitable—

or in favour of simply saving resources and enabling all taxpayers to pay less tax. Administration systems which display this feature that mistakes, at least in one direction, may be of life-or-death importance, e.g. the pension to the widow, merge into other administration systems where even the worst mistake in either direction (i.e. against or in favour of the applicant) can occasion no more than irritation or minor pecuniary loss to the citizen. There are, therefore, varieties of administration system in which the cost in resources of pursuing 'mistake-avoiding' objectives in their full rigour begins to become a factor which is, or could be, relevant to decision making.

If public opinion concurs, the possibility arises of designing procedures which, while perhaps continuing to insure completely against error in one direction accepts, in order to save resources, a risk of error in the other (less important to the citizen) direction. If necessary defined bounds can be set to limit the size of error which could arise: an estimate will be made of the probability of such errors occurring. In the least judicial or least 'life-or-death' areas of administration consideration of the rate of trade-off between the use of resources and occasional minor mistakes in one or both directions could then be relevant to the procedures adopted. In many 'internal' administration activities the relevance is great, e.g. in the use of staff time on detailed checks of travelling claims to make minor adjustments, in both directions, to the calculations of the sterling equivalents of sums expended overseas in foreign currency.

Such possibilities do not change the nature of administration systems. The opportunities I have mentioned will tend to arise at the margin: looked at as a whole these administration systems will still contrast sharply with the management systems which we shall next consider. And development along these lines would involve changes in the public attitude to administration systems from which at present 'infallibility' tends to be expected: deliberately accepted fallibility within defined limits in any area might seem highly undesirable. It has begun to appear, for example, in the random sample, rather than complete, checking of accounts. But it has still far to go.

CONFORMITY AND CONSISTENCY

But we have touched on what many see as one of the main characteristics of all public service activities—the emphasis on conformity and consistency. Conformity derives from equity and takes the form of the proposition that a citizen in any part of the country should obtain precisely the same decision (in approximately the same time) as any other citizen in precisely similar circumstances, on an application to central government. Similar considerations apply within a narrower area where a local authority has the ultimate power of decision. Consistency implies that where different circumstances produce different decisions they should be 'consistent' or 'fair', e.g. if a widow with several young children receives a different pension than a widow in otherwise identical circumstances but with no children, the pension of the former should be larger than that of the latter by an amount regarded as 'reasonable'. Conformity and consistency are certainly regarded as criteria of efficiency in administration systems. (Oddly they are expected in this to be *plus royaliste que le roi* since, although the citizen expects his guilt or innocence to be independent of the location of the court in which he is charged, public opinion accepts a far wider range in penalties imposed on the guilty—and even the emergence of regional or local differences in the seriousness with which particular magistrates treat certain offences—than they would be inclined to tolerate in decisions made by government departments or local authorities.) Another criterion of efficiency in the public service is compatibility. Whereas we look generally for conformity and consistency between decisions of the same kind, i.e. made by the same system, compatibility is expected between decisions made by different systems. Detailed comparisons of different systems are difficult and frequently only a broad order of compatibility is needed, but different decisions in different systems should at least have the same sign (positive or negative) in relationship to objectives. It sounds simple: in fact it is very difficult to ensure in government and the effort absorbs significant resources.

Certainly the bureaucratic hierarchical system of organization has as one of its main strengths the ability to produce conformity and consistency. But although conformity and consistency are important in administration systems they are not features found only in such systems. They exist to greater or less extent in other kinds of system—education, hospitals, etc., and for different reasons in management systems including those run by private industrial corporations. We shall consider later why management systems may also seek conformity.

OBJECTIVES IN ADMINISTRATION

Finally, but not of least importance, we have the tendency for objectives in administration systems to be as general, as infrequently reviewed and as little used in day-to-day decision making as the mottoes which form part of the crests of the oldest British families. Even more permanent are those of judicial systems often engraved in stone over the entrances to courts. In some administration systems there may even be no explicit objectives to be discovered and the existence of implicit objectives has to be argued from the proposition that every activity must be intended to contribute to some purpose, or must at any rate have been started at some earlier period with some end in view. In this situation it is not surprising that, although administration systems may often generate vast quantities of data, there is often a lack of information which provides feedback to the system on the extent to which objectives are being fulfilled. Changes in structure and process tend to be marginal and associated with the need to find solutions to 'problems' and will often involve amendments to legislation or administrative regulations.

THE IDEAL SPECIFICATION OF A MANAGEMENT SYSTEM

I shall now analyse the requirements of an ideal management system before discussing how far in practice these features exist at present. To take up the subject of objectives which ended the review of administrative systems, we would hope to find that in management systems there was much attention to aims, goals and targets, to their definition from the highest level down to those needed as criteria for decision making at the lowest levels, since only by constant measurement against objectives can decisions involving alternative uses of resources be made better. In the definition of these objectives, in their review in the light of information feed-back on the results being achieved by the implementation of current plans, a management system would be expected to be more 'active' than an administration system. When I compare, in a later chapter, public service and business management I shall return to the implications of an 'active' approach and how far this can reasonably develop in the public service. At this stage it is sufficient to illustrate the point by saying that if a government department responsible for the design and procurement of furniture had produced a chair which was being manufactured in bulk at a very competitive price, it would be entirely consistent with an active managerial attitude for the organization to approach also, say, those responsible for schools or hospitals to see whether the same contracts could meet their needs at a saving in cost. But an 'active' approach in management should not be equated with expansion or 'empire-building'. A reputation for management should be capable of achievement in the public service, as it certainly had been in business, by contraction of unrewarding activities or by redeployment of resources. What distinguishes the active approach here is the decision to stop or reduce the use of resources on certain activities before rather than after this action has been recommended by some outside investigation and before resources have been used unrewardingly for long periods. But whether in expansion or contraction, management requires a degree of involvement and a conviction not necessarily that the objective or the plan is ideal but that at any rate the strategy (i.e. objective/plan relationship) is capable of success. Within administration systems a far more detached view of the structure and processes is compatible with success. It is not rare to find such a system in which all operating there are more conscious of its shortcomings than of its virtues. But change is not possible: time for legislation is not available or the state of public opinion makes desired changes impracticable to introduce. In the meantime administration proceeds: maladministration is avoided.

MANAGEMENT AS A SUCCESS-SEEKING TASK

The management system should also show a different attitude to 'mistakes' than an administration system and a different attitude to risk. Management systems are liable to make 'mistakes' although we need to analyse more clearly what essentially this means in a management context. But management which is judged like administration by its ability to avoid taking any decision which could later be described as a mistake, will by definition prove incompetent management. Management is concerned with success. This needs to be measured net, i.e. successes minus failures equals net achievement. The best and most highly rewarded buyers in departmental stores make some purchases which even in the January sales fail to find buyers at prices well below that paid for them. The explanation does not lie in the incompetence of all buyers which might be eliminated if, say, they were all graduates and had had to acquire a master's degree in purchasing. It lies in the existence of risk and uncertainty.

RISK AND UNCERTAINTY IN MANAGEMENT

Risk and uncertainty are seldom absent from management decisions and cannot be eliminated as risk can in administration by the use of adequate time and of the complete range of procedures or consideration at sufficient hierarchical levels. What Professor Wilson wrote[2] of management in business is also relevant to management in the public service:

'. . . at the top levels . . . the main responsibility is almost the opposite of passive safeguarding of assets; it is that of trying to increase the assets by making estimates of probability and by sharing decisions about the complex risk taking, the organized "gambling" which makes up such an important proportion of top management work.'

It is therefore essential in evaluating management decisions *ex post* to take account of the part played by risk and uncertainty. An unwelcome outcome is not synonymous in these matters with a 'mistake' any more than when the captain of a cricket team loses the toss—or even when he loses it five times in succession. And an apparently satisfactory outcome may conceal a 'mistake'—a failure by faulty analysis, delay in decision making or other reason to take full rather than partial advantage of highly favourable circumstances. And no outcome at all, because nothing has been done and no resources used, may be the worst 'mistake'—if it is ever identified. A rational approach to, and acceptance of, risks is essential to a management system in a way which contrasts strongly with that appropriate to a judicial or to an administration system. But analysis of risk and acceptance of it, is not, as is at times assumed in the public service, synonymous with recklessness. Quite the contrary—it could be argued that those who implicitly take the greatest risks in resource decisions may be those who believe that in some way tisk can be totally avoided. The problem of understanding risk and uncertainty is fundamental to management in government.

TIME AS A VARIABLE IN MANAGEMENT

This situation contributes to the different attitude to time which could be expected in good administration and in good management systems. As we have seen time is not normally critical to administration or to judicial decisions: to reach correct decisions on difficult cases time can (within certain limits) be used. Of course, an indefinite deferment of a decision in the most delayed case—or a substantial increase in the period required to reach decisions on all normal cases—could eventually come to be regarded as forms of maladministration or of miscarriage of justice. Public opinion on what are the extreme limits of what is reasonable seems to vary considerably from country to country, with opinion lying in both judicial and administration matters at the impatient end of the range in Britain by comparison with, say, some European countries. But even in Britain time will seldom have the same significance for the man operating in an administration system as it will for his colleague in management. In the latter to use time may be a way of reducing risk or uncertainty, but at the same time the opportunity which success in management is seeking to seize may be diminishing over time. Trade-off situations of this kind with time as the variable are common to management: rare (although not totally unknown) in administration, and even rarer in justice (an application for an interim injunction to prevent some imminent act is perhaps the exceptional case). A common source of irritation between businessmen and civil servants operating administrative processes arises from their quite distinct attitudes to time. To the former the latter seem unreasonably dilatory: to the latter the former seem unreasonably impatient.

CONFORMITY IN MANAGEMENT SYSTEMS

I have said earlier that an interest in conformity is not incompatible with management. Certainly one would expect to find a greater willingness to experiment in certain areas or with certain groups (the trial marketing approach) than is normally possible—or has often been attempted—in administration. But conformity in the shape of standardization, by permitting the economies of large-scale production, has an essential part to play in using resources to best advantage in the public service as in business.

ORGANIZATION FOR MANAGEMENT

I shall next consider the form of structure and the personal qualities appropriate to a management system. The traditional long hierarchical structure with limited delegation, specialists like doctors and lawyers used as advisers, divisions concentrating on finance and personal management involved in decision making rather than advisory roles, is well suited to administration. In management few if any of these features are likely to be suitable. If management is to be opportunity-taking, to be quickly responsive to changes in output needs or input variations becoming possible, more delegation is needed: this suggests shorter hierarchies for, within a hierarchy of the length which has become normal in administration, headroom for effective delegation at each level cannot be found. And whereas administration is essentially an impersonal process, management needs at times to be more personal— what can be achieved depends on the people available and a structure may need to be designed to suit the managerial style of those with exceptional ability in management. The fact that differences in management style exist has been established by studies of business: one is not necessarily to be preferred to another. Of course at times areas of management would settle down over a period and more stable and conventional forms of organization would come into being. But within large management systems one would expect to find some sub-systems organized on what writers in organization have described as 'organismic' rather than on 'mechanistic' lines. And in the former and perhaps also in the latter, we might expect to find specialists working in teams with general managers to analyse particular problems, to carry through particular projects rather than operating in separate specialist hierarchies. In management systems we would expect to find finance and establishment specialists becoming advisers to managers to whom substantial financial and personnel management authority had been delegated rather than exercising the direct decision making (or decision vetoing) authority found in administration systems. The references to 'accountable management'[3] in the Fulton Report on the Civil Service discusses these and similar criteria in some detail. There can be no doubt that a substantial measure of delegation is essential to accountability. If power without responsibility is the prerogative of the harlot, responsibility without power is that of the fool.

What of the officials needed to operate management systems? Are they likely to be much the same kind of person as those who will succeed in administration systems? It seems improbable that they are. Partly it seems a matter of temperament—the patient and prudent on the one hand: the innovator and the taker of calculated risks on the other. The herbivore and the carnivore. Partly it is a matter of interests and training—the administrator concerned with law and legal processes, with his mind turning back to precedents, the manager concerned with economics, the behavioural sciences and quantitative analysis, his mind mainly on future events and recalling the past only to act on the economist's dictum 'bygones are bygones': his interest in the law limited to ensuring that he acts within it. Some skills will be useful in both areas; those of negotiation for example. The interest of the administration system in the written word, in seeking unambiguity in the legal sense, the willingness to sacrifice ease of communication to achieve it, will not be found in the management system. The manager will put less in writing (happily realizing that to do so involves a cost and the reading of it a further cost). He will be interested in communication rather than in legal enforceability. His rules will be in the form of the 'drills' intended to ensure the safe take-off and landing of aircraft: they must be unambiguous and clear to those who act on them rather than to courts. He may doubt the value of those rules which, if observed, produce a paralysis in resource using activity. He will care little for finer points of style. But the manager will be very interested in numbers and their relationship. He may do the calculations himself (or use a terminal giving-on-line access to a computer) while delegating drafting as far, or until, literacy is found.

Despite the unfashionability of the doctrine of the all-rounder, it would be futile to deny that experience has shown that there have been, and still are, able men who operate equally effectively in each of these very different systems—and for that matter in some of the intermediate systems of the public service spectrum. But I doubt if there are many: I believe that the distinction between the administrator (as I have defined administration) and the manager (as I have defined management) is real. The Fulton Committee suggested[4] that a division of a future graduate entry to the civil service might be between those concerned with 'economic–financial/administration' and those concerned with 'social administration'. This is in some ways similar to the administration/management distinction but in other ways it differs from it. For example Fulton saw personnel management as part of social administration. I would define it as a management rather than an administration sub-system for its *raison d'etre* is surely to acquire, deploy and develop to best advantage an important category of resource—the employees of the public service. But in any case since the public service embraces far more species of system than the administration and management systems which I am contrasting here, it is likely to need men with far more than two basic kinds of skill and temperament.

MANAGEMENT SYSTEMS: THE IDEAL AND THE REALITY

So far I have been describing the ideal characteristics of a management system in the public service. This is not to claim that the public service today reveals such a marked contrast between management and administration systems. Most administration systems when identified would reveal the structures and processes I have described. But it is more difficult to generalize about management systems. If I were to choose my examples I could certainly pick out, from central and local government and other public corporations, examples of all the features I have suggested as necessary in management systems. And, although I might be hard-pressed to do so, I might even find a system or two which possessed all the required characteristics. However it must be admitted that taking central and local government as a whole an outside observer obtaining information on a random basis would be far less likely to comment on the existence of clearly differentiated management systems but on their non-existence or rarity. He might well conclude that the dominant characteristic of the public service—or at least of central and local government—was of the prevalence throughout all systems of structures, processes, success criteria and attitudes based on what I have described as appropriate to administration systems.

THE SPILLOVER FROM ADMINISTRATION PROCESSES INTO MANAGEMENT

There are a number of reasons why this situation has arisen. Administration is the older function in the public service and an increasing volume of management has over time been given to organizations planned originally for tasks appropriate to administration. It should not be thought that the growth in management in the public service has been at the expense of administrative work for this has also been increasing greatly over time. A reluctance until recently to analyse the different nature of the tasks by the systems approach or some other method has resulted in much work which is basically management, e.g. primarily concerned with the use of resources in pursuit of objectives, being regarded within the public service as suitable for regulatory and control processes. In the past, the concept of inputs in the form of resources being devoted to outputs intended to achieve defined objectives by a plan consciously selected from among alternatives and subject to review was alien to almost all sectors of the public service.

Management is basically a 'flow' concept whereas the man working in a government department or local authority has tended to think in 'stock' terms. On taking up a post he inherits a stock of employees, equipment, accommodation, implementing agreed plans and processes. The broader long-term concepts of output and of objective are often obscure. The short-term output and short-term objective is only too clear: to deal as well as possible with the daily work-load generated by factors beyond control. If the short-term pressure of work is high enough—and in the public service it usually is high enough—neither the opportunity nor the need to see the whole operation in managerial terms may arise. It is true that the need arises to think about inputs at least in the shape of money and men (other inputs like accommodation, office equipment, telephones, etc., were traditionally often treated as 'free goods'—which does not mean freely available goods). But here too the system reduced these to regulatory and control processes. Many decisions were covered by a wide variety of regulations embodied in a financial control code. Staff decisions were covered by an even greater variety of regulations embodied in a separate code of instructions. It was important in the 'mistake-avoiding' climate appropriate to an administration system that all these regulations should be followed. By this means the public service has in the past—change in this respect is now rapid—translated many managerial (resource-using) functions requiring a positive success-seeking approach into regulatory functions requiring mistake-avoiding approaches. In the public service systems the need for conformity and consistency came to be as great in its internal activities as it may have had to be, for different reasons, in its external relations: decision rules taken by some civil servant twenty years earlier but embodied in some 'code of instructions' came to be regarded as mandatory as if they formed part of an Act of Parliament. It was, I believe, primarily this development which made the public service until recently such an unfavourable environment for management and limited the development or even the identification of management systems operating quite differently from administration systems.

OTHER HISTORIC FEATURES HOSTILE TO MANAGEMENT

But there were many other factors to reinforce the traditional submergence of management. Until the reforms in the control of public expenditure began in 1960 following the Plowden Committee report, the whole process of settling financial provisions and staff complements on a short-term *ad hoc* basis with little forward planning produced much negatory work on preparing abortive schemes and tremendous emphasis on 'incrementalism': the concept of stocks as sacrosanct but subject to adjustment at the margin.

External considerations all exerted influences in the same direction. The interest of Parliament in public expenditure was basically regulatory: the worse offence was the need for an 'excess vote' after expenditure had been incurred beyond the total approved, or for purposes not authorized by Parliament. Exchequer and Audit and the Public Accounts Committee in central government and the District Auditors in local government provided a formidable machinery for the discovery, publicizing and at times punishment of 'mistakes'. No similar process for the discovery of 'successes' existed although from time to time the Select Committee on Estimates exerted a benevolent influence in this direction. The external environment was as unfavourable to management as the internal.

Finally we should note that another reason why 'mechanistic' bureaucratic organization has become dominant in public service organizations is not only because, as I have argued, administration processes have overlaid management but because this kind of organization is normally associated with great scale and with a need for conformity. Some public service organizations are very large even by comparison with business corporations and, as we have seen, conformity may be a genuine requirement of a managerial system rather than one forced on it by inappropriate administration attitudes of mind.

For all these reasons, management systems did not develop historically in the public service as clearly identifiable units with structures, processes and success criteria contrasting sharply as they should have done with those of administration systems. In a later chapter I shall refer to developments involving management which have occurred since 1960 and will show that what I have described in this chapter as the historical or traditional development is now subject to challenge and change. The Fulton Report on the Civil Service, which is strongly managerial in spirit, is likely to increase the rate of change. Indeed the problem in the future may be the reverse of the past: to ensure that what is appropriate to management systems does not become a new standard pattern forced on systems with very different tasks.

DIPLOMATIC SYSTEM

I have analysed at some length the contrast between the more extreme varieties of management and administration system. It would be tedious to analyse here in the same detail every species of system found in the public service—the research system, for example, or the professional system as illustrated by say legal advisers to a government department. But one species must be discussed in more detail for its role is decisive to any analysis of management in government—the diplomatic system.

The diplomatic system was, as I commented when I first referred to it, difficult to name. It is as difficult to describe. It is easier to state with confidence what it is not, than what it is. Certainly, if we list all the attributes of the management system, we find that the diplomatic system displays few, perhaps none, of them. The attributes of an administrative system are equally lacking in the diplomatic system. So, I am sure, are those of the research, the professional, and other species of system. The diplomatic system is certainly distinct and it must have positive characteristics as well as negative. If the man working in an administration system arrives at the office intending to deal with cases correctly, the manager hoping to use resources more efficiently, the diplomat's ambition for the day is perhaps to see an advance in the affairs in which he is involved. In some varieties of the diplomatic system—the Minister's Private Office or the secretariat of Cabinet Committees—the 'advance' may amount to little more than to keeping abreast of developments, to end the day with no more business awaiting decision: with no more, and hopefully a few less decisions 'bogged down' than at the beginning of the day. In other varieties of diplomatic system 'advance' may have a more positive implication. There would be hope of some progress in negotiations—'progress' embracing of course, the prospect of frustrating the plans of an 'opponent' (often, of course, a colleague).

In many matters to which the management and administration systems reveal different attitudes, the diplomatic system will be found to have an approach distinct from either of them. On time, the administration system is insensitive within wide limits and inclined to patience: the management system strongly committed to that time-scale which seems likely to produce the best return on the resource use, and often impatient. The diplomatic system is both less committed to a prevailing attitude and more sensitively attuned to the opportunities of fine adjustment. It will choose to operate at times with more speed than any management system: at others more slowly than any administration system even of the most judicial variety. The diplomatic system knows not merely the pros and cons of an announcement on a Tuesday rather than a Friday but those between one at eleven in the morning or four in the afternoon. On the use of the written word, the statements emanating from the diplomatic system will convey meaning more readily than those from administration, in a style to which more attention has been devoted than in those from management. There will be no apparent ambiguity. If subsequently some is found, it will not have occurred inadvertently in the competent diplomatic system. The diplomat will find statistical data and quantitative argument of less relevance to a decision than the manager, but will be more inclined to become involved with such data than the administrator—learning enough about, say, discounted cash flow to use such calculations when favourable to his case and to point out their limitations when the reverse situation arises. In personal relations, at which those successful in administration systems may be inadequate and those in management systems effective but possibly abrasive, the diplomatic system is likely to display the qualities needed to succeed in negotiations—and sooner or later every system finds that it needs to succeed in negotiation. In objectives, the diplomatic system will often emphasize very broad, long-term aims and detailed short-term tactical goals—which may not only change but can be reversed readily. Flexibility is thus another characteristic of the diplomatic system. With flexibility, the diplomatic system brings also the ability to keep a variety of middle-term strategies in a meaningful relationship to long-term objectives while continuing to be concerned in detail with the immediate interface between these strategies and the public. These areas of interest, and the attitudes and skills which they encourage, contribute to the effectiveness of most large-scale systems whether in business or in government. The relationship which develops between the diplomatic, administration, and management systems determines the character of the total system.

THE INTERRELATIONSHIP OF SYSTEM

We have observed earlier that systems and sub-systems are interrelated and that major systems may comprise sub-systems of many different species and varieties. Each may have been chosen as the most suitable form of sub-system for the task in hand. There may have been, at one stage, an evenly balanced choice between alternative strategies each of which would need to be implemented by a different form of system. There are therefore occasions to which Sisson's comment, which I quoted earlier, is apt—that the government 'provides a service' or 'applies a regulation' because it thinks that that is the best way of governing. But the character of a particular sub-system may never have been the subject of any explicit decision—it may merely have displayed a capacity for evolution in response to pressure from the environment. Or it may reflect the inclinations of those who are working in, or who once worked in, the sub-system to operate the form of system to which their own skills and experience were best suited.

But different species of sub-systems, however they have acquired their present character, may co-exist and co-operate in a stable society. Each knows its role and its place. It could be a society of parity of esteem and of parity of opportunity. We could for example, imagine a government department, comprising five major systems of distinct character, with five deputy heads, comprising say, a manager, an administrator, a diplomat, a scientist and a doctor of medicine, and of the five most recent Permanent Secretaries of the Department, one had come from each of these different species of system. As I said, we could imagine such a possibility. . . .

A more probable situation, which I would find it easier to illustrate by example, would be a system in which, despite the presence of sub-systems of many different species and variety, one sub-system had established hegemony over all others. This fact could be established by examination of the structure, by analysis of major decisions, or by a study of the background and particular skills of those appointed to be in charge of the whole system. This too could be a stable society: all know and accept their role and status. Or there could be a degree of conflict and tension between sub-systems of different kinds: within limits this too could be consistent with stability.

But we can also imagine sharper conflict: a struggle between sub-systems to establish authority. Here we can see that in such a struggle each species of system has both strength and weakness. Victory may depend on the sequence in which successive challenges are made as in the childhood game in which the hands of the two contestants represent 'stone', 'paper' and 'scissors'. And thus a common—although not universal—outcome in the public service might perhaps be a system in which the 'stone' of administration sub-systems at the middle level of the service (particularly in establishment and finance) blunts and restricts to lower levels the 'scissors' of management sub-systems, while the 'paper' of diplomatic sub-systems (I had not appreciated that this simile would prove so apt when I embarked on it!), wraps up the administration sub-system and exercises effective control at the top. In business, the imaginary outcome might be different. Here it has been conventional for administration sub-systems to be restricted to lower level clerical tasks where detailed rules allow for the work to be highly programmed—and eventually taken over by computers. Diplomatic systems are most common around middle levels in 'staff' functions such as those of personnel management and training. And at the top, the sharp blades of the management system's scissors keeps the 'paper' of these diplomatic 'staff' sub-systems under control.

If there is any substance in this fanciful concept of a traditional pecking orders of system in the public service and in business, the past decade must have seen the established order under challenge in both spheres. In business the growth of scale of the business corporation has led to a development of bureaucracy in which administration systems begin to prevail over management and in which 'staff' functions begin to influence the highest levels of decision making. And at these levels the nature of the decisions and the skills required to implement them in, say, a major international corporation begin to seem more appropriate for the man brought up in a diplomatic, than in a management, system. Civil servants may even be recruited by such corporations.

In the public service the challenge has been different. The management sub-system (in one of its several varieties) has sought to take over and transform sub-systems of other kinds or to shake itself free of their constraints by acquiring sufficient delegation (perhaps by being hived off) to take over or to influence the taking of decisions at the highest level. So far, this challenge has met with but modest success. The administration system has, as always, proved strong in defence. And the diplomatic system is well-placed to resist challenge; a fact (or a hypothesis) for which there are two alternative explanations. The first is that the diplomatic system prevails on Darwinian principles as being that best adapted to the environment. If we recall the many criteria which may, in some loosely related way, determine whether one use of resources is better than another, we may also remember that only some of the criteria are likely to reflect the interest, experience and analytical skills of the man who has developed solely within a management system. The man trained in the diplomatic system finds it easier to acquire sufficient understanding of management or economic criteria to operate in a multi-criteria environment, than the manager to acquire the knowledge and skill appropriate to the 'pluralist' criterion. If this is so, it is perhaps an inevitable consequence of a democratic society and leads to the kind of solution favoured by James Robertson in which at the centre 'secretariat' organizations (in all probability 'diplomatic' by my classification) exercise control over 'hived off' management or administration systems of substantial size and much authority but nevertheless subservient on major decisions.

The other explanation attributes the survival of the power of the diplomatic system not to any inherent suitability for the environment of the public service, but to its ability to adapt the environment to ensure its own survival. Certainly the skills of the diplomatic system would not be incapable of exercising some degree of influence over the environment if it were to prove necessary. And if I personally attach less significance to this latter possibility, it is simply because I believe that, in practice, the necessity seldom arises.

SYSTEMS AND MANAGEMENT

In this chapter I have emphasized the differences between three important species of system; how these differences affect the attitudes of those working in the systems; how these attitudes in turn influence the approach adopted to the use of resources. But nothing could be more unreal or unrewarding than to imagine that in any public service each system will be found to have in full measure all the characteristics that I have attributed here to one or other species of system. Such examples can be found. Cross the Channel and in most West European countries the administration system is available for study. It was a distinguished French civil servant[5] who described the attitude of his citizens to such systems in 1970 in such terms as:

'the slow reactions of the administration where the idea of time and its growing value for the decision or its execution are assessed by the criteria of another age. The cost of delay for the citizen ... is not entered on any file.
'the frequent loss of any faculty of initiative or any creative imaginative virtues which are submerged in the uniformity of rules and the cumbersome procedures.
'the imprecision and obscurity in the distribution of responsibilities for a decision. ...'

These remarks were made in the context of an address on the allocation and use of resources. Assessed against the performance of tasks appropriate to administration, the strengths of the French system are great and, in the opinion of some commentators, include features which Britain could with advantage copy—at least for certain administrative work. In Eastern Europe also, no more than a brief visit to a government organization is required to allow it to be placed clearly in the administration or management category. If the casual visitor encounters few diplomatic systems, it is perhaps because government departments are the wrong place to look for them. In the U.S.A. the multiplicity of agencies has allowed some to develop as single species systems and to reveal clearly their management or administration character. The visitor abroad can also track down the systems through the training provided. Identify the graduate of the *École National d'Administration* and he is likely to be employed in an administration system—unless he is in the Ministers' *cabinet* where the highest skills of the diplomatic system are evident.

By contrast the graduate of the *École Polytechnique* will be bringing professional management skills to bear on the tasks of any system in which he is employed.

Britain is not the best place to identify systems in their purer forms. There are many multi-system departments and authorities and many varieties and hybrids of system. Particular officials are less easy to identify as clearly, and perhaps irretrievably, committed to the attitudes of a particular system. But some are so committed. They find a particular work culture sympathetic and can influence their careers sufficiently to keep always within this form of system even if moving between organizations. Others feel less committed to any system but are regarded as having the attributes needed in one system but not in others. On the 'horses for courses' principle they are never posted to other forms of system. But in British central government there has been extensive cross-posting at the higher levels between the administration, management and diplomatic systems which has served to blur the outline of systems and to conceal the fact that some officials, however often they move, retain basically the same approach which may incorporate the attitude relevant to the administration, to the management or to the diplomatic system. Less frequently, a man can be found in one of these three systems who retains all the attitudes appropriate to a research system or to a professional system. The fact that there is a great variety of not precisely defined systems in government in Britain does not, in my view, make it less important to seek to discover the identity of systems and the attitudes of those within them. These in the end determine the quality with which resources are used. No amount of exhortation, instruction or techniques will have much effect if the main structure of systems does not provide a significant role for management and a rewarding career for managers.

At this stage two of the three characteristic features of management in government have been explored—the complexity and inevitable controversy associated with many decisions on the use of resources and the complexity and diversity of the systems within which the resources are deployed. It follows that, if better management is to be anything more than a catch-phrase, it can develop only from accepting and attempting to understand and master this complexity; from accepting controversy and seeking to ensure better participation by the public in management processes. It can only be discredited by efforts to impose a crude simplicity where none exists or by evading participation in the vain hope that this will avoid debate and criticism. Similarly, systems analysis makes clear that progress will be evolutionary. Management will develop from changes at the margin, by which the administration system becomes a hybrid with management, the diplomatic evolves into the diplomatic-management system and eventually perhaps into a management-diplomatic system. And, at the margin, management strategies will more often be preferred to administration or to other strategies.

In the next chapter the third important feature of government management will be considered—the difficulty of measuring success in management precisely and the lack of any sustained effort to identify it even imprecisely. I shall then consider how the public service can carry through the innovation management needs before discussing recent British experience and current prospects.

NOTES ON CHAPTER 5

1. The resemblance between administration and judicial systems has, of course, been noted much earlier, e.g. W. A. Robson, *Justice and Administrative Law*, 3rd edition, Stevens, 1951 and C. Sisson, op. cit. (Notes to Chapter 1).
2. A. T. M. Wilson, *Journal of Management Studies*, February 1966.
3. The Civil Service Report of the Fulton Committee, op. cit. (Notes to Chapter 1) Volume 1, Chapter 5, pp. 51–54.
4. The Civil Service, op. cit., Volume 1, Chapter 2, pp. 19, 20.
5. M. Philippe Huet, 'The Rationalization of Budget Choices in France', *Public Administration*, Autumn 1970. The French approach, RCB (*rationalization des choix budgetaires*), as described by M. Huet seems both to have a more logical title than the Anglo-American equivalent and to be as well-based on rationality as the title promises.

CHAPTER 6

ASSESSMENT OF PERFORMANCE IN MANAGEMENT IN GOVERNMENT

I do not greatly care whether I have been right or wrong on any point but I care a good deal about knowing which of the two I have been.

Samuel Butler

INTRODUCTION

There are some critics of the public service who would find the first part of Samuel Butler's aphorism relevant to public service management. They believe that one of the main problems lies in the low correlation between success or failure in using resources and success or failure in careers. But many in the public service would see the problem as lying in the second area—unless it can be known whether a management decision proves right or wrong or, as it would be preferable to say, for better or for worse, the basis for either the system or the individual 'caring' hardly exists. In Chapter 3 I was concerned mainly with the problem, which arises at the point of decision, of assessing whether one use of resources, one management decision, will be better or worse than another. The problem that now needs to be considered is whether, after the decision has been implemented, the new outcome is preferable to the previous one; whether hypothetical outcomes which would have resulted from alternative strategies can still be compared with the actual outcome; and whether the result of change in the use of resources can be measured in any way and degrees of improvement or deterioration quantified. And in more static situations, how is the level of efficiency in management to be evaluated?

There is no general law which associates complexity at the decision making stage with complexity in evaluating the outcome. Some find calling on the toss of a coin a 'difficult' decision. Most of us would find complex a decision on a best strategy for submitting bids for auction by tender of lots which may yield oil. But the coin falls. The tenders are opened and oil is or is not found later under a particular lot. The outcome is less difficult to determine than was the decision to take. In other cases the position is reversed. There may be a clear case for investing in some new piece of heating equipment which has well-established claims to save fuel. It is installed. But next winter is not identical to last winter, more buildings are attached to the system although some existing accommodation is less fully used. Has the investment yielded the expected

114

return ? It may have done so although the total fuel bill increases—or have failed to do so even if fuel costs fall. Evaluation is not impossible but it will be more complicated and imprecise than at the decision stage. This last example is typical of a common situation in public service management and indeed in many experiments in the social sciences. Conceptually it is possible to analyse in advance the probable effect of changing one variable assuming that others remain constant. In real life and when the decision is implemented or experiment conducted, the other variables change also. Nor are investment decisions in business exempt from this particular problem. The analysis *ex ante* is often far more sophisticated than the evaluation *ex post*—if indeed the latter process occurs at all For however thorough the ante-natal examination, the post mortem is dispensed with while the subject seems in reasonable health or can be asserted plausibly to have died of natural causes.

But despite the absence of any general law to the effect, experience suggests that the problems of evaluating decisions on resource use in the public sector will on balance be greater, rather than less, than those on taking the decisions. There are exceptions. As we have seen in Chapter 3 some changes to achieve first level improvement in management of the constant output/lower input kind seem simple to evaluate although, as I have indicated, the apparent simplicity may be misleading. And measurement of success may not always possess the precision claimed. A scheme proposes that a constant output of typing can be achieved with fewer staff by transferring some 'allocated' secretaries to typing pools. The change is made. The output in volume is maintained. Success, measured with precision in savings achieved, is claimed. But perhaps some marginal loss in time to managers or in accuracy of output has been overlooked and the fact that over a period some of the most competent secretaries, who do not like working in pools, may leave and be replaced by less competent may also fail to be brought into the account. So that even the simpler kinds of evaluation may need 'confidence limits' or 'error estimates' set against quantitative results. And the outcome of a rejected plan cannot normally be assessed *ex post*—whether in this example contracting out all the typing to an agency would in the event have been more successful.

WHAT IS TO BE ASSESSED?

Before exploring more complicated forms of evaluation there is one more simple issue which needs to be considered. Traditionally evaluation of performance in resource use in the public service has been based on the search for mistakes—either of the *ultra vires*, failure to obtain the required parliamentary authority, kind in central and local government, or the failure of budgetary control system kind, e.g. a project estimated to cost *a* in year *x*, was actually costing 2*a* in year *y*, and 3*a* on completion in year *z*. And certain proposals for improving evaluation of the type sometimes described as 'efficiency audit' would often better be described as 'inefficiency audit' for, if not conducted on a random basis, the tendency seems to be to direct these audit resources to areas where it may seem *prima facie* that something is wrong rather than to areas where efficiency seems to be high and where therefore there might be lessons of more general application to be learned. All of these 'critical' activities are necessary in the public service. Their equivalent can be found in business where, however, certain checks and balances are found which are missing in the public service. For example, while the production of a film like *Cleopatra* may be a nightmare from the point of view of budgetary control the emphasis placed on this in any final evaluation could hardly be unaffected by whether in the end it produced a high return on the investment. And throughout business the hunt for inefficiency can be conducted against the background that good management will reflect itself usually (although not inevitably) in good, measurable and attributable results. But owing to problems of assessing, measuring or valuing outcome or even output in many public service activities this background of achievement recording is absent and a concentration on the search for and exposure of failure or error creates an environment in which mistake avoidance becomes regarded as the equivalent of success.

BALANCE IN EVALUATION

I start therefore with the proposition that management evaluation in the public service must develop on the principle of 'balance'—as much effort must be devoted to establishing, publicizing and learning from efficiency as from inefficiency, from success as from failure. Of course externally a balance of publicity is unattainable. Public servants waste money will always be man biting dog: public servants save resources will always be dog biting man. This must be accepted. But internally it is of the greatest importance that efficiency in management should be as identifiable as success has been in some of the tasks appropriate to diplomatic or administration systems.

IMPLICATIONS OF RISK AND UNCERTAINTY FOR EVALUATION

Secondly it is important to establish that evaluation is concerned with the assessment of good or bad management, better rather than worse decisions in the use of resources, competent rather than incompetent implementation of decisions. This is not the same as to seek 'success' or 'failure', if we identify such terms with 'a predicted satisfactory outcome' or 'an unpredicted unsatisfactory outcome' respectively. Many decisions on resources in the public service are made, as in business, in the terms of game theory against an opponent—a state of nature or a person, group, perhaps a nation. Their actions and reactions cannot be known but can only be forecast subject to varying degrees of risk or uncertainty. In such situations good management will always produce some bad outcomes: bad management some good outcomes. What better management hopes to achieve is an increase in the proportion of good outcomes to bad. This recognition of risk and uncertainty as an element in public service management is again, I suggest, fundamental to any helpful development of evaluation. It is a point to which I shall return.

FORMS OF EVALUATION

Evaluation can be made of outcome or, if too difficult, of output (with assumptions that the output–outcome relationship is that predicted); it can be based on effectiveness of outcome (or of output) or of efficiency (either outcome–input ratio or output–input ratio); and will usually fall into one of three varieties:

> measurement against an absolute standard
> comparative measurement of achievement
> measurement of direction and extent of change over time.

And the scale of evaluation can range from, say, the whole public service, through the civil service or a government department or through major and minor systems down to sub-systems or one component of a sub-system performing a single task.

A study of this wide range of possibilities is needed to decide firstly the form and scale of evaluation which would be most relevant to good management and secondly the kind of evaluation which is likely to be practicable. It will be found that the slight coincidence between the two is a major problem. But to start with the ideal, I suggest that the most meaningful form of evaluation would be outcome efficiency measured against an absolute standard. To know of any resource use that it is 80 per cent or 20 per cent efficient against an absolute standard would be as useful to the manager as such knowledge is to the engineer in certain fields, even if for both the ideal of 100 per cent efficiency will in practice always be unattainable. With this knowledge the evaluation of both comparative and temporal change would be far more meaningful than without them. For to know no more than, that in some resource use, Britain seems to be about 5 per cent more or less efficient than France or

2 per cent more or less efficient than it was twelve months earlier provides reassurance similar to that which a car driver can get from looking at the car ahead or at his speedometer when his main anxiety is that at the last junction his wife, who was reading the map, diverted him down the wrong road!

But however desirable absolute standards of performance might be they neither exist nor are they likely to exist. Conceptually it might be possible to envisage the level of efficiency in which all staff were as competent as the present level of the best, the organization so effective that even management consultants recommended no change, the best strategies were being pursued by methods incorporating all the most relevant techniques with as much and as accurate information as was attainable. But it is only necessary to consider in more depth and detail even a single element in this 'ideal norm' for the vagueness and imprecision to emerge, and its unsuitability as a base for any quantitative assessment of performance to become clear. In practice it is as necessary to settle for second best measures of performance as it has proved to be to seek second best solutions in allocating resources.

ENQUIRY AND MEASUREMENT

The process of evaluation may be based primarily on the production and publication of quantitative data which conveys, or purports to convey, information about performance with no, or little by way of, explanatory statement in support of the figures; or it may be primarily by way of enquiry or investigation in which information, much of which may not be in quantitative form, is collected, discussed and analysed and a judgement on performance formed. The two approaches are not mutually exclusive. Rarely will quantitative data in itself provide sufficient information for evaluation. The accounts of business companies, for example, normally need to be interpreted in the light of the Chairman's statement and frequently to be subject to detailed study and comment by business investment analysts before conclusions on the standard of performance can even begin to be drawn. Similarly enquiries will often benefit from quantitative data on certain matters, even when the basis of evaluation is not predominantly quantitative.

I suggest that in the public service much more emphasis will need to be applied to enquiry and investigation and less to judgement based on quantitative data than is the case, say, with the evaluation of management in business corporations—or as would be the case if company law in all countries required published accounts to reveal the detail required now in some countries. In almost all systems and sub-systems where management is not the primary task, enquiry is likely to be needed to establish the degree of efficiency in the use of resources. Even for management systems where the criteria on which decisions are taken include, with significant weights, 'the national interest' or 'a consensus in negotiation' evaluation is likely to need enquiry. It is difficult to envisage any form of quantitative data revealing the extent to which the fulfilment of these particular decision criteria had reached, exceeded or fallen short of that expected. To eliminate these criteria from the assessment of performance, while basing decisions on them would, as I have suggested earlier, be a form of irrationality. In the end, therefore, it is only where the sole or predominant decision criterion is B (the business or commercial) or E (the cost–benefit analysis) that quantitative assessment with some explanatory material may in theory provide a valid basis for evaluation of management efficiency. But even in these areas, when we study the type of quantitative data actually available, the validity of the information will often be suspect.

The forms which quantitative data may take are many, but among those most commonly found are:

Annual Commercial Accounts

Clearly these are likely to be most useful where the B (business) criterion predominates. They could also be appropriate for E (cost–benefit) criterion systems provided that social benefits not reflected in direct receipts are the subject of cash payments into the system and vice versa for social costs. If these 'social' payments are not made but introduced into the figures as notional adjustments or as footnotes to the accounts, the whole operation is likely to acquire a high degree of unreality.

Even if this risk is avoided it seems unlikely that such accounts will ever convey unequivocal information about management efficiency. They will be the outcome not merely of the efficiency of management but of price and investment decisions which may have been imposed on the organization (perhaps in the national interest), of the capital structure and of changes in the market and in other parts of the environment. In the end, therefore, valid evaluation is likely to demand enquiry to distinguish, if it is indeed possible to distinguish, the effect of these various factors.

Ex Post *Appraisal of Investment Projects*

This is certainly one of the most meaningful and realistic forms of evaluation since precisely the same criteria may be applied *ex post* as *ex ante*. But it is not one of the more simple for, as I have mentioned, variables which were assumed constant at the decision making stage will have changed when the return on the investment comes to be measured. Changes in price levels over time demand complicated adjustments to figures. It would certainly be unwise to take at face value the claimed rate of return if assessed by those who had originated the investment. Here too some form of enquiry is likely to be needed.

Unit Costs—Measured against Output (Commonly) or Outcome (Rarely)
These may consist of a time series of comparative costs within a single sub-system or a single date comparison between unit costs of producing an identical (*sic*) output in different sub-systems. Data of this latter kind in the public service are the equivalent of those made available through various forms of inter-firm comparison to business management. The general approach extends down to forms of clerical work measurement[1] where the output of the individual rather than the system is evaluated. This form of quantification (other than of the clerical work measurement variety) may raise difficulties:

(a) Temporal comparisons, if one or both parts of the ratio are in money terms, encounters the problems of changes in the levels of prices. If comparisons are to be at a 'constant price' level, it may be difficult to find the appropriate price deflator. A general index of prices may seem irrelevant to a single specialized activity, while a price index confined to the particular output concerned could produce some paradoxical results if the public service were the sole, or virtually the sole, producer of the output concerned. For an index of school building costs, for example, an index of wholesale prices might be too general, of school construction costs so narrow as to involve circular argument. An index of costs of all construction projects might be the best available.

(b) Single-period inter-system comparisons avoid the price problem, but only to encounter the difficulty found in some inter-firm comparisons that the unit of output is not in fact identical, that the figures are not, as hoped, all calculated on exactly the same basis (particularly on matters like the allocation or non-allocation of overheads) and may reflect differences in technology rather than differences in efficiency.

In both forms of comparison the problem of defining 'quality' is serious.

In general, unit costs will provide a haystack of data concealing a few needles of information which diligent search may reveal.[2] Provided that the figures circulated or published represent data prepared for other purposes, e.g. for internal management or for 'regularity' forms of accounts, it may be worthwhile circulating them even on the assumption that 90 per cent of the data will convey no meaning to anyone, and that 5 per cent will be either ambiguous or positively misleading. For instance what conclusion should be drawn from data which show that the daily cost of feeding a patient is 50 pence in one hospital, only

40 pence in another or that the ratio of staff costs to total expenditure in a public authority has fallen from 14.2 per cent to 13.7 per cent? If, however, additional costs are to be incurred in collecting and analysing such data specially in the interests of evaluating efficiency, 'costing the costing' becomes relevant. After a trial period, the significance of the data for evaluation needs to be investigated; by enquiry.

THE NEED FOR NEW PROCESSES OF ENQUIRY

I return to the point that while more and better quantified information may help investigation to evaluate management efficiency, it will seldom be a substitute for it. The main need is therefore, for more and better processes of enquiry. At present the Public Accounts Committee fills the role in Britain but mainly in the 'regulatory', 'budgetary control' fields and from the 'error discovering' approach appropriate to such work. I have already argued the need for 'balance' in evaluation. An extension of processes of enquiry must not only concentrate on management efficiency but seek to establish success and publicize the results as fully as failure.

The process is likely to need two elements—evaluators and analysts. The evaluator could be a person or a group such as a committee. He or they should certainly take evidence both from the decision makers in the system or sub-system under evaluation and from those affected directly or indirectly by the outcome produced by the use of resources concerned; and from independent observers who believe that the decision criteria or the strategy are right or wrong. Analysts would work in support. Various ways in which the two main requirements could be met include:

Evaluation

Public Accounts Committee
Select Committee on Estimates operating in Sub-Committees
Management Consultants
Ad hoc enquiries conducted by a specially appointed person, Committee or, say, University Department.

Analysis

The development of an efficiency audit capacity in the Exchequer and Audit Department
> or in some specially constituted central units for central and local
> government or the health service
By management consultants (including, of course, the capacity in this area of some of the leading firms of accountants)

By individual advisers or analysts appointed by the evaluation body
By university departments or research organizations.

Another important development in this area is that of PAR (Programmes
Analysis Review) which I shall return to discuss in Chapter 9. This will
provide for the review in depth of continuing programmes for the use of
resources for given ends. It is likely to allow past achievement, as well as
future plans, to be evaluated.

If success is to be established, failure exposed, what is essential is that
the enquiry capacity should be adequate to look into *all* forms of resource use with sufficient frequency to generate the attitudes of mind
appropriate to efficient management. This certainly does not mean
annually. But intervals of five years or more would mean that managers
would be posted into and out of sub-systems without any external
evaluation. Nor does it mean that every sub-system will need investigation in the same detail or at the same frequency.

Assuming that the present work of the Public Accounts Committee,
which would in no way be diminished by the proposals under discussion, would continue to absorb fully the time available, the most likely
form of development would be through the Select Committee on
Estimates[3] which has in the past carried out this type of investigation
into certain forms of resource use. The establishment of a committee to
concentrate on the nationalized industries[4] has within this area undertaken a task very similar to that proposed generally. But no analytical
capacity has been available to committees, although recently a single
consultant has been appointed *ad hoc* as adviser to some sub-committees.
Such appointments might continue to be valuable even if facilities for
detailed analysis and investigation became available, either through the
development of the Exchequer and Audit Department into efficiency
audit (for which E. L. Normanton has argued in a recent book[5]), through
other central audit units or through the commissioning of consultants
or research organizations. Perhaps all have a role to play, with university departments or research organizations concentrating on areas where
there is a complicated decision function and where the weights given to
the different criteria need to be brought under review, while management consultants report on some of the main B and E criteria based
areas of resource use, and the Exchequer and Audit Department on
others.

But the use of parliamentary committees has been subject to certain
constraints associated with their appointment for a single session which
in some subjects may provide insufficient time for the commissioning
and discussion of essential research and analysis. A two-year 'rolling
programme' of enquiries would overcome this problem. In the past
decade public expenditure control has been converted from a single

year to a rolling programme basis. The infinite flexibility of the British machinery of government is no doubt capable of achieving the same benefits in evaluation. For local government, and any other parts of the public service not subject to even the degree of parliamentary control appropriate to the nationalized industries, special processes would have to be worked out.

My conclusions are that performance in management is at present subject to inadequate evaluation other than on the 'first level' basis of trying to achieve a given output with fewer resources. We are moving into a period in which far more quantitative data in the form of accounts or unit costs may become available. I am sceptical whether these will in themselves contribute much to the evaluation of management, although they may provide some of the information needed for enquiry which seems the most suitable form of evaluation. It will be imprecise. But it need not be unfair. Above all it needs to achieve a balance between recording success and exposing failure.

NOTES ON CHAPTER 6

1. For an account of clerical work measurement in the public service see L. C. Harmer, *Clerical Work Measurement*, CAS Occasional Paper No. 9, HMSO, 1968.
2. The Treasury published *A Selection of Unit Costs in Public Expenditure* (HMSO, 1968). The figures attracted less attention than expected. But as the introduction by the Management Accounting Unit of the Treasury stated: 'It would be easy in a number of cases to draw wrong conclusions about either efficiency or standards from a comparative study of cost figures only in different years or different regions. The factors underlying the differences may be complex. The costs are simply an important starting point for further enquiry.' It may be doubted whether some of the data even stimulated enquiry.
3. This section was written before a major development of the select committee system of the House of Commons was announced early in 1971.
4. On the valuable role of the Select Committee on Nationalized Industries in compelling a public discussion on criteria see the article: 'The Government must pay the public piper' by Ian Mikardo, MP (Chairman of the Committee 1966–70) in *The Times*, April 19, 1971.
5. E. L. Normanton, *The Accountability and Audit of Governments*, Manchester University Press, 1966, Chapters VI, IX and XIII.

CHAPTER 7

CHANGE IN THE PUBLIC SERVICE

In government change is suspected, though to the better.
Francis Bacon

CHANGE AND MANAGEMENT

Better management will require change. Different strategies will produce different outputs to achieve a better outcome. The change involved will concern both those within the system and externally those affected by the outcome. Or the same output may be produced by a different organization, using different processes. The consequences of change will be felt mainly within the system. There are some who see the public service as designed to have, or as having acquired, the maximum possible resistance to change and thus to improved management. Within the public service the position may seem different with change, in one form or another, as not merely a common but as an over-frequent event which in itself may inhibit efficient management. This issue should be explored in the light of the growing theoretical and descriptive literature on change or innovation (I use the two words as synonyms) in large organizations.[1]

I shall explore first whether the public service is an environment more hostile to change than other forms of organization and, if there are factors which discourage change, discuss how they can be overcome. I shall then consider problems of determining the right scale of innovation and of the degree of importance to be attached to avoiding sub-optimal change. Then I shall consider whether all organizations have a limited capacity for change over a given period, for it has been suggested that in the public service this capability tends to be pre-empted by political or major forms of organizational change not directly related to better management. I shall suggest that the indirect costs and benefits of change need to be assessed in considering proposals and refer briefly to some problems of the relationship between time and change.

MAJOR AND MINOR CHANGES

I shall be concerned with major identifiable changes requiring a considerable time (in some cases several years) to implement. But this is not to be taken to imply that I believe them to be generally more important than the cumulative effect of the innumerable minor day-to-day changes in organization, process, staffing or the quality of decision making, many of which escape attention entirely, while others receive no more than momentary notice in circulars of even more ephemeral interest than most. Minor changes occur continuously—sometimes inadvertently, sometimes with intent. From a management point of view, some prove to be for the better; some are intended to be for the better but prove for the worse; and some are just for the worse (the loss of a man who cannot be replaced by one as able). If over time the proportion falling into the first category can be increased at the expense of the other two, the result, 'the small increment of extra performance diffused over a large number of individuals at all levels of the organization',[2] may be as valuable as major changes. But it is on major changes that I shall concentrate in this chapter.

THE ENVIRONMENT FOR CHANGE

Professor Kenneth Arrow has described[3] as 'an important empirical truth, especially about legislative matters' that 'the *status quo* does have a built-in edge over all alternative proposals'. He was referring to the situation that can arise through voting procedures when no one of several proposals for change can command a majority but to continue the present course of action (or inaction) does not require a majority (or a vote). Similar circumstances may occur widely in the public service, not merely in legislative matters or by way of formal voting processes, through the need to ensure a wide measure of consistency in decisions internally (e.g. between government ministries or different departments of a local authority) and the frequent need to debate proposals for change publicly and win a sufficient degree of support for them. This internal and external support may be lacking in the required degree, even where satisfaction with the present situation is slight or non-existent. And the cost (in terms of resources to be used) of seeking to acquire, by persuasion and negotiation, the internal and external support needed may, in cases of proposed minor improvements, make it irrational to pursue them, for the expected benefits may not exceed the combined costs of negotiating and implementing the change.

Some academic writers see this situation not only as one that exists but one that should rightly continue to exist. Professors M. Buchanan and G. Tullock,[4] for example, have claimed that:

'We must sharply differentiate between two kinds of decisions: (1) the positive decision that authorizes action for the social group and (2) the negative decision that effectively blocks action proposed by another group.'

On this Arrow[5] commented that:

'The asymmetery between action and inaction is closely related to their [Buchanan and Tullock] support of unanimity as the ideal criterion of choice: under such a rule the *status quo* is a highly privileged alternative.'

and that:

'There is a fundamental divergence of opinion, which has not been fully recognized, on whether or not social choices should be historically conditioned or equivalently, whether or not inaction is an alternative different from other alternatives.'

Arrow expresses his own opinion that:

'. . . there is no special role given to one alternative because it happens to be identical to or derived from a historically given one'.

My own position on this is the same as that of Arrow. I believe that processes to counteract any bias in favour of the *status quo* are likely to be valuable.

DECISION MAKING AS A CONTINUOUS PROCESS

To overcome this constraint on change, it is necessary to encourage in the public service an attitude to decision making which sees it as a continuous series of choices made over time rather than as an exceptional and infrequent event which occurs only at the point in time at which a decision initiates a change. Under any control system, say, at a very simple level, a thermostat in a heating system, information about temperature is being processed continuously against the objective of maintaining the temperature at a given level. 'Decisions' to operate or not operate the equipment are made continuously not merely when it is switched on or off. In the same way, in public service decisions, it would be more accurate to speak not in terms of deferring a decision until . . . but of taking a decision to continue the present strategy (or to do nothing) until. . . . It is surprising how, if the choice is presented in this way, the balance of advantage can sometimes seem different. The bias the *status quo* enjoys over alternative proposals may not survive a demand that its continuation be affirmed positively. At least that has been my experience.

HEDGES IN PLANS

Another approach which can benefit the prospects of change against the built-in advantages of the *status quo* is the development of strategies for change which contain built-in hedges against future risks and uncertainty. On this, I agree with James Schlesinger,[6] 'a good plan should be viewed as a complicated structure to foster intelligent hedging. It ought not to be viewed as a prescription of future activities.' It is a characteristic demand made of proposals for change that they should be able to be proved effective against every possible future event—even if the existing strategy can be seen to be ineffective even in the event of the sun rising tomorrow. The use in change of a phase by phase approach to decision making (decision tree), in which at each stage two or more options are open as further information becomes available, can greatly increase the prospects of starting a strategy of change—particularly if one of the options open at the end of phase I is a return to the *status quo* at no, or minimal, cost in resources. However unlikely it may seem that the option will be exercised, its existence is as reassuring to the decision maker as the life-boats on a ship to the passenger.

THE ZERO BASE REVIEW

A third approach designed to offset bias in favour of the *status quo* in the allocation of resources is what the Americans describe as the 'zero base review'—a refusal to regard the present use of resources as being largely outside the field of review and thus to confine debate to incremental adjustments. Under this approach the assumption is that no resources will in future be allocated to the particular programme unless it can be shown to be justified, and the scale of resource use justified, in relation to alternative uses of the resources. This is a painful process which even in the most favourable circumstances will generate far more emotional conflict and friction than incremental negotiations. To be worth doing at all such reviews need to be based on thorough preliminary analytical studies. They cannot, therefore, be repeated frequently. Professor Robert Anthony[7] suggests at five-yearly intervals, but I suspect that there are a number of areas where a major review of this kind once a decade would be sufficient. To generate such reviews as normal rather than exceptional procedures it has been suggested that approvals to use resources in pursuit of a given end should, like passports, lapse automatically after a defined number of years. It would not normally be appropriate for statutory authority for a service to lapse also: the 'cost' of renewing it might be even more substantial than that involved in negotiating agreement to use resources on it for a further period. Here, too, the approach described as PAR (Programmes Analysis Review) should be helpful for it incorporates the 'zero base' attitude.

So far I have been discussing the possibility of a bias in favour of the *status quo* in the use of resources and suggested how it could be overcome. But a further obstacle to change of one kind—in organization and the deployment of human resources—may arise from the scale, and the bureaucratic characteristics associated with it, of many public bodies.

Michel Crozier points out[8] that bureaucratic organizations resist change longer than non-bureaucratic and that limited delegated authority will frequently require a decision in favour of change to be taken at the top of the organization. But 'people on top theoretically have a good deal of power. . . . But these powers are not very useful since people on top can act only in an impersonal way and can in no way interfere with the subordinate strata. . . . If they want to introduce change they must go through the long and difficult ordeal of a crisis.' Crozier points out that wars and social and political crises provide favourable opportunities for long overdue change. Quite so: but since some social disbenefits arise, there is need of an alternative. Fortunately it exists in the form of one of the many bodies of independent or external enquiry, for example, the royal commission or the Select Committee on Estimates. These bodies, like the management consultants who advise large business corporations, often recommend changes that some of those responsible within the organization wished to implement but in order to do so needed the weight of external support, or pressure, to overcome opposition or inertia.

In public service bureaucracies, although not necessarily in business bureaucracies, another factor that discourages change is that the work culture and the reward system (which does not of course mean exclusively or even primarily pay) is discouraging to change in which risk is involved, in which success may be difficult to quantify and evaluate particularly where the goal is an improvement in efficiency rather than in effectiveness—the quality of the output. Let sleeping dogs lie is persuasive when one is on a bite to nothing. This is one reason why change is less likely to be initiated within public service organizations than in business.

FACTORS FAVOURABLE TO CHANGE

But the public service has some factors favourable to change to set against the obstacles mentioned. It has been suggested[9] that a new government department can be created from parts of several existing ministries more quickly and smoothly than a similar re-organization could be achieved in a large business corporation. This is attributed to the career structure, pay and grading of the civil service, which not merely safeguarded employment and salary level of those involved in a change, but also safeguarded their status. A grade like 'Assistant Secretary', whether in one department or another, conveys unambiguous information about status in a way that the use in a business corporation of a title like 'Divisional Manager' does not. And the fact that transfers between departments at the higher levels has now become normal rather than exceptional has created a 'task force' attitude which allows human resources to be re-allocated much more easily. Within a department the regularity and frequency of transfers between posts at most levels, at least in the civil service (less so in some other parts of the public service) may in the past, as the Fulton Committee claimed, have made the average time spent in a post too short for maximum efficiency. But this has at least reduced the personal, as opposed to professional, involvement of those critical of proposed changes in opposing their implementation.

It is also the case that, in Britain, the environment is far more favourable to innovation in the public service than in most other countries. The remarkable informality of British procedure allows many changes like the creation or abolition of government departments, changes in recruitment, training, pay and career development practices, changes in contract and purchasing procedures to be made more quickly and without the elaborate legislative formalities that in certain countries makes the cost of introducing modest changes outweigh the benefits expected from them. Even such few formal constraints as exist, including one as apparently formidable as the fact that annually Parliament authorizes the Government to raise taxation and to incur expenditure for no more than one year ahead, which could be inimical to the effective use of resources if applied rigidly (e.g. that no government department could enter into leases or contracts extending over more than twelve months), are not in practice applied in this way. In management Britain should be able, therefore, to achieve better results than many other countries: there are no constitutional excuses for failure.

Another factor which not only helps the British public service by comparison with those of other countries but favours it over business corporations is the Whitley tradition of consultation between the 'official' and 'staff' sides, which is found in varying forms in central and local government and in the health service. Although the Fulton Committee suggested[10] that the Whitley system had been 'allowed to operate in ways that hamper effective management' they thought 'these defects . . . in no way inherent in the Whitley system itself'. Certainly it would be difficult to maintain that staff associations or Whitleyism constitute hurdles which are difficult to clear by those who can establish that change will improve the use of resources. Indeed there have been some changes in the civil service, e.g. the expansion of management training, where the staff associations were the protagonists. Some business corporations would be willing to exchange their constraints in this area for those of the public service.

My conclusion is that as an environment for change the public service has, by comparison say with industry, some advantages and some disadvantages. The latter, if recognized, can be overcome, in part at least, by methods such as those I have mentioned. And if in the end a degree of resistance to change survives, it need not be regarded too tragically. A cult of change can develop in which those who support every proposal for change seem clearly qualified to be promoted while those who oppose any proposal for change seem obsolescent. A certain minimum level of resistance to change within organizations fulfils the same purpose as the force of gravity on planets: its total absence would increase not decrease problems. A public service operating on an Orwellian maxim 'Any change, good: all change, better' would be unlikely to seem an improvement to the community. But the probability attached to this risk need not discourage an interest in change in present circumstances.

SUB-OPTIMAL CHANGE

The scale of change is another problem that has acquired importance particularly in business management circles. In some business management schools the rooting out of sub-optimal change seems as important as the eradication of heresy seemed to the Inquisition. The changes in the public service in the past decade can be said to have been sub-optimal in the sense that they have affected the part rather than the whole of systems and that their co-ordination and integration has often been absent. But the public service should not confess and recant too readily for the fact that improvements in its management have been recently, and may continue to be, sub-optimal. Any strategy of change qualifies for the term sub-optimal if looked at from sufficient breadth of view, and in the history of the human race only perhaps the change described in the first verses of the Book of Genesis can claim to be free of sub-optimality. Even that did not rule out difficulties arising subsequently in the system—as those who have read on will know.

But, while I do not personally use 'sub-optimal' as a term of abuse, it is certainly true that the return from an investment in change may be highly sensitive to scale, composition and sequence. At the experimental stage very small changes directed to a single or narrow range of variables may be justified but once the information from this equivalent of a pilot plant, a test marketing, has been attained, the scale may need to be substantially increased to produce the best outcome. Here as elsewhere there may be economies of scale but beyond a certain point diseconomies arise for reasons I shall discuss later. Judgement on where this point lies is both difficult and critical.

In considering the best scale on which to implement change, it should be kept in mind that there may be thresholds in the scale of change which have to be crossed if effectiveness is to increase. An interesting point of view[11] is that of Dror:

'A less optimistic implication of the systems view of public policy making is that improvements must reach a critical mass in order to influence the aggregative workings of the system. Improvements which do not reach the relevant impact thresholds will at best be neutralized by countervailing adjustments of other components.'

Both parts of this comment are interesting—the threshold concept and the idea of countervailing adjustments tending to neutralize minor improvements which would suggest a running-up-the-down-escalator situation for the unfortunate public service in which the *status quo*, wherever it survives, produces a gradual deterioration in performance. Certainly in management training it is possible to see the validity of the threshold concept—the occasional man attending a course from one level of an otherwise untrained hierarchy may have little effect: if the whole hierarchy or better the whole sub-system or system understands the new concepts, techniques or approaches the impact of the training on effectiveness could be considerable. But I am not aware of evidence which would tend to confirm or refute the general validity of the threshold concept in management change, although intuitively—thinking of the need to change a work culture—it seems plausible. Even less is known about the evidence of 'effectiveness drift'—in either direction—in the public service. In industry, operatives using the same machines for some years show increased not reduced productivity over time since familiarity breeds minor skills and know-how, not contempt. It seems plausible that the same considerations would apply in many areas of the public service particularly in administration systems where familiarity with often complicated regulations and decision rules should over time increase output. It does not therefore seem obvious that an improvement in, say, the allocation and use of resources in a single system like defence takes place against a background of a gradual decline in management performance or should generate reductions in performance elsewhere (if this is the implication of Dror's use of the word countervailing).

It is also important to consider whether change in the interests of better management should concentrate on one of the many 'areas' to which innovations could be directed, with a view to dealing sequentially with other areas if indeed they are seen to need change. Or whether it is better to pursue from the outset a strategy in which several or all the areas are changed at the same time. These areas of change include:

(i) major organizational change at the higher levels of the system;
(ii) minor organizational change at one or several lower levels of sub-systems;
(iii) changes in senior appointments;
(iv) changes in junior appointments;

(v) changes in personnel management—recruitment, career development, training;

(vi) changes in process to bring objectives and major strategies under review and change where necessary;

(vii) changes in process or decision making within given strategies (first level improvement in management).

Ideally major changes should often affect all these areas. But the problems, of planning and implementing change which is large both in scale and breadth, are so severe that often change will be planned and implemented sequentially. If this occurs, the logical sequence would seem to be

(vi)—because from this will emerge the species of system needed to carry through the strategies adopted

(i) and (iii)—so that those in charge of the organization will be associated with its planning

(ii) and (iv)

(v)

(vii)

It would perhaps be rare to find change in the public service which followed at all closely the order which I have suggested as logical. Almost every permutation can be found in practice with perhaps a tendency for (v) and (vi) to start rather than complete the sequence. On occasion they both start and complete it!

DISECONOMIES OF SCALE AND INTEGRATION

The resources needed to implement a series of integrated large-scale changes may be far greater than that needed to introduce an equal number of non-integrated changes. Innovation directed to a single area may involve resources which increase in arithmetical proportion to scale, while the resources required for integrated schemes tend to increase in geometric proportion to scale. The tendency towards such a situation arises from a number of factors:

(a) as more and more sub-systems, of different species and variety, become involved in a change, it is likely to be necessary to produce a growing number of possible solutions within which what is best for one or more sub-system is traded-off against some loss in potential benefit to others.

(b) To change even one sub-system may require two or more negotiating hurdles to be cleared—at the minimum in the public service the 'official' and 'staff' sides. As the number of systems involved, and the alternative schemes under review, increase, this process grows rapidly in difficulty. Two systems may, for example, involve eight negotiating stages, whereas change in a single system only two. This arises from the necessity of negotiating a provisional agreement in one system which cannot be confirmed until, perhaps after revision, the basis of agreement with the second system is known. It is the same problem which arises in negotiating on pay with two trade unions who will not negotiate jointly but between which relativities are important. Of course if joint negotiations are possible the number of stages will be reduced, but not necessarily the length or complexity of negotiation.

(c) All proposals for change are likely to include estimates of cost or other estimates measured in physical units which if honestly presented are likely to be 'range' figures indicating risk (for which probabilities will, desirably, be made explicit) and uncertainty. The risk and uncertainty may affect the cost or the time required for the change or be associated with say the environment and affect the benefit side of the calculation. While two or three range estimates, two or three probabilities of risk which might be involved in a scheme involving a single sub-system can probably be handled, ten or twelve of each which might be involved in major integrated schemes can prove almost impossible to handle even with computer support. So the solution will be to settle for single middle-of-the-range estimates and ignore all but the most important risks. There is a 'cost' in this: some worthwhile hedges may be omitted from the plan; the full range of possibilities on expenditure and time are obscured.

It can be seen, therefore, that while the potential benefits of larger-scale integrated schemes may be greater, costs and delay may increase to offset these in part if not in whole. Indeed it could be argued that the best strategy today for those in favour of the *status quo* is not to oppose a proposal for change but to welcome it provided it is evaluated and, if successful, implemented on a sufficiently large scale. The rationality of this argument is difficult to oppose by those favouring innovations. Indeed it is one which they at times advance themselves and thus ensure that the *status quo* survives at least into the long-term (as defined by Keynes). As optimality in scale and integration is approached the decision maker develops the attitude of mind so well described by Shakespeare:

> 'And thus the native hue of resolution
> Is sicklied o'er with the pale cost of thought
> And enterprises of great pith and moment
> With this regard, their currents turn awry
> And lose the name of action.'

This tendency for scale and complexity to breed delay and indecision is reinforced by the fact that since all major changes are likely to require the support of those at the top of the organization this becomes increasingly at risk with time. As the planning period for change increases from beyond, say, two years to three, four or five years, so the probability increases that in a government department the Minister or Permanent Secretary or both, and in the local authority the Chairman of the Committee concerned or the Principal Officers or both, will leave for one reason or another and be replaced by those less committed to the change in hand or even opposed to it. This could create a situation in which public announcements of proposed changes become a surrogate for change. In an environment which seems to be heavily engaged in innovation, the *status quo* like paradise is lost and regained.

One final argument against seeking too large a scale, too perfect an integration, in schemes of innovation is that advanced by those who see a positive virtue in a measure of overlapping and redundancy between public authorities on the argument that in communication systems and in some physical engineering systems the need is now recognized to 'build-in' an appropriate degree of redundancy, for 'fail-safe' and other reasons. In the public service 'a policy of redundancy permits several and competing strategies to be followed both simultaneously and separately'.[12] This approach is seen as providing an insurance against a breakdown or overload in any single part of the machinery of government[13] which otherwise might have cumulative effects and as a hedge against backing the wrong plan—which might happen even if aims and the environment remain unchanged. It is somewhat different conceptually from the kind of hedging which Schlesinger recommends, which is intended to give a single plan sufficient in-built flexibility to adjust to changes in aim or environmental factors over time. There are circumstances where the 'redundancy' approach—the backing of two competing strategies—may be preferable. But while planned and accepted redundancy may on occasions make sense, it is quite another matter to argue that whatever the extent or the nature of the redundancy and overlapping, which has developed without conscious intent over time, represents an effective use of the resources involved. And the criteria by which the former situation is to be distinguished from the latter have not been defined precisely by those seeing merit in redundancy.

A CAPABILITY FOR INNOVATION

As the public service in many countries moves into what is likely to be a period of larger-scale, more fully integrated change intended to improve the use of resources, the question arises whether there is in organizations with heavy on-going responsibilities a limited capacity to undertake change. If so, what determines the size of the capacity and how can it be used to best advantage if, as a limit would imply, the opportunity cost of a change undertaken is the benefit of the next best change which has to be foregone (or delayed). Certainly most people employed in the public service believe that there is a limit to the number and extent of changes that can be planned or implemented at any time. Whatever the conceptual difference between a widely held belief and an objective fact, in operational terms for those planning and implementing innovation both may need to be given much the same weight.

What are the resources involved in change and which, if any, are likely to be in inelastic supply in the short-term, thus creating a fixed fund of resources that limits what can be attempted at any time ? They can be divided into physical resources (including computers—both hardware and the programmes and other software—and accommodation) and human resources. The human resources tend to be needed for four kinds of activity:

(i) analysis of system(s), selection and evaluation of alternative schemes
(ii) provision of knowledge of the internal and external environment
(iii) negotiation and decision making
(iv) implementation

and can be found from three sources:

(a) externally by recruitment or commissioning an organization, e.g. consultants or computer software specialists;
(b) internally by allocating staff full-time to the work;
(c) internally by the part-time involvement of staff in the scheme while remaining responsible for their existing work.

Innovation is a form of investment in that outlays are incurred in early years in the expectation of a flow of benefits over a later (and normally longer) period. The provision of resources for change is like the provision of finance for investment. It can be obtained externally (from the market) or internally (from the organization's own resources) and will frequently be financed by a mix of these two methods. And as a company urgently needing to undertake new investment may lack the cash flow to finance the investment, even in part, internally, an organization needing to change can face a similar problem.

The physical resources should not constitute a serious problem. A public service organization, like a private, might at any time lack the finance needed to acquire the resources. But since change is investment, if the present value of the net flow of benefits expected is at least as high as from alternatives in the form of physical investment (e.g. in operating plant)—and if it is less it is difficult to make a case for the change—the resources should normally be available. There may be physical problems of supply over certain resources—lack of suitable accommodation in a particular town, a long delivery date for the model of computer required. But again these problems should be the exception rather than the rule and constrain action in the short-term only.

Turning to human resources, similar short-term problems may arise over particular scarce skills being sought by external recruitment or commission. But a more severe and continuing constraint on change is likely to be the human resources needed from within the system or organization. Even if as much use as possible is made of outside consultants and of external recruitment, some allocation of full-time staff from within the organization is likely to be essential to plan and implement major changes. By definition these are likely to need to be among the most able people in the organization: change planned by those who could most easily be spared would itself be likely to prove expendable. And their withdrawal from operating posts (where they are replaced with more or less difficulty) adds to the problems created for those in these jobs of providing information, contributing to the discussion of alternatives, taking part in negotiations, becoming involved in the implementation of the selected plan—and in curing the teething troubles which are usually if not inevitably associated with change. And these part-time demands on staff time must, if major change is involved, include to a significant extent the time of those at the top of the organization for whom the opportunity cost of time is highest (which does not, of course, imply that they must be frantically 'busy').

If there is one fact, which has emerged clearly from the study of major changes in business, it is that any which proceeds without the close and effective involvement of those at the top or which is planned entirely outside the system has little prospect of success. And it is in the extent to which these at the top of the organization, and at senior levels in the particular system(s) concerned, can devote their time to change, having allocated some people to work full-time (often in association with consultants or external organizations), which effectively determines the capacity for change. It is a military maxim that to regroup, a unit must break contact with the enemy. It is an advantage enjoyed rarely by the public service (which has in any case no enemies!). It may occasionally be possible in business when, say, a plant can be closed temporarily. And it creates the paradoxical situation that where change may most be needed it may be hardest to implement because of operational pressures on those running the systems. Nor would it necessarily be right to seek to give priority to top level involvement in change to improve management. James Schlesinger has observed:[14]

'The [U.S.A.] Department of Defense has done an effective job in considering appropriate middle-level inputs for middle-level objectives ... these are the current issues which absorb so much energy that comparatively little is left for considering such issues as the shape of the world and how it is changing and the appropriate higher-order objectives and how they will be influenced by external change. Achieving efficient management, while desirable in itself, may not be the most important thing in the long run.'

It is clear therefore that in any organization at any time the capacity for change is limited. It is the conclusion reached by March and Simon:[15]

'Action programmes are related to each other primarily through the demands they make on the scarce organizational resources available for initiating and carrying on action.
'... if all the resources of an organization are busily employed in carrying on existing programs, the process of initiating new programs will be slow and halting at best.'

The implication of this is that proposals for change are in the short term like mutually exclusive schemes of physical investment—it is not sufficient to show that a scheme yields an adequate pay-off on the investment, but it must be shown that it gives a higher rate of return than that which would have been obtained from any alternative plan of innovation which has to be forgone or postponed. This has important consequences for the public service where the tendency is for decisions on change to be taken sequentially and without full awareness of the opportunity cost.

COSTS AND BENEFITS IN CHANGE

We have so far considered only the direct costs and benefits arising from change. Are there also for change the equivalent to the 'externalities', the indirect 'spin off' effects which economists may identify as costs or benefits in other uses of resources? Some believe that there are and that, to take the benefit side first, there are indirect advantages associated with change which justify the implementation of what on a direct assessment of costs and benefits would seem sub-marginal schemes. To quote Schlesinger again[16]

'No organization is quite right and, without prodding, organizations will grow typically less sound over time. To avoid growing stale, any organization needs an occasional shaking-up or breath of fresh air.'

This general and unquantifiable benefit (some may not agree that change has this virtue and consider organizations to be like old cars where the replacement or overhaul of one sub-system serves only to produce stress and breakdowns in the remainder) should be distinguished from a more limited and quantifiable indirect benefit in that a scheme can embrace retirements, transfers or promotion of staff as presentationally part and an inevitable part of the change, even if, in fact, the relationship is slight. As against these indirect benefits we need set certain indirect costs (other than those attributed above to the old car school of thought). I have mentioned that teething troubles and some short-term loss of output through unfamiliarity with new processes are normal to schemes of change. They are normally foreseen in plans and minimized by such methods as preliminary training of staff. A residual value for such short-term factors is left in the estimates. But by definition the unforeseen is not foreseen and contingency plans to minimize all problems cannot be prepared. Yet experience shows that the unforeseen in some form can reliably be expected to occur. These costs may need to be brought into the reckoning by the decision makers: they are unlikely to be incorporated fully in proposals submitted to them.

But to understand the indirect costs of change in organization we must turn to the behavioural sciences where the subject has been studied more intensively than in most other disciplines. Although Laurence Sterne wrote that 'nothing is so perfectly amusing as a total change of ideas', behavioural scientists, and others more closely associated with management than Sterne, do not find that a complete change in organization, or in process, produces a similar effect on those concerned. It is more typical to report[17] that 'managers and operating personnel . . . can suffer frustrations, emotional disturbance and loss of motivation'. Indeed study of the behavioural sciences can easily produce in those contemplating change another reason for finding virtue in the *status quo*. But while those who have undertaken research into this subject have emphasized the dangers, they have developed normative theories which should allow the innovation to avoid or minimize them.

Professor A. T. M. Wilson defines[18] three main forms of anxiety over change:

(i) Fear of change in the ways in which things are done and the impact of this on customary ways of working ('work culture') and over customary levels of effort and satisfaction in one's job.

(ii) Fear of loss of job or loss of career prospects.

(iii) Fear of a relative diminution of the power or prestige of one's functional group, or of the category of employees of which one is a member.

Plans for change do not always make provision for all three areas of difficulty. The third of these fears is familiar at craft level in union demarcation disputes. It is no less common, in different forms, at technical and managerial levels. Professor Wilson suggests plans to minimize these anxieties:

(a) The first type of anxiety is greatly influenced by slow and deliberate build up of general awareness of the situation and of the external factors which compel innovation and change (for example, technological developments, increased international competition, etc.).

(b) The second type is best handled by manpower planning and, especially, by a systematic scheme of management development which will attempt to foresee changes and their effect on career prospects, and in providing opportunity or frustration.

(c) The third type of anxiety—change in the political system—is essentially a matter for the top management of a company. Major changes in the power structure need careful planning and timing. Leadership is a main factor.

With the public service, anxiety of the second type is much less common than in many business firms. But it can arise, e.g. in a major reorganization of local government which greatly reduces the number of authorities. But in general attention can be concentrated on overcoming the first and third forms of anxiety.

TIME AS A CONSTITUENT OF CHANGE

Change is a process through time and the role of time in change is seldom less than important, often decisive. Time may even be regarded as an alternative to change as, having in itself, through the process known as 'the effluxion of time', remarkable powers to solve problems and resolve conflict. This point of view is not unknown in the public service. Although it is not one which by temperament I am inclined to share, I have to admit that there are occasions when its validity is established by events.

All change is intended to affect the future but is inevitably rooted in or influenced by the past. Strategies are based on information and even the best real-time computer information is providing information about 'yesterday' (using this as a generic term to cover the range of time from five seconds ago to fifty years ago). From this information, conclusions are drawn, forecasts made, strategies developed. And thus even when we believe ourselves to be reacting vigorously and quickly to changing circumstances, we seldom succeed in living in other than what has been described as 'the recent future'.[19] And it is not at all difficult to be heavily involved with the not-so-recent future, i.e. to be implementing changes which are already obsolescent, perhaps even obsolete. There are many reasons for this. As we have seen, objectives do not and should not remain constant over long periods and may need to be revised while change is in progress. Much of the interpretation of information, on which plans for change are based, lies in detecting trends developing in the recent past and making assumptions about their continuation into the future. Uncertainty is involved, at times heavily, in the process. And the environment about which assumptions have been made may itself alter in unexpected ways. For all these reasons, it is likely to be the exception rather than the rule for change to produce in the future the results expected of it. Departures from expectation may be favourable as well as unfavourable: there is no bias here towards the *status quo*.

There are also cycles, even fashions, in change: centralization/ decentralization; specialization or generalization; geographical or product basis for delegation. There may be advantages in following fashion or cycles rather than trying to opt out of them. But to join in at the wrong time may be worse than either. The British civil service may observe with interest ideas now developing in American business management, such as 'diagonal pattern of career progress in which aspiring managers are systematically moved across frontiers among divisions and between line and staff positions in preparation for general management roles';[20] or the opinion that the general manager will in future need the qualities of leader, administrative planner, extrapolitic planner, entrepreneur, statesman and system architect, which is seen to raise the question whether it would be better to train a general manager as such from the start or whether a specialist with one of the required skills can develop the remainder.[21]

CONCLUSIONS

I have suggested in this chapter that the public service is, or could be if some bias towards the *status quo* is countered by known strategies, a favourable rather than an unfavourable environment for change and in Britain to a greater extent than in many countries. I have argued that, in seeking the 'best' degree of sub-optimality in change, the large claims likely to be made for scale and integration on the benefit side need to be measured against costs which take full account of increased risks and uncertainty inevitable. And that, if a large measure of integration seems impracticable, it is essential to achieve the best sequence in a series of non-integrated changes. I have supported the view that plans extending over several years should have built in to them, even at some cost, a series of hedges or options, phased over the implementation period as far as possible, since objectives and the environment may change, the interpretation of information may change, those in charge of the organization may change. I have suggested that public service organizations have a limited capacity for change at any time due to the demands made on the time of certain key personnel within the organization and that the cost of any change must be seen as the opportunity cost, i.e. the next best change which must be forgone or deferred. We have seen that change can have a beneficial effect on people and morale or the reverse and that part of the cost of a scheme of change is the hard work needed to achieve the former rather than the latter.

The public service has undertaken many changes in the past twenty years but, with few exceptions, there has been little research into the process and results. Less experience is available to aid future innovation. This kind of research might confirm some of the views which I have put forward in this chapter. It would be as valuable if it refuted them.

NOTES ON CHAPTER 7

1. Bennis, Benne and Chin (eds.), *The Planning of Changes*, Holt, Rinehart and Winston, 1964; Professor Tom Burns and G. M. Stalker, *The Management of Innovation*, Tavistock Publications, 1961; J. G. March and H. A. Simon, *Organizations*, Wiley, New York, 1958 (Chapter 17, Planning and Innovation in Organization).
2. My notes attribute this expression to a senior consultant from the McKinsey organization but he may have been quoting from another source.
3. Professor Kenneth Arrow, *Social Choice and Individual Values*, 2nd edition, John Wiley, New York, 1963, p. 95.
4. J. M. Buchanan and F. Tullock, *The Calculus of Consent*, The University of Michigan Press, 1962, pp. 258–59.
5. Arrow, op. cit., p. 119.
6. James Schlesinger, *Organizational Structures and Planning*, CAS Reprint Paper No. 1, HMSO, 1969, p. 6. (This paper was published earlier by the Rand Corporation and included in *Issues in Defence Economics*, National Bureau of Economic Research, New York, 1967.)
7. Speaking to a seminar on Planning Programming Budgeting Systems, London, 1969.
8. Michael Crozier, *The Bureaucratic Phenomenon*, op. cit. (notes, Chapter 4).
9. By Mr, now Sir, Frederick Catherwood, speaking to a civil service course.
10. The Civil Service: Report of the Fulton Committee, op. cit., Volume 1, pp. 88, 89, 90.
11. Yehezkel Dror, 'PPB and the Public Policy-Making System', *Public Administration Review*, March–April 1969, p. 153.
12. Martin Landau, 'Redundancy Rationality and the Problem of Duplication and Overlap', *Public Administration Review*, July–August 1969, p. 347.
13. An interesting example of the existence of 'redundancy' of this kind was provided in 1965 by the ability of the British Government to introduce the Selective Employment Tax without having to use either of the main taxation departments (the Board of Inland Revenue and Customs and Excise) who were over-loaded at that time.
14. Schlesinger, op. cit., p. 17.
15. March and Simon, op. cit., Chapter 7.
16. Schlesinger, op. cit., p. 2.
17. John F. Mee, 'Matrix Organisation', *Business Horizons*, Summer 1964.
18. At the London Business School.
19. Drucker, *The Age of Discontinuity*, op. cit.
20. S. M. Linowitz, 'The Demanding Seventies', *Public Affairs*.
21. Views expressed by Professor Ansoff.

CHAPTER 8

MANAGEMENT IN GOVERNMENT AND IN BUSINESS

the (Civil Service) staff college would concentrate on management and administration in government. This is not the same as management and administration in business. It can be similar to it but it will never be the same. . . .

The Rt. Hon. Edward Heath, M P, speaking in the House of Commons, November 21, 1968.

EARLIER COMPARISONS

In an earlier chapter, I drew a sharp contrast between the objectives, structures, processes and success criteria appropriate to an administration system and to a management system in the public service. Is the contrast as great between public and private sector management ? It is a question which has interested many commentators, one of whom, Sir Josiah (later Lord) Stamp, in an address in 1937[1] foresaw that a dichotomy would develop in the public service between the work cultures of administration and management (as I have defined these terms). But he also believed that public and private management would remain sharply contrasted:

'The task of the administrator in the future much more than in the past will, therefore, be to secure the maximum social net product and the disposition and training best adopted for this will be that most valuable to the public. Two classes of people are clearly marked out as unsuitable at once. First the forceful push-and-go business man of the single management type, accustomed to fixing his goal and achieving it in a competitive world. Second the exactly trained civil servant given to the analytical application of a legislative programme in a statute . . . co-operating with other departments similarly bound, working to the elaboration of a complete static programme to be generally applicable by principle and precedent. . . .'

The same writer had much earlier in an article published in 1924[2] developed this theme of a sharp contrast between the public service and business. In his analysis he concluded that it was the requirement of the public service to secure consistency between decisions over wide areas of government which was the most important single cause of difference from business.

But this is but one of many explanations which have been advanced for differences between public service and business management. And as we have seen in the opening chapter there are some who do not see any distinction of real significance. Among those who do, the distinctive factors on which the main emphasis has been placed are:

1 The scale, complexity and the 'integrative and allocative functions of a society wide basis' of public service operations in contrast to business.
2 The political element in public service decisions.
3 The immeasurability of public service work, i.e. the impracticability of quantifying or evaluating the activities of public bodies in the way possible for business corporations and commercial firms.
4 The concept of 'accountability' which subjects public authorities either to detailed control by elected bodies or to general control over objectives, resources used and performance.
5 Differences in organizational form and employment practices with a hierarchical, bureaucratic organization, life-time career structures, inflexible pay and promotion practices regarded as typical of the public service contrasted with a flexible organization, hire-and-fire philosophy and a lack of constraints on pay and promotion regarded as characteristic of business.

Before examining in more detail each of these areas of contrast, it may be helpful to limit the area of debate. I doubt the value of a comparison between a generalized concept of the public service as a whole and business as a whole. Since I hope the contrast between that part of the public service concerned primarily with administration and a business firm will be at least as obvious, from what I have written in the earlier chapters, as the distinction between, say, a hospital or a university and a business, I propose to concentrate on a comparison between business organizations and the systems of central and local government which have management as their primary task. A comparison between nationalized industries and private industries would be less meaningful for the opposite reason: the similarities would be too great. Although nationalized industries could have been organized differently and given different objectives from those now characteristic of these bodies—and few of those who in the nineteenth and early twentieth centuries proposed the nationalization of industry probably expected them to be as they now are—their present operations are broadly comparable to those of large, private industrial organizations and are increasingly subject to similar criteria of performance.

We need also to be clear, since there exist for both the public service and for business myths which differ greatly from realities, whether we intend to compare myth with myth, reality with reality or, as sometimes happens, a realistic view of the public service and a largely mythical concept of business derived perhaps from ideas about the role of the entrepreneur in classical economic text-books, garnished by pen pictures of businessmen from nineteenth-century novels or biographies. It is characteristic of such a simpliste attitude to business to think of an individual businessman as the decision maker rather than a large and complex organization, to assume a single basic objective 'to maximize profits', to imagine that the profit and loss accounts and balance sheets prepared by accountants provide a uniquely correct and unambiguous quantitative statement of the extent to which the objective is being achieved, to believe that 'hiring and firing' is one of the main activities (and occupational risks) of businessmen. This view of business as a very simple, very rough game with winners clearly identified is often held by those who see the public service in terms of almost indescribable complexity, subtlety and sophistication in which the score resembles that of a Mahler symphony more than that of a football match. The comparison which I wish to draw is between the public service as it exists—a spectrum of different systems which although complex are by no means beyond analysis and appraisal—and business as it exists today in the age of the large private corporation controlled not by a single brash entrepreneur but by a 'techno-structure' in which complexity, subtlety and sophistication may be far from unknown qualities. In short, as far as I can, to compare reality with reality.

CONTRASTS IN SCALE AND COMPLEXITY

I wish first to exclude from the comparison two important managerial functions of government—those of managing the economy and of allocating resources between major systems such as defence, health, education and the Arts. In scale and complexity these tasks have no parallel in business. The planned annual allocation of total capital investment and of total resources for current expenditure made in the public service is not the subject of any equivalent decision-making process in industry and commerce. Total investment and its distribution emerges from a multitude of decisions made company by company: the resources available in any company for investment and current expenditure being dependent on a number of factors such as cash flows available from sales revenue, retained as depreciation provisions or undistributed profits, possibilities of raising new equity capital and/or fixed interest loans, availability of short-term credit, etc. And the extent to which a company will seek to obtain resources for investment from one or more of these sources will be determined by its assessment of the investment opportunities open to it. But macro-economic management and the allocation of resources between major systems in the public service occupies the time of only a very small proportion of those engaged in management in the service. To most managers in central government, and to all in local government, public corporations and the nationalized industries, these major decisions tend to be exogenous variables much as they are to their colleagues in business. We should not be justified in regarding this kind of decision on the use of resources as the yardstick by which we measure public against private management and in concluding that the contrast in the scale and complexity of decision making is a decisive difference. Let us rather think in terms of contrasting say the Stationery Office and the British Printing Corporation, the Ministry of Defence and British Petroleum, the supplies division of the Ministry of Public Buildings and Works and the John Lewis Partnership, the housing activities of a London Borough and those of Span Houses.

On this basis it seems difficult to see scale, or the integrative/allocative nature of the work as significant points of contrast between such pairs of organizations. Within the Stationery Office, the defence system or the supplies purchasing system, resources are not allocated 'on a society wide basis' but to achieve the best use of resources in pursuit of the objectives of the particular system. At the headquarters of a large industrial corporation, particularly one operating internationally, the decisions are as likely to be of an integrative/allocative character as in a public service system involved in management.

But what of complexity, particularly on the argument that the typical public organization is claimed to have multiple objectives, all of which are difficult to describe while typically business has but a single objective—to maximize profits? It is true that multi-objectives will often be found in major public service management systems. The difficulty may be less in describing them than in relating them quantitatively. But lower down in sub-systems fewer goals, even a single aim, may be found which can be expressed precisely and for which criteria of efficiency can be devised. And in business the belief in the single objective, profit maximizing, decision maker of classical economic theory, has on an analysis of the modern large public corporation by many writers since Berle and Means,[3] for example, Marris,[4] Shonfield,[5] Galbraith,[6] come to seem more myth than reality. On examination it seems that the private corporation is as likely to have multiple objectives as the public organization and among them some including achieving maximum survival strength and growth may be more important than profit *maximization*, although there is likely to be a level below which profits or, more accurately, the rate of return on assets must not be allowed to fall as this would threaten the survival of the organization.

Perhaps, if growth is more important than profit maximization to the large business corporation, this in itself constitutes a significant point of contrast with public bodies whose explicit aims do not commonly include growth whether from motives of self-preservation or for other reasons. It would be difficult to argue that no central department, no branch of a department, no local authority or part of one, has ever been known to have ambitions towards growth. The public equivalent of the takeover bid is not unknown. Some are pursued intermittently and inconclusively over half a century. But in general the criteria associated with growth or an increased share of the market do not have as general an appeal in the public service where the former may be seen as a creator of increased problems and the latter as increasing rather than decreasing vulnerability to continued survival.

To sum up, both large public and business organizations have multiple aims at the top, more frequently single goals in sub-systems. The important distinction is that most if not all of the main aims in business are related in some way to resources and can therefore be integrated. In some public bodies the aims are far more diverse, only some concern resources and their integration is difficult: at times impossible.

CONSISTENCY AND CONFORMITY

If we turn to consistency and conformity, seen by Sir Josiah Stamp as the most important contrast, further differences appear. Within the Ministry of Defence the need for uniformity between pay and conditions of its employees in different parts of the world is likely to be greater than is the case of those of employees in different subsidiaries of an international corporation. More important would be the need of the Ministry of Defence to co-ordinate many of its activities to achieve consistency with those of other government departments, e.g. to ensure that its use of training facilities in a particular country is in line with Foreign Office objectives in that area. However on reflection it seems doubtful whether the differences here are fundamental. Large industrial corporations operating throughout the world may need to keep in touch with their embassies overseas to ensure that decisions on resources to be used in particular areas reflect conditions and likely developments in the countries concerned. And may not international oil companies co-ordinate their plans in negotiating with national governments, or may they not, if left to their own devices and free of constraints imposed by monopolies or restrictive practices legislation, pursue consistency and conformity in negotiation with other firms operating in their industry almost as whole-heartedly as public organizations ? Perhaps in the end, therefore, while a difference in the extent to which consistency and conformity are pursued can be seen to be a real point of difference between public and private management, the contrast between the attitude of society to such practices in either area is even more pronounced. We can also note that as industrial organizations grow in scale they tend to become more bureaucratic in structure and process. Their employees may demand consistency and conformity; as may their customers. So one can see in this area too a trend towards convergence but not one which has, or probably ever will, eliminate entirely the greater concern of public bodies with conformity and consistency.

POLITICAL CONSIDERATIONS

What then of the claim that a public service management system must be highly sensitive to political considerations, or to pressures from outside interests like amenity groups, while public corporations are relatively immune from such pressures ? Here too the distinction can, in my view, be exaggerated. When it originated, the comparison was perhaps being made between, say, the local builder or the owners of a single small coal mine and a public authority. But the large public corporation has seen the need for sensitivity to public opinion, nationally and locally. Frequently their activities will need the approval of national authorities, local projects may be subject to planning enquiries. Pressures from interested groups may affect even the strongest public corporation as much as public bodies. Indeed a case could be made out for the proposition that in some cases they may be more responsive to such pressures. Even if this pressure, if ignored, might at the worst cause no more than delay, it will often be the right managerial approach to pay to avoid the delay by a concession which will increase costs or by appeasing the opposing interests in some other way. And in a period when nationalization is a real possibility in many countries, the public corporation may be much concerned with its 'image' as an important factor in preserving the independence and safeguarding the future of the public corporation—which many writers now see as the objective of the highest importance in business.

Has the private firm the same interest as the public organization may have in the democratic objective (D)—the involvement of the public in decision making and in the minimization of conflict (C) as an objective ? On the former certainly not, unless it will either benefit the E objective variable, e.g. preliminary discussion in the local press of future plans to open a new store in the area may start to build up a group of potential customers or where it promises to benefit the C objective variable, e.g. an announced and phased withdrawal of spare parts for an earlier piece of equipment may achieve this as contrasted with the alternative of a sudden unannounced withdrawal. The large private corporation taking a long term view of its future development and concerned to safeguard its own existence may have an interest in minimizing conflict as great, and at times even greater, than that of a public authority although it will seldom have an interest in open public involvement in decision making on resources. Considerations of commercial secrecy may often make the corporation antipathetic to any public knowledge or involvement prior to a decision. Three quotations from views expressed in the spring of 1970 in Britain may illustrate a trend towards the large business corporation becoming increasingly involved in the complexities which affect decisions on resources in the public sector:

> 'If the corporation is to survive ... management would have to modify its traditional practices. ... Old criteria ... would be replaced by a new ethics and a new management, able to deal with conflict and fully aware of social and political factors.[7]
>
> 'Managements in British industry would increasingly have to justify their decisions to their employees and the community as a whole—they do not have a divine right to manage.[8]
>
> '... international corporations have now a massive power, not only financial but industrial. ... Because there is a two way interest the firms themselves bend over backwards to show that they are sensitive to national interests. ...[9]

In these three quotations, we can see emerging in the business sector in embryo form the three objective variables—N (the national interest); D (open participation in decision making) and C (reducing social conflict) which, with the economic criterion, may be present in public sector decisions on resources. But while convergence may be starting here it is far from complete. It may never be complete: the contrast will become less sharp but not disappear.

MEASURABILITY

How significant is the claim that there is a major distinction between business and public authorities (other than nationalized industries) in that for the former all inputs and outputs are quantified objectively and precisely in monetary terms by independent auditors in the profit and loss account and the difference provides a precise measure of success or failure (profit or loss) while in government, since neither inputs nor outputs can be quantified, success or failure is no more than a matter of opinion? The first point to be made here is that the objectivity of company accounts has been questioned: their precision would be generally agreed to be illusory. On matters like say the valuation of fixed assets and stock, depreciation, provision for bad debts or future settlements of claims there is scope for wide variations in practice. Nor, despite appeals for this to be done, have company accounts overcome the problem of using a standard of measurement—money—which in most countries loses a varying proportion of its value year by year. Since inter-year comparisons form part of the precise quantification attributed to business management this is a serious handicap to any objective assessment of performance—indeed it has been said that if allowance is made for this factor some audited 'profits' would in fact be 'losses'.[10] It might indeed be argued that in the presentation of figures of public expenditure to Parliament showing comparisons between years in 'constant price' terms and in the *ex post* adjustments of this nature (but not identical in method or concept) embodied in the National Income statistics, the public sector has a lead over the private in realism and in quantification which is meaningful.

The problem is sometimes presented, particularly in Britain, as due to a lack of standard conventions in accountancy practice. More standardization might help—at least in making inter-firm comparisons. But the problem cannot be 'solved' in this way for the fact remains that a number of the variables involved are not by their nature precisely quantified—the values of assets and stocks for example are functions of future expectations discounted for risk. By definition this is an imprecise concept: a matter of opinion in the last resort. We can see both the value and limitations of conventions in national income accounting which is as strong on detailed precise standard conventions as accounting is weak. This enables figures of impressive precision to be produced for say gross national product. But if one looks behind the conventions to the assumptions and imprecisions underlying them, it is only too clear that these statistics provide a rough indication of changes in economic output within a country, an inadequate basis for comparisons of economic wealth between countries and no basis at all for an assessment of changes in national welfare. More accounting conventions will not therefore give business activities an objectivity or a precision which public bodies cannot hope to approach.

It should also be recognized that within a large business corporation only a small proportion of the management sub-systems dispose of their output by sale on the market and will therefore have sales revenue to set against costs and can therefore use 'profit' as a guide to decision making within the sub-system. It is with this fact in mind that someone, probably Drucker, has said that in business there are no profit centres, only cost centres. It is true that in some business firms output is 'charged out' as it moves from one sub-system to another but the values attached to such outputs are to an extent arbitrary: they will seldom if ever establish whether the organization as a whole is in fact operating currently at a profit or loss.

If, therefore, we compare the reality rather than the myth of quantification in business with that in the public service, the contrast is not razor-sharp. For the inputs to public service systems can be, and are, quantified in the form of annual estimates. It is true that the conventional form of these may fail to reflect or fail to reflect fully the 'cost' of using land, buildings and equipment which were bought outright in a previous period (and which have an opportunity cost) or which were leased at fixed rents at some date in the past which do not fully reflect current opportunity costs. But these exclusions may be as common (except where equipment is still subject to depreciation provisions and when these reflect replacement costs) in company accounts. Nothing, therefore, prevents the public service developing cost centres as fully as business organizations: their relative scarcity reflects the fact that conventionally estimates in central and local government and in some public corporations have been prepared and presented in such a way that they do not provide comprehensive or valid figures on cost for use by management sub-systems. And those running such systems, if they have realized that they were in fact responsible for a management sub-system, did not require, or were unable to get, meaningful cost information.

When we look at output the contrast is certainly much greater. How is the output to be valued in monetary terms of a hospital, a prison, an aircraft carrier, the Cabinet Office, a television programme? These are the kinds of question which are frequently asked, often rhetorically, by those in the public service inclined to find management irrelevant. But we need to break down the problem before deciding that it is insoluble. The first point is that some of the 'outputs' mentioned do not arise in management systems but in other kinds of system and are not therefore strictly relevant to the comparison I am making. The second is that there are within the public service considerable transfers of goods and services, many arising in management systems, to which charges could be applied much as in business. Even when it was a government department the Post Office charged other departments for postal and telephone services and paid the Ministry of Public Building and Works for buildings, including architectural and engineering services and supplies, procured for it. If it were thought desirable in the interests of management, such procedures could be extended. Accommodation, training, management services, use of computer time, use of vehicles, all subsystems of this kind have outputs which in the outside world have a market price. In some, but not all, companies, internal charges are levied for some or all of such services. The reason that output is not valued or seldom valued, in such public systems (all of which would seem to me, if not to all of those in charge of them, as basically management systems) is that there has been in the past a general decision rule that such charges are wasteful. In the words of the Report of the Ramsay Committee 1927 'it was most undesirable for Government departments to develop clumsy and very intricate accounting machinery at great cost in order to transfer money from the left pocket to the right pocket in the same pair of trousers'. After the war the Crick Committee was hardly more encouraging to such procedures.

In the terms used by the Ramsay Committee even
business would support their conclusion. But the key
'clumsy', 'intricate', 'great' and perhaps 'transfer'. Th
whether management might be improved by simple a
of charging or even, in many cases, by 'book-keeping' transac
than by actual payments. At this point, I need do no more than s
that there could be much more monetary valuation of output than there
is at present. Its relative absence is not inherent in the nature of the
public service but reflects past decisions and practices. However, even
after assuming that everything practicable had been done to charge
for, or value, outputs in the public sector it must be admitted that there
would still be a significant gap between the outcome and what is
possible in private business.

ACCOUNTABILITY

This is often seen as the main factor in a contrast between public and
private management. To some, the principal element is the right of
elected central and local government bodies to seek information on and
to challenge every decision, every proposal however detailed, for the use
of resources in a way from which private companies are entirely exempt
and, within the public service, nationalized industries are largely free—
although legislation may require them to justify certain managerial decisions, e.g. on prices to special consultative bodies, and in these and
other important matters to obtain the approval of the Minister concerned. To others, it is the personal responsibility of the Minister to the
House of Commons for all activities of his department which is the
most significant aspect of accountability in central government in
Britain, although no precise parallel exists in local government. This is
seen as drastically limiting the scope for delegation of decision making in
management in central government. A third group would see financial
constraints, e.g. annual budgeting processes or constraints on personnel
management, as the worst features of accountability. In all these respects, the public service is contrasted sharply with the public corporation which, on the Galbraith–Marris hypothesis, is regarded as no
longer accountable at all in any real sense to an external authority—the
'technostructure', i.e. those running the corporation at the top having
learned how to keep the shareholders quiet at the annual meeting of the
company.

I believe that this contrast, in the black and white terms in which it is
often presented, is more stark than reality justifies. It is true that seldom
if ever is a Chairman or a Managing Director of a corporation subjected
to the kind of detailed interrogation which a Minister may face in the
House of Commons or a Permanent Secretary receive at the Public

Accounts Committee. But only a tiny percentage of decisions on resources in the public service become the subject of a debate in Parliament or discussion by the Public Accounts Committee in any year—if ever. Nor is it true that in central government most of those responsible for management decisions on resources are subjected to a continuous barrage of Parliamentary Questions, letters of enquiry and complaint to the Minister, or Adjournment debates in the House of Commons. Some are for some of the time: research would be needed to establish the proportions involved but I suspect that they would be found to be much smaller than is commonly believed. Nor is it true that the doctrine of ministerial responsibility prevents a high degree of delegation in the public service: indeed in some respects, e.g. capital investment decisions, civil servants often enjoy a much higher degree of delegation than their opposite numbers in business corporations. And the constitutional position of Ministers as being subject to the control of Parliament and unable to spend a penny without parliamentary approval, while true in a sense, hardly presents an accurate account of decision making on resources. Finally the past twenty years has seen a transformation in the constraints on the use of resources imposed by the annual budget system and by what was once over-detailed Treasury control. The process is incomplete but progress here is real.

If the position in the public service is not what it seems—at least in central government, for in local government detailed control and intervention by elected representatives is greater—the same is true for the private corporation. It may be that most bodies of shareholders are passive and relatively easily satisfied for most of the time: but not all of them all of the time. And if it is unknown for a Minister to shelter behind an official if a decision is attacked in the House of Commons, it is surely almost equally unknown to find the Chairman of a corporation replying to a shareholder's complaint about an unsuccessful project by attributing the blame to the Director of Marketing or of Production. Nor do public corporations ignore enquiries or complaints: indeed they may devote as many resources to dealing with them as a government department: the main distinction here is that those at the highest levels will normally wish, and be able, to keep free of detailed involvement in this work.

This last fact gives rise to what some with experience of both business and government see as one of the most interesting points of contrast, which is the difference in the direction of the flows of information.[11] In business the 'front-line', where the battle is being won or lost, is seen as at the point of sale or on the production floor and much of the volume of flow of information is from higher levels to these lower frontline levels. The reverse flow of information is, even when a well designed information system is in operation, small in volume—although highly important in content. The result is that some senior civil servants moving to posts at Board level in large corporations have assumed at first from their near-empty in-trays, by contrast with their experience in government departments, that their new colleagues were boycotting them. For in a government department the battle is seen as being fought on two fronts, and the one where the clerks are communicating over the counter or by letter with the public is often seen as less important than the proceedings in the House of Commons or in the Cabinet. The weight of information flow may therefore be greater towards than from those at the top of the organization. This does not mean that there is little or no delegation: many decisions may be being made at all levels—it requires only a tiny proportion of these to become the matter of parliamentary or inter-ministerial debate for the load at the top to become heavy. There is no doubt, therefore, that for those at the top, a government department seems quite different from a large business corporation. But for those lower down where many management decisions are made the contrast is less, although it does not disappear entirely.

ORGANIZATION AND PERSONNEL MANAGEMENT

Some see the main difference between government and business as lying in this area. Government organizations are seen as inevitably large, bureaucratic in organizational form, staffed by those who join direct from school or university and stay in the service until retirement, are promoted by seniority within a particular 'class', and remunerated at standard rates bearing no relation to performance which, however poor, still enables the man concerned to continue in post since it is impossible to get rid of him. By contrast business firms are seen as smaller, flexible organizations, continuously hiring and firing staff and rewarding those who stay with completely flexible pay and promotion strategies.

Here again the extreme contrast is much exaggerated. We have seen there are two reasons why many government organizations are bureaucratic: it is an organization form well suited to handle administration and most large organizations become bureaucratic. In business, the latter applies: the former may not. But as private corporations increase in size they too are tending to become more bureaucratic. Differences here are becoming smaller. And in the public service small flexible organizations have been and are being set up to tackle particular managerial tasks. There is no constraint which prevents this: all that is needed is a recognition of the possibilities and the will to implement them. In promotion, too, the contrast is not of black and white. On balance it seems true that seniority, although not of decisive importance, still carried more weight in the public service than in business, at least up to and including middle levels of management: beyond that very little. Probably the constraints which have been in the past greatest are those in the civil service created by the class system (and by somewhat similar professional boundaries in local government) and in pay. Following the Fulton Report at least the first of these barriers is being broken down. Whether all contrast with business will disappear remains to be seen. Finally movement in and out of the public service at all ages is much greater than it was in the past—those who are incapable of effective work are removed from the service in larger numbers than is often believed—while statistics relating to large business corporations suggest that the proportion of managers who serve until retirement is much larger than the public may believe. Here again we find the contrast has been exaggerated. But it still exists.

THE CONTRAST BETWEEN PUBLIC SERVICE AND BUSINESS MANAGEMENT

I am inclined to select, as a most important point of contrast, the difference in what is meant by the 'best use of resources'. In the public service the criteria are more numerous and complex. 'National considerations' may be involved at least in some of the most important decisions. Economic analysis will need to be based on social costs and social benefits rather than on expenditure incurred and receipts earned as in business. And the best decision may in the public service need to be one which trades off some economic benefit for open participation in decision making and minimizes conflict. The public corporation may also at times give weight to national considerations. Some are beginning to take account of social costs (which affect the company's 'image') and the safeguarding of the future existence of the corporation may increasingly suggest that some price is worth paying to reduce conflict with society or some sector of society. But even allowing for these trends, the differences in complexity (but not on the whole in scale) of decisions on resources seem among the most important points of contrast. Another most significant distinction between the public service and industry or commerce is that a substantial proportion of the resources used by the public service is in systems which are not management systems—the best use of resources is a secondary rather than a primary task. For large parts of the public service this creates varieties of systems which in management cannot be compared directly with business—it is like asking whether Manchester United or the Harlequins is the better team.

I believe that there is some relevance in most of the other points of difference—the greater need of the public service to secure consistency

and conformity, the political environment, problems of measuring inputs and outputs, accountability, greater constraints in personnel
management. But none of these seem in isolation or even collectively
to make every management system in the public service totally distinct
from that in business. In short, in a public service management system,
where 'national' considerations did not affect significantly decisions on
resources, where social costs and benefits could be disregarded and
monetary costs and receipts measured inputs and outputs accurately,
where decisions need not be discussed openly with public participation
and where the activity did not generate conflict in society, management
in the public service would resemble closely management in business.'
And where exceptionally an example can be found in the public service
of a system which meets the conditions I have set out, for example, the
Supplies Division of the former Ministry of Public Building and Works
with a turnover of £70m. annually, I believe that it resembles a business
corporation in all essential respects. Certainly it is far closer to one than
it is to an administration system in the public service. But a high proportion of the resources used by the public service are in systems where
these conditions do not apply and where there are significant points of
contrast between management and that found in business.

NOTES ON CHAPTER 8

1. Sir Josiah Stamp, later Lord Stamp, in an address on 'The Administrator and a Planned Society', October 1937 (reprinted in *Public Administration*, January 1938).
2. Sir Josiah Stamp, in an address, 'The Contrast between the Administration of Business and Public Affairs, February 1923 (printed in *Public Administration*, No. 3, 1923).
3. Adolf A. Berle, and Gardner C. Means, *The Modern Corporation and Private Property*, Macmillan, 1934.
4. Robin Marris, *The Economic Theory of 'Managerial' Capitalism*, Macmillan, 1966.
5. Shonfield, *Modern Capitalism*, op. cit. (Notes on Chapter 2).
6. Professor John Kenneth Galbraith, op. cit. (Notes on Chapter 4).
7. Dr Lindon Saline (of the General Electric Company, U.S.A.) speaking in London; report in the *Financial Times*, March 12, 1970.
8. Campbell Adamson (Director-General of the Confederation of British Industry) in a newsletter: quotation from *The Times*, April 9, 1970.
9. Hugh Stephenson in a review entitled 'Implications of transnationalism' in *The Times*, April 9, 1970.
10. Professor Ralph C. Jones, 'Effect of Inflation on Capital and Profits: The Record of Nine Steel Companies', *Journal of Accountancy*, January 1949. D. R. Myddelton, 'Inflation and Accounts', *Accountancy*, December 1965; and 'Accountants Beware Currency Debasement', *Financial Times*, March 11, 1969.
11. It was Mr, now Sir, Frederick Catherwood who called attention to this distinction.

CHAPTER 9

BRITISH EXPERIENCE AND PROSPECTS

Your glazing is new and your plumbing's strange,
But otherwise I perceive no change.
Rudyard Kipling: *A Truthful Song*

CHANGE AND STABILITY

The public service is large. Even the constituent parts such as the civil service, local government and the health service much exceed in scale even the great business corporations. Neither the public service nor its constituent parts are homogeneous. It is not surprising that both change and stability can co-exist: either or both can be found by those who seek them. Thus books, and the opening chapters of reports, have been published in which the lack of adaptation over time has been seen as the dominant characteristic of some part of the service. If the conclusions of these works have to be summarized in three words: 'perceive no change' would be as fair as some alternatives I have heard.

But in 1969 when I was asked by a French review of public administration to write an account[1] of developments in the British civil service in the sixties, I found no difficulty in identifying large areas of 'new glazing' and 'strange plumbing' without, however, deceiving myself or, I hope, my readers into believing that it had been a decade of universal or revolutionary change. I selected for mention three main areas of innovation. The first was a series of developments (I wish I could have reassured my French readers that they had been planned and co-ordinated—or met Cartesian criteria in full) in organization and in the development of, and relations with, staff. I referred to the growth in central co-ordination of the civil service through the Pay and Management part of the Treasury—later transformed into the Civil Service Department—which came to provide far more central co-ordination in personnel management and more training, particularly in management, advice on computers, and a central source of expertise in management techniques. I described the trend towards large departments and the experiment in organization such as integrated hierarchies in the Ministry of Transport. And there were continuing efforts throughout the decade to improve the development and the morale of staff by methods such as the appraisal interview.

The second area of innovation that was noteworthy in the sixties was the transformation over the period of the planning and control of public expenditure to give it depth (over time by projecting commitments and plans five years ahead), breadth (by incorporating all public expenditure making claims on resources), and a greater measure of consistency over time by minimizing sudden short-term changes in direction leading to the cancellation or postponement of projects. The third important area of change was the growth in analytical capacity and in the use of computers. Within this expansion there was a growing trend towards experiment with—it would be difficult to claim that there was ever any firmer commitment—the more sophisticated analytical approaches such as operational research and cost–benefit analysis.

In other parts of the public service, developments in the decade were remarkably similar to those in central government, although they were adopted independently with differences in the timing and in the degree of innovation. But in both local government and in the health service the trend was towards greater co-ordination at the centre, towards an increase in the scale of organizations, towards a greater use of analytical techniques and computers.

In the past two years most of these trends have been reinforced. The Fulton Report encouraged a further development of the central co-ordination of the civil service and in its recommendation of a unified grading structure, which was accepted, set in train a new direction of change which might possibly pre-empt a not insignificant proportion of the total resources available centrally for innovation. More large departments have been set up. Some that were already large have been so greatly expanded in scale that 'giant departments' has now become a respectable generic title. More analytical units have been set up: more computers installed and the control of public expenditure has continued to evolve—displaying a growing concern with the validity and significance of the statistical data and of the constant price convention on which the procedure rests.

I shall not describe in detail these many developments: all, or almost all, are well documented elsewhere. I shall however need to comment on them in an effort to predict the prospects for management in the public service. But although the word 'management' appeared in many of the statements explaining or introducing the various forms of innovation I have described, it is essential to keep in mind that management, as I have defined it, was not the sole, and in some cases not even the primary, reason for the changes. I have emphasized that the management role is but one of those falling to government and a change may be justified under some valid criterion even if it contributes nothing to better management or is inimical to it.

My own analysis of the state of management in government suggests that the forms of change most likely to lead to an improvement in management would be those:

- which increased the status of the activity of seeking positively a better ✕ use of resources and thus gave it higher claims on the time of decision makers at all levels.
- which made explicit the decision criteria, the objectives and the weights by which they were interrelated, and thus increased the prospect of a better strategy for the use of resources, when found, being recognized as such both within the service and by the public.
- which, within a recognition of the identity and characteristics of systems, served to discourage 'administration drift'—the tendency of public authorities to convert all discretionary tasks into regulatory; to encourage systems which were administration for statutory reasons to acquire at the margin discretion of the *de minimis* variety; which encouraged diplomatic systems involved in the allocation or use of resources to develop the knowledge and attitudes relevant to integrative–allocative management; which in systems which were not, and could not appropriately be converted into, management systems, allocated a responsibility for the efficient use of resources to a person and sub-system and encouraged an interest and appreciation of management throughout these systems where some other task or tasks has primacy.

which encouraged thought about the 'resources' used and about their 'cost'.

- which provided for those in all systems a flow of current information on resource inputs and outputs and provided for the monitoring of output against the outcome sought.
- which created an environment both within and outside public authorities in which success was identified at least as fully as error and where the ability to use resources efficiently was regarded as at least one important attribute of officials operating in management.

If we consider some of the main developments in government in the past decade, it is clear that few of them have any direct or certain effect in creating improvement in any of the directions I have described above. This is hardly surprising. In many cases the aim of the change was primarily to improve an aspect of government other than management as I have defined the concept. The centralizing and co-ordinating trend in central and local government, the growth in scale in government departments with the tendency for local authorities to follow this trend, and the reorganization of the control and planning of public expenditure were all motivated by broader aims than solely to improve efficiency in the use of resources, although this was certainly a consideration in some of these innovations.

It may, however, emerge that these changes have had indirectly a clear and beneficial effect on management. This could certainly be said of the reform of the planning and control of public expenditure, which I described earlier as a necessary, if not sufficient, condition of any worthwhile development in management.[2]

When we contemplate the likely effects of scale of giant departments —for whatever these are it is certain that they cannot yet have worked their way through in full—no clear conclusions emerge. In two respects the prospects seem encouraging. Firstly the result is to bring many of the large disparate blocks of public expenditure under the control of a single organization. This should encourage the sub-allocation of resources within each of these areas by methods in which analytical techniques contribute more, and the more extreme form of creative conflict less, than in the past when there has been divided control. Scale will also mean that in the case of systems which in the past have comprised subsystems from two, three or even four government departments the whole may in future form part of a single organization. Better co-ordination and more co-operation might be expected. It may also permit flexibility in the transfer of resources within a system if all expenditure in future falls on one vote instead of being divided between several votes.[3] And there may be economies of scale in government as in industry despite the very different weights technology has in the two areas. In management services, for example, there are certainly increasing returns to scale—at least up to a point which in the sixties no more than two or three departments reached.

But in all these respects there are less encouraging possibilities. The allocation of resources may improve but it is possible to reflect that, when historians come to study the use of resources in government in Britain in the period 1945–70, it would be surprising if they do not find cause to criticize some of the distribution of resources over the period even within the field of responsibility of a single department throughout that time. And if allocation were to be based mainly on pluralist negotiation, rather than on analysis, the view that greater rationality emerges from such processes if conducted within a single organization than in several organizations is not, as far as I know, a hypothesis which has been tested. Again the hypothesis that all sub-systems co-operate amicably within a single organization, while generating friction and lack of co-ordination if they are part of several organizations, would seem to require research. I shall be happy to provide evidence for and against both points of view.

In any case there is no prospect in government of bringing many major systems under single organizational control, for the sub-systems span the fields of central and local government, of the nationalized industries and the health service. Nor, if we look at the scope for economies of scale, will everyone be convinced that in, say, the function of personnel management the few people involved in a small organization who can know personally a significant proportion of the staff will necessarily be at a disadvantage in efficiency in comparison with the large establishment unit in a giant department, where a lack of personal acquaintance with staff is made good by on-line access to a computer-based data bank. And turning from the large organization to the growth of central co-ordination in the civil service there are some commentators like Mr Peter Jay who believe that advantages of more centralization may at least be reduced by the division of a central concern with the use of resources between two ministries—the Treasury and the Civil Service Department. Sir Richard Clarke in a series of lectures[4] in 1971 saw the central role divided into three—for the Cabinet Office now exercises some analytical functions. He proposed a different division between a Central Management Department (responsible for all 'resource use' control functions, whether expressed in terms of finance or manpower) and a National Economy and Finance Department (exercising the macro-economic and taxation functions of the Treasury). This would certainly seem deserving of study in any country which has options open and is primarily concerned with efficiency in the use of resources.

But the giant department and central co-ordination are mainly aspects of the machinery of government: that was to be taken as given as a parameter within which I would discuss management in government. In Sir Richard Clarke's words '. . . when one has finished machinery of government one should then start on the substance of government'. Certainly there is a risk that macro-change in organization and macro-process in the allocation of resources (such as that of the PESC procedure) may leave unaffected to a surprising degree the use of resources within systems and sub-systems. To a general in war, a decision to transfer a division from one corps to another or to attach a tank brigade to every infantry division is important. He will also profit by studying the large-scale map in which pins and flags identify the position of major units. But the wise general will, like Horrocks in the Second World War, spend, what may seem to some, a disproportionate amount of his time in neither of these activities but in moving around the forward areas, observing how effectively units are actually controlling ground which maps show them as 'occupying'; in discovering the real state of morale, and the attitudes of those he commands. In these the general may see the battle being won or lost. The same view may be taken about management.

In the same way, there is a risk that as the allocation of resources 'improves', supported by ever larger and better flows of information, the effect may be disappointing in actually producing a better or even an acceptable use of resources on the ground. A time series of past, and proposed future, allocations may indicate that one system has suffered what are sometimes described as savage cuts while another has received generous increases. Let those making the allocation get away from their offices—if for no other reason than to escape the angry or anguished protests from the former system and the over-effusive expressions of gratitude from the latter. They may find 'in the field', visiting units *randomly selected*, that the former system still has the resources to maintain the lawns of its establishments to a standard about twice as high as that thought appropriate for Parliament Square, while in the favoured latter system those who look out of the windows of their premises would be unable to see the sky because of the height of the weeds in the grass, even if the windows had been cleaned in the past three months. Of course no single example of variation in a single standard of this imaginary kind forms a decisive index of the efficiency of allocation. It cannot be said that the resources allocated to the maintenance of grounds in the two systems represent the marginal use of resources. Indeed, throughout the public service, the problem is one of finding ways of identifying the true margin from 'false' or 'negotiating' margins. A degree of inefficiency or prejudice produces in all systems areas of output which are either grossly favoured or neglected. To treat either of these false margins as generally valid could lead to wrong conclusions in either direction on allocation. By negotiating margins, I mean the kind of 'imputed' information about margins collected by asking systems how they would use a marginal increase in funds and what they would have to abandon if a marginal reduction in resources were made. The law of negotiating margins ensures that all answers to the former enquiry will sound highly attractive and involve clear additions to social benefit, while all replies to the latter question will be unappealing and sound socially harmful. There is always a 'quantity' and a 'quality' margin in each area which it is also useful to distinguish.

Improvement in analytical techniques and in information which, even if far more disaggregated than in the past, is bound to have an element of aggregation, seems unlikely to allow a system responsible for allocation to dispense with first-hand visual observation of the output of the resources used. To the cybernetician this will seem amateur, obsolescent advice. In the example I quoted, electronic devices could today monitor the height of the grass, detect and count the number of weeds and the degree of opaqueness of the glass in the windows. Through feedback the flow of financial resources could be directed or diverted to remedy situations, to print out orders to the work force and turn on the sprinkler system if the grass is failing through drought to reach the rate of growth for the time of the year defined in the programme. Quite so: but, while this equipment is still on order, first-hand information may, if still crudely collected by visual inspection, have a small contribution to make to the science of allocation.

This has been by way of a digression from my reflection on the benefits which management in government has enjoyed, or can expect to obtain, from major change in organization, from improvements in the planning and control of public expenditure, while noting that the effects on systems, on attitudes within systems and on the actual use of resources may fall short of what at first might be expected.

It may seem to some readers surprising that I do not offer at this point advice on how systems and sub-systems should be organized to achieve efficiency in management and on how morale and attitudes in sub-systems be improved. I do not do so, because I doubt the existence of universal or even general solutions to these problems. My conclusion is rather that if government provides a favourable environment for management, if the structure of systems and sub-systems is appropriate to carry out strategies selected after rational analysis, those in charge of the systems and sub-systems would find forms of organization suitable to the task and to their own style of management and that, if they did not know how to do this or how to achieve the best results from their staff, good advice is ready to hand. It is on these grounds that I shall not use this opportunity to commend, for certain systems, an approach like management by objective,[5] useful as I believe it and indeed other techniques to be, but turn to consider developments which may lead to a better selection of strategies and to a more appropriate structure of systems.

Turning to the future, it is possible to see in several of the ideas and approaches, which constitute the agenda for change, direct effects on many of the factors which I set out earlier as relevant to more efficient management. I should like to consider three of these in some detail: Accountable Management; Programming–Planning–Budgeting (PPB) which incorporates Programme Analysis Review (PAR); and the general growth in the capacity for analysis in government (both operational research and cost–benefit fall within this area). I shall refer under each of these heads to developments or experiments which have occurred. But it is true of each that their full contribution to efficiency and management lies, if it lies anywhere, in the future.

ACCOUNTABLE MANAGEMENT

The Fulton Report stated[6] that 'accountable management means holding individuals and units responsible for performance measured as objectively as possible'. This makes one part of accountable management clear, but not another, which is at least as, and perhaps more, important. As it stands the statement is reminiscent of Orders of the Day issued by a commander-in-chief to battalions on the eve of a battle for which they are inadequately equipped and are under tactical orders which have only the most remote prospect of success. To complete a definition of accountable management there needs to be added the phrase '. . . and where the person in charge of the unit regards himself as so responsible'. Since management is so largely an attitude of mind the latter condition will favour efficiency even in the absence of the former: the former without the latter will create only a collapse in morale and confusion.

If accountable management is seen in this light, it will not be found to be a phenomenon entirely unknown in government until recently. Here and there circumstances have provided conditions, including an appropriate degree of delegation, in which accountability could develop. But this has been exceptional. Generally, even in management systems, responsibility has been too evenly diffused over every level of long hierarchies, with too little delegation at any level, to allow any individual to feel a personal responsibility for the efficiency of the system as a whole.

Accountability is sometimes seen as the antithesis of a situation in which nobody cares. There is no justification for this assumption: caring and feeling responsible are two different attitudes. In the hierarchical situation the problem for management—it is not, as I have argued earlier, a problem for administration—is that too many people at every level care too much in the wrong way. They all care that no mistakes are made and as few risks as possible taken which might involve themselves or their organization in criticism. Accountable management does not therefore produce caring where none existed but a different form of concern better suited to management.

A recent Civil Service Department memorandum[7] commented that 'The Fulton concept of accountable management . . . is primarily concerned with defining management responsibility in quantifiable though not necessarily formal terms, so that managers can be held responsible for their performance measured as objectively as possible'. Certainly one would expect to see inputs to accountable sub-systems valued in full —the cost centre concept, and where outcome (or at least output) can be valued or quantified it may provide information relevant to the evaluation of performance although it may not in itself be decisive. But Fulton, rightly in my view, did not insist on quantification of output as a necessary condition of accountable management and I believe it can exist, as an appropriate attitude of mind, with a suitable measure of delegated authority, even where outcome and output are imprecise.

The main pre-requisites for accountable management are:

(i) Involvement of the manager in decisions on strategies or if he has not been involved, e.g. takes over on-going responsibilities that he has sufficient confidence in the practicability of the plan, and

of the probability of the plan having the desired effect on outcome, to feel accountable.

(ii) The cost centre approach: a budget within which the manager
enjoys as much delegation as possible to switch resources.

(iii) Authority of the manager to organize as he thinks best and in personnel management:

    (a) To be involved in new appointments, to be able to veto those
he thinks unsuitable, to be able to have transferred (within a
reasonable time if not immediately) those who prove unsuitable. 'Hiring and firing' powers are certainly not needed
for accountable management.

    (b) Not to have staff transferred from his system without consul-
tation and adequate notice to find a replacement. The power
of the manager to promote, or reward by allowances when
increased responsibilities are accepted by members of the
system (although acceptance of a proportion of 'external'
promotions could reasonably be required of him), and to
make reports on all members of his staff which might influence their career development.

    (c) A process by which success or failure of the system, whether
quantifiable or not, is assessed impartially with the main
emphasis on efficiency (outcome/input ratio) rather than on
effectiveness (outcome only)—although the level attained in
the latter is also relevant to the evaluation of performance.

Several factors can encourage the development of accountable
management. They include the physical decentralization of a sub-
system. Or the introduction, into a hierarchy of grades, of titles like
Controller, Director or even Manager which leads someone to feel a
sense of responsibility for the whole of the operations of the sub-
system, including the use of resources.

The main potential advantages of accountable management are that it
will help identify management systems and, even more important, other
systems which could operate better as management systems but which
are currently of a different species. Accountable management should
allow the systems to which it is applied to develop attitudes, to seek
opportunities for improvement, rather than solve problems which
arise, and create a success-rewarding environment for the efficient
manager in government. A risk is that accountability will be seen as, or
will be distorted over time into, a concept which exists primarily to
identify responsibility for mistakes and to penalize failure—with neither
mistakes nor failure defined in a rational way (if at all). Over-emphasis on
detail, or a perfectionist approach to matters such as the extent to which
commercial accounts or self-financing can be applied, may result in no

more than a few systems being regarded as accountable and all others continuing as before. It will also fail if increased delegation proves more shadow than substance with the result that those in charge may be held to be accountable while never feeling more than frustrated. The more able will soon migrate to the more congenial climate of the administration or the diplomatic system leaving behind in management the bureaucratic equivalent of the American 'fall-guy'. But even to refer to these risks is to call attention to the absurdity of imagining that they are not all foreseen and will be easily avoided.

PROGRAMMING–PLANNING–BUDGETING

(alias Output Budgeting and incorporating Programme Analysis Review (PAR))

Few approaches to efficiency in management in government have been launched with as much publicity, or marketed so aggressively, as PPB in the U.S.A. in the mid-sixties. It appeared in what Bernard Gross described as 'a burst of grandiose claims of breakthroughs and exaggerated application to irrelevant situations'. Charles Schultze, at the time Director of the Bureau of the Budget, spoke in similar terms to a Congressional Committee;[8] 'Much has been published on PPB. Learned articles have treated it sometimes as the greatest thing since the invention of the wheel.' Predictably, the force of the initial impact generated an equal and opposite reaction of the kind described by Schultze (continuing the previous quotation): 'Other articles attack it, either as a naive attempt to quantify and computerize the imponderable, or as an arrogant effort on the part of latter-day technocrats to usurp the decision-making function in a political democracy.' Schultze sees PPB as neither one nor the other of these extremes but as 'a means of helping responsible officials make decisions'. I shall not advance any different view in commenting on PPB, although I would suggest that PPB can also be seen as helping responsible Ministers and even responsible legislatures to take decisions. As we have seen, many decisions in government on the use of resources are complex and controversial; the question for consideration is how, and how far, can PPB assist to make these decisions better.

PPB is difficult to define. It requires for understanding a fuller description.[9] It has a chameleon-like character which allows it to adjust itself in name and content to the demand of the environment. It comprises several conceptually distinct parts which are interrelated but not, in my view, to a degree which justified the initial presentation of PPB as a system (this was when the initials PPBS held the stage). Among the components of PPB it is possible to separate out and identify:

a process by which resources are identified, costed and assigned to the objectives, which their use is intended to serve, through a series of 'programmes', each comprising a number of programme elements.

A planning process by which strategies within the public service are costed, and proposed expenditure over several (commonly five) future years estimated and made available as information for decision making on resource allocation and for macro-economic planning and control.

A budgeting allocation and control process by which resources are mobilized and authorized for use in particular ways within a definite period of time, e.g. the coming financial year.

A process for introducing measurement of outcome achievement, or where impracticable, of output attainment for each programme (or programme element).

A framework within which analytical studies in depth can be commissioned for programmes where *prima facie* they seem likely to be useful and carried out as a regular normal procedure rather than as a special inquisition.

Two questions arise on this prospectus. Is PPB in fact a system or integrated process which must be accepted or rejected as a whole ? Who, among the many parties involved in decisions on the use of resources in the public sector are likely to enjoy the benefits (or disbenefits) of PPB ?

PPB AS AN INTEGRATED APPROACH

It is, of course, possible to define PPB as embracing all the elements set out in the prospectus and to assert that anything which falls short of the entity cannot be described as PPB, e.g. 'Output budgeting (an alternative British title for PPB) has to be considered as a system and not just as a new way of setting out the tables of figures in respect of public expenditure'. But the issue, if we do not define it away, is whether like the thirty-nine articles the approaches incorporated in PPB must all be accepted; and whether all must be introduced together in a series of related changes. I see PPB as consisting of several processes which neither are, need be, or can be, fully integrated at the interface. PPB is a group of sensible propositions (on some of which rational men may entertain reservations) which are neither mutually incompatible nor so logically interdependent as to make it necessary to accept all or none. On this view it is not a system.

If we look first at the relationship between the budgetary (single year) and planning (five year) processes it will be found in most countries that the former is not merely, as might be supposed, an integral part of the latter but a distinct process with different ambit, purpose, and unit of measurement. These differences arise in a number of ways. The annual budgeting system found in many public authorities is basically a process of authorization to allow resources to be used to defined extents for defined purposes. This may require proposals to be classified in a different format with boundaries erected between categories, as the basis of the 'regularity' forms of audit. These categories may differ greatly from the classification best suited to planning purposes. So far, for example, in the U.S.A. the form in which Congress approves appropriations has not been brought into line with the programme classification of PPB introduced by the Administration (and translator programmes or 'cross walks' between the two are necessary).[10] In Canada the new programme classification seems well on the way to replacing the previous form, after co-existing with it for several years. In Britain, discussions by the Select Committee on Procedure seem to leave the options open on this. Another factor is that the ambit of the annual budget authorizing process may differ greatly from that appropriate for planning resource allocation. In Britain for example the five year planning of public expenditure which has come into existence in the past decade in advance of PPB covers *all* public expenditure, including the investment although not current expenditure, of nationalized industries. Much of this is not subject to the day to day control of central government departments. Little more than one-third of it is required to be voted annually by Parliament or is subject to audit by the Comptroller and Auditor General. This divergence between planning ambit and budgetary ambit is unlikely to disappear, even if Britain adopted PPB generally, since the motive behind the longer term planning of public expenditure has been only partly to achieve a better use of resources. At least as important has been to achieve better management of the economy and from this point of view local authority expenditure, whether financed from rates or loans, and expenditure by other public authorities does not differ significantly in effect from central government expenditure.

The costs or inputs appropriate to an annual budgeting authorizing process and those appropriate to a longer term planning process differ conceptually. Clearly an authorizing process will tend to limit itself to resources needing authority to be used: typically such systems do not provide at all for the use of such resources as property in public ownership or equipment (including computers and other plant) which has been bought in an earlier budgeting period. Of course the process could be adjusted to do so by setting up some property and/or equipment-holding agency to lease it out to users at market rents. But since these would be internal, financial transfers, the total of the 'expenditure' presented by authorities would no longer equal the net expenditure to be authorized.

More formidable problems have been overcome. But at present in Britain the full opportunity cost approach to the use of resources, which is not merely preferable but essential for the rational longer term planning of resource use, is not identical with 'expenditure' authorized in annual budgeting systems.

There are three other reasons why a 'plan' for a given future year will need to be adjusted as the time comes to translate it into a budget for the coming year. Plans frequently represent the financial implications over time of decisions taken rather than the possible implications of proposals yet to be approved—certainly this is the basis on which PPB developed in the U.S. Department of Defense. At, or shortly before, the stage at which a forward plan is translated into an annual budget, new decisions will be taken and will be incorporated in the budget. The second factor is that five year plans, certainly in Britain, have been based on assumptions about the general state of the economy. Even if those assumptions are fulfilled precisely by events at the budget stage a degree of 'fine tuning' is likely to be necessary. If the economic position differs from the assumptions (a not unknown occurrence), the degree of adjustment may be greater. But the magnitude of what may be popularly described as 'slashing cuts' should not be over-emphasized. In evidence to the Select Committee on Procedure, Treasury witnesses estimated the reductions in total public expenditure made in the exceptional circumstances of the aftermath of devaluation at no more than $\frac{3}{4}$ per cent in the first year and $2\frac{1}{2}$ per cent in the second year. Thirdly there is the problem that five year plans will be based on some price convention, for example, all estimates will be in terms of constant prices measured at the price level prevailing in a base year—commonly the year in which the plan is prepared or reviewed. This price level may not be that appropriate for translating the first year of the plan into the budget for the coming year. The latter will need to ensure that it provides the public authority with the command over resources needed in that period—in other words it may need to anticipate future price changes at least to the extent they are known firmly to be due to take place. Conventions differ on how far anticipation should extend: the point here is that plan/budget price level conversions will be needed.

All these distinctions show that planning and budgeting are different processes in purpose, ambit, concepts and conventions. The most one can ensure is that the two processes are mutually consistent in a general way. Integration is not, and perhaps should not or cannot be, complete.

But whatever the differences between budgeting and planning they have at least some basic similarity which distinguishes them from the other activities of measuring outcomes (or outputs) and of analysis in depth of resource-using strategies. Both budgeting and planning are concerned with flows of resources over time and are deeply rooted in a particular unit of time—that of the financial year which determines the budgeting process and makes it convenient to roll forward the five year plan by one year once each financial year. Both processes are likely to operate within closely prescribed timetables—the budgeting process to conform with statutory or other requirements of the legislature or authorizing body and the planning review process so as to achieve the best 'fit' with the budgeting, both from the point of view of load-spreading for the staff concerned, in so far as some are involved in both processes (it would be difficult to imagine this not being the case), and to ensure that data on the outcome of one process is available when needed as information for the other process. But the measurement of outcomes or, if impracticable, of outputs, is not related inherently to annual reviews or, where they are, e.g. education, the appropriate year may not coincide with the financial year. Nor is it necessarily an activity that conceptually needs be, or in practice can conveniently be, timed to coincide with budgeting or planning timetables. To force it into this mould may lead to the adoption of those measurements of output which happen to be available at the right time of the year at the expense of better which would be obtained later. And it could lead to the use of ready but superficial, if not misleading, indicators of outcome being preferred to those appropriate to the evaluation of outcome by analysis in depth which the complexity of many public programmes may need.

We may also note that the programme (made up of programme elements) is specifically designed as a form of classification to throw light on a particular activity—that of allocating resources between objectives over periods of time. There will be certain kinds of decision, e.g. converting the heating system of all buildings owned by a particular local authority, or all hospitals in an area, from one fuel to another which needs evaluation *ex ante* and *ex post* for which programme classification will not be meaningful. There are others such as the electrification of a part of a railway system where the costs might form a programme element but which would not provide a basis for annual reviews of outcome or output because of the impracticality *ex post* of separating out annually the effects to date of this investment from the operations of the system as a whole.

If next we consider analysis or special studies, the closeness of integration with such time-dominated process as budgeting and planning is even less than with outcome/output measurement. Indeed it could be said of analysis, as has been said of corporate or strategic planning, that it is in essence an irregular and unprogrammed activity. Indeed nobody suggests that under PPB analytical studies in depth would be directed to every programme annually, but merely that decisions on how analysis could best be used would be integrated in some way with the decision making processes on plans and budgets. This might mean so little as to be innocuous, but if it is intended to imply that, from the point of view of timing, the decision making periods on budgets or plans is also the appropriate time to commission analysis one may doubt whether the pressure of such activities make the periods the best time to reach rational decisions on other issues which need not be taken concurrently. And if it implies that analysis is to be regarded as primarily a tool of central resource allocators, rather than that of those at the head of sub-systems or systems, the proposition also seems suspect. Analysis is a tool of management and the initiative to use it should come frequently (although not exclusively) from the managers of systems and sub-systems when the time seems appropriate for them. We see, therefore, that when Aaron Wildavsky[11] wrote of 'a shotgun marriage' between PPB and analysis he was if anything being charitable about the degree of compatibility between them—after all most shotgun marriages arise through the relationship of the parties having at least on some occasion been close.

Not only is the relationship of analysis to time as different as possible from that of budgeting and planning, but analysis needs to be based on different concepts of inputs or costs from those appropriate to budgeting or, as I have described, the somewhat different concepts appropriate to planning. As in the latter, the concept of cost in analysis will be an opportunity cost, but in many areas of analysis the far broader concept of social opportunity cost (measured against social benefits) will be relevant. Indeed the case for commissioning analysis—as in the case of the cost–benefit study into the Victoria Line Tube in London—is to discover the existence and extent of costs and benefits which are not incorporated in, or brought to light by, information flows relevant to budgeting or longer term planning processes. This kind of analysis can be attempted twice—once *ex ante* once *ex post*, but it cannot throw up measurable streams of information on social costs and social benefits (for example, the effect on road congestion which the additional underground railway capacity causes) which can be incorporated or at all readily related to the annual flows of financial or 'adjusted', e.g. constant price information relevant to the budgeting and planning processes. The Appropriation Accounts, local authority accounts and similar accounts for other public authorities provide *ex post* information which can be directly related to the budgetary allocations. In Britain it is difficult to provide information flows on resources used which can be related directly to the forecasts of the five year plans. There are both theoretical difficulties and practical problems of adjustment for changes in the value of money. But if the latter is difficult, any idea of incorporating figures of social benefits and social costs with financial data in annual information flows seems totally beyond the bounds of possibility. Most of the former are conceptual and are not represented by any 'hard' transaction of a kind recorded as data. So that for this reason too, the integration of analytical data with those appropriate to budgeting and planning can never be achieved. The latter are based on actual financial transactions adjusted, particularly for the planning process, by a series of 'conventions' similar in character to those, and in part identical with them, incorporated in national income statistics. Analysis is concerned to extend and use financial and other data not by standard *conventional* adjustments but by *unconventional*, i.e. devising a methodology appropriate to the problem.

Analysis and outcome/output measurements are intended to improve decisions on how resources can best be used while budgeting and planning are concerned with how the resource use arising from such decisions can best be phased over time. Budgeting, planning and analysis will all define 'costs' differently. It is nevertheless a virtue of PPB that it prevents these processes becoming regarded as totally distinct and a situation arising as it tended to do in British central government expenditure before 1960 when proposals for using resources were approved sequentially 'in principle' and 'on their merits' to an extent well beyond the practicality of funding them. If 'capital rationing' and 'current resource rationing' is likely to be normal in most areas of public expenditure, this implies that resource-using proposals cannot be authorized in a meaningful way even if investment schemes have a positive present value when discounted at the standard discount rate in operation in the public service, or even if current expenditure schemes show a surplus of social benefits over social costs, but only if they can find a sufficiently high place in a ranking order to obtain a ration of the resources available in particular years. This factor does provide more justification for the grouping of the various approaches under PPB without, however, eliminating the many areas of non-integration I have described.

It would seem, therefore, that what PPB offers is not a system in the sense of a group of closely integrated components, but several good ideas all relevant to the better use of resources and loosely interrelated—that strategies and their use of resources should be planned over a period of years, that inputs should be related to outcomes, that outcomes (or, second-best, outputs) should be measured, that strategies should be evaluated or reviewed by analytical studies in depth from time to time. What PPB offers is in effect what business management would describe as a marketable package. It is like an airline operator who offers not only a return flight but, for an inclusive price, a hotel reservation, a season ticket to the ancient monuments and a tour of the night clubs with their resident hostess. In public service terms PPB is an approach which has presentational advantages in negotiation. In Britain analysis has spread rapidly in advance of PPB (as indeed it did in the U.S.A.). In planning public expenditure over a number of years the British system was as advanced as in any country. The measurement of outputs and even of outcomes had started. But in Britain there are few if any areas of resource management where all the ideas incorporated in PPB are well advanced and some where none is operating fully. Much the same was true of other countries and the sudden, dramatic decision on the general adoption of PPB by the Federal Administration of the U.S.A. in 1965, and the different and slightly slower process which Canada has adopted, can both be seen to have at least short-circuited the time and negotiating cost in getting each organization independently to consider separately each of the ideas comprising PPB. The position after the general adoption may be untidy and the outcome at first disappointing. But it may provide a far better base for rapid improvement in the use of resources than the previous situation. As against this, it can be argued that a system-by-system approach to persuade those in charge of a particular system that PPB is in *their* interests, not those of some external authority, is more likely to give these ideas roots in the management system and ensure survival and growth.

It will be seen therefore that any public authority approaching PPB has at least four options open:

1 To follow the American example of the quick dash by seeking to introduce rapidly all elements of PPB in all parts of the organization —and to tidy up the confusion and eliminate the superficial subsequently.

2 To seek the adoption of all elements of PPB in single sub-systems at a time, after careful preliminary preparation (hoping perhaps that, as experience increases, confidence will grow and the later stages of the process of change proceed more quickly than the earlier).

3 To seek the general adoption quickly of programme classifications for budgeting and planning purposes (thus saving time and resources in negotiation of this change department by department); to clarify and improve the classification in the light of experience; and then to consider the role and form of outcome/output measurement and of analysis sub-system by sub-system.

4 To concentrate on necessary analysis in depth and develop a study of resources under programmes, without changing the planning and budgeting processes. (This is basically the Programmes Analysis Review (PAR) approach.)

In Britain there was never in the sixties any sign of an inclination to adopt the first option. Much care was taken to avoid the faults of which those concerned with introducing PPB in the U.S.A. are now accused— over-enthusiasm and over-selling, a premature decision to introduce it throughout the Federal Service at short notice, a failure to establish agreement on the role of PPB between the Administration and Congress. By 1970[12] Britain had achieved in central government some familiarity with the concepts through publications and training, at least two valuable preliminary studies, an improved system of resource allocation in the Ministry of Defence which incorporates some but not all of the features of PPB, and the opening of a dialogue between the House of Commons and the Government which suggested that a measure of agreement might be capable of achievement in Britain. But there was no PPB in central government, although in local government the Greater London Council had started to implement it. In Canada[13] and France[14] progress by 1970 had been greater in central government without repeating the difficulties which had occurred in the U.S.A.

Clearly there is no one of these options which will be 'right' for all public authorities at all times—there are trade-offs between advantages and disadvantages in all these approaches which will need to be evaluated in each case.

As this book goes to print, the British seem to be taking the fourth option and concentrating on PAR and analysis, leaving planning to the existing PESC system and budgeting unchanged.

THE BENEFICIARIES OF PPB

PPB does not provide better decisions on the use of resources or any guarantee of improved management. Each of the elements of PPB provides better information and since the quality of information is one variable determining the quality of management it should, other variables remaining constant, result in a better use of resources. But, as we have seen, the better use of resources involves complex not simple criteria. There are at least five parties with an interest in the decision making process: the public; elected representatives nationally or locally or the elected or nominated Boards or Councils of certain public authorities; decision makers with central co-ordinating responsibilities for resource allocation or use (e.g. in central government the Cabinet, the Treasury; in local government the Council, the Chief Executive, Treasurer); decision makers with similar central co-ordinating responsibilities in major systems (e.g. central finance units in, say, the Ministry of Defence or the integrative/allocative system of the Department of Education or Health); the managers in charge of sub-systems in government departments, local authorities, hospital boards.

If PPB is concerned with information it must also be relevant not only to better decision making but to power and authority. There is a wide measurement of agreement among those who have conducted research in this area that, irrespective of where power or authority may seem to lie in, say, an organization chart, in practice they are found where the information is and are not found where the information is not. The sharing of authority for decision making would also be seen by some as a zero sum game—there is a limited amount and if one party acquires more, by definition one or more of the other parties must end up with less. The friction which introducing PPB has caused in certain countries can only be explained in terms of such concepts. In the U.S.A. the initiative for PPB has come from the 'centralists'—the third and fourth of the five groups listed above—in the shape initially of the central organization of the Department of Defense and subsequently of the Bureau of the Budget. This may explain the relative, and in some ways surprising, lack of welcome for it from Congress and what would seem to be a sullen if not positively hostile response in some management sub-systems. The latter reaction may have been magnified by what would seem on this side of the Atlantic to have been the predominating attitude of centralists in the early days of PPB in which it was presented as the key which would unlock dusty attics and cellars of resource management and allow a task force of highly intelligent, fully trained, well motivated and public-spirited centralists to sweep them out and expose the inadequacies of the caretakers notable for their lack of all the above mentioned qualities—the Ariel–Caliban confrontation. This approach seems certain to be counter-productive, for it is of the nature of a sub-system manager to cast himself in the role of hero rather than villain in schemes for improvement in the use of resources (a fact well understood and exploited by management consultants and O. & M. specialists) and he will, if he can, re-write the script to achieve this. In Britain so far no one of the five interested groups mentioned is so closely associated with PPB as to arouse the suspicions of the other four. Strong support for PPB (and some opposition or apathy) can be found in each of the five groups. Particularly important may prove to be the fact that through training and publications a significant degree of interest (although not unanimous enthusiasm) has been built up among system managers *before* they have come under any external pressure to use PPB.

The role of the sub-system manager in PPB is critical. Efficient management in the public service has to be based on the internal efficiency of the sub-systems—it cannot be enforced from outside by external enquiries, analysis or other means, however useful the latter may be in contributing to the achievement of high standards. One of the important contributions which PPB can make to management is in its effect within all systems of forcing resources to be seen as flows over time intended to achieve stated outcomes, with the results being measured against objective where appropriate. I have referred earlier to the fact that in much of the public service the historical spillover of procedures and attitudes appropriate to administration systems into management systems has not produced this basic approach to the use of resources. PPB could, therefore, help create an attitude of mind which is certainly a large part of efficient management.

Consequently I see the better information flows that PPB will provide as a positive sum not a zero sum game. All can benefit from it since all five interests from the sub-system manager to the general public have distinct and important roles in decisions on the use of resources which more information should allow to be better fulfilled. Of course PPB would not allow those who now ratify or discuss decisions *ex post* to take decisions *ex ante* in future, or those who now delegate to refuse in future to do so, without friction resulting. Within the framework of established roles the information which PPB can provide should allow the total system to operate more effectively. But in one respect PPB, by throwing more light on choice and alternatives, may sharpen conflict in an area where in the past ambiguity has minimized it. This will arise if and when both central and local government (and possibly regional authorities) are using PPB. As each comes to know more about the objectives resources are serving, each will have the information, and in all probability the inclination, to re-deploy them to better advantage from its own point of view. Both, or all three, cannot however do so without conflict or compromise.[15]

PPB AND SYSTEMS

Since the structure of programmes and programme elements are concerned with the use of resources to achieve major aims and limited goals respectively, it might seem that there must be a coincidence with the pattern of government that emerges from a systems analysis. The major system finds its motivating and unifying force in the pursuit of a particular major objective: the sub-system in a more limited goal. This would seem to imply that the structure of programmes and elements was merely the representation, in resource allocation terms, of the system structure. In a sense this is true. PPB encourages and, indeed, almost compels thinking to proceed in terms of systems and away from organizations. It is, therefore, a favourable influence indirectly for better management, irrespective of whatever improvements in decisions on resources result directly from the sum of the PPB processes of planning, budgeting and analysis. But the coincidence between programme and system structure is not exact or complete. It is closer between sub-systems and programme elements. The reason for the lack of identity between systems and programmes is that for neither is there any uniquely correct, single set of relationships, valid for all purposes, to be found by examination. I emphasized earlier that a sub-system may belong at any time to more than one major system. This fact means that there will often be a number of equally valid and rational ways in which the use of resources within sub-systems can be brought together to constitute a 'programme'. And while in some cases it is logical to analyse the collective outcome of a related group of uses of resources in pursuit of an objective, there may be occasions where it would be an exaggeration to claim that the sub-systems concerned had sufficient degree of interrelationship needed to constitute a system. Some programmes are neither under the control of any organization nor deployed within a system.

An example may serve to establish this latter point. All the resources directed to the minimization of, and the consequence of, road accidents are divided between a wide variety of organizations and a great number of systems—police systems, hospital and ambulance systems, judicial systems, social security systems, as well as the more obvious road construction, road maintenance or traffic control systems. But it is difficult to regard this entity as a system. There is lack of relationship or communication between many of the parts. But it is meaningful and an aid to rational decisions to analyse together all these inputs, although there would be found to be severe constraints in trying to allocate them in a better way within the 'programme'. Some of these uses of resources will be found to be 'open-ended', for example, police, ambulance, hospital, social security. They will be used or not used according to circumstances, not according to plans or budgetary controls. And although it could be argued that, say, the resources to provide more and better road signs could be 'found' by the resulting savings in hospitals, police or social security systems, the transactions could neither be relied on to be self-balancing in this way, nor expected to be, for alternative claims on the resources becoming available within the hospital or police systems will have greater priority than their 'release' to some national 'system' responsible for the road safety programme.

In the example given, what is attractive in logic may be impraticable to operate. But other superficially rational programmes, e.g. gathering together all the resources used in training (central, departmental, external) in the civil service to set against the objective of say 'a better informed, motivated and skilled service' would be both deficient in logic (since training can more appropriately be grouped with other forms of investment in staff development as a programme element in fulfilling the objectives of particular systems) and in practicality (since no central system exercises control over the total resources used in training throughout the service).

In general, care is needed to ensure that programmes and changes in total allocations to, and sub-allocations within, programmes are meaningful. Someone (some sub-system) should be clearly responsible and in control of each programme element. If the total programme is not and cannot, as in the case of road safety, be made the responsibility of a single system a 'programme committee' might be useful to advise on the balance of allocation between programme elements, while recognizing the limits of their influence over out-turn and of their power to switch resources between certain elements. Indeed such a committee might wish to bring within its area of review resource uses closely related to, but outside the scope of both the narrower budgeting and the wider planning ambit of PPB. Public authorities can often 'secure' the use of resources in pursuit of an objective without themselves needing to mobilize the resources in full if at all, for example by legislation requiring the use of resources by individuals or firms, by percentage grants or subsidies to achieve leverage on the greater use of private resources, by financially self-balancing measures. For instance the regular inspection of vehicles in the interests of road safety could be achieved by legislation and carried out by private garages without any of the resources entering into PPB figures (other than perhaps a minor contribution for enforcement) or by providing state vehicle testing centres towards the cost of which vehicle owners paid inspection fees which met the cost in part or in full—or which even made a profit. Probably, therefore, the most useful basis of PPB is where a programme element is effectively under the control of a sub-system and the programme of a major system. If the latter is impracticable the alternative is the co-ordination of a committee which would bring closely related uses of resources within the private sector within the scope of their review. But in assigning resources to objectives there is no unique categorization that is better for all purposes than another. The capacity to reclassify inputs in several ways is an option worth preserving—by the 'building block' method of estimating and recording expenditure.

Even if programmes and programme elements coincide with systems and sub-systems, problems of allocation will remain. Is a dam carrying a road and providing hydro-electricity to be shown against the programmes for roads, flood control or power generation or is the cost to be allocated between them? (negotiations on a 'fair' allocation could themselves use significant resources). Or is it to be charged in full against the programme of the principal beneficiary—if clearly identifiable? Some experts favour the latter solution, but at times it could result in programme totals misrepresenting significantly the objectives to which resources were assigned and experience suggests that this is unlikely to be overcome by attaching explanatory notes to the figures. As against this, allocation will immediately produce programme or element totals which are not under single control since, while the total cost of a project can be allocated, control cannot be—or cannot sensibly be. Probably therefore the balance of advantage lies in non-allocation except where the resources contributed to another programme represent a significant —say in excess of 1 per cent—part of that programme in which case allocations might be preferred, but the sum allocated should be separately identified as a sub-total within the programme total. And if allocation is pursued it would be essential to have a PPB office with arbitrary power to make instant judgements on 'fair' allocations—and fair assignments in cases of dispute. Nothing would be more discreditable than for resources in staff time of £100 to be spent in debating whether the air fare of £70 to send a road engineer to a United Nations conference on transport in developing countries should be charged to the programme for road construction, to that for supporting the work of the United Nations or that for aid to developing countries.

Another form of allocation problem is that of 'overheads'. To what extent, if at all, should, say, the cost of Ministers, Permanent Secretaries, Finance and Establishment Divisions be 'charged out' to the various programmes and elements for which they are responsible? In general, since these costs are not under the control of sub-systems managers responsible for programme elements it seems better not to allocate them but to retain them as a separate 'supporting' programme element. Similarly with most research expenditure, except that directly commissioned by a sub-system. But management services, training, typing, transport should not only be charged out to programmes but made the subject of actual payments by the sub-systems receiving the services. The sub-systems providing the services would operate as service units generating income. And of course all costs of accommodation, printing and other services of this kind, even if provided by a central agency, would be charged to programme elements.

Both in the definition of objectives and in establishing measures of performance for each programme difficult problems will arise on PPB. On objectives the interest and skill in drafting which exists within the civil service could easily absorb an undue amount of time. It is not that objectives are anything but important, but the difficulties of defining them precisely, particularly at the highest levels of major programmes, and of trying to define the relationship between multiple objectives, are likely to be resistant even to the best drafting. Indeed I have seen very few examples of true objectives in PPB schemes in other countries. I mentioned in an earlier chapter that 'policy' is at times used to mean no more than a brief description of an activity. An objective in PPB is often little more: as if a fishmonger were to define his objective as 'selling fish'. While, therefore, it may be useful to bring together all resources being directed to some particular military force, for example, 'a defence force east of Suez', this is hardly in itself an objective. If the purposes for which it existed were stated, alternative possibilities of achieving the same end by different means could be brought within the field of analysis. Civil expenditure contains many similar examples. All of this suggests that initially a rough and ready approach to objectives should be adopted with those of the major programmes inclining towards the rough, and those of programme elements to the ready. Exposed to public discussion, some improvement in objective definitions could be expected in time.

Even less should implementation of PPB be delayed by seeking comprehensive and effective measurements of performance for every programme and element at the outset. I have suggested earlier my doubts as to whether some such measurements will ever be meaningful and whether they may not do more harm than good. Deciding what weight to attach to measures of performance of the weights and measures department may be a useful and worthwhile activity: but it could be tackled at a later stage in PPB.

The introduction of PPB requires staff of intelligence and imagination to be devoted full-time to the work. But it is only in the field of analysis or special studies, which, as I have argued, have no more than a loose relationship to the main structure of PPB, that numbers are likely to be large, or rare and esoteric skills may occasionally be relevant. Knowledge of the other elements in PPB could be taught in a course of four or five days to those possessing the higher forms of common sense. Any branch of the public service that lacks staff with the ability to plan PPB has more serious problems than the lack of PPB. It is in analysis, and in planning information systems to support both PPB and the whole decision making process within systems, that the problem of qualified and sufficient staff will arise.

To sum up, there may be advantages in introducing the main structure of PPB even in advance of perfectly defined objectives, acceptable measures of performance for all programmes and elements, a sufficient analytical capacity or an ideal information system (although of course some method of allocating out-turns to the estimates in the programme classification is needed at the outset). Even such an incomplete Mark I version of PPB will generate throughout the service attitudes of mind favourable to management by clearly associating the use of resources with objectives. And bringing together expenditure at present subdivided among many different estimates may reveal at least some examples like that in the country where it was found that the total support from a variety of agencies to a particular industry amounted annually to twice the annual net income of the producers concerned. No large or sophisticated analytical capacity is required to find grounds for reflection in such cases.

Exactly the reverse sequence to the introduction of PPB is that embraced in the concept of PAR. PAR concentrates initially on the analysis of programmes and was largely conceived for the purpose of analysis rather than arising out of any general reorganization of the classification of resource uses into programmes for budgeting or planning purposes.

This can be justified either on the grounds that the budgeting and planning processes are too difficult to change or that they are already at an acceptable level of effectiveness, although not based on a programme classification, and that priority should be given to bringing analysis to the same level. At this point, therefore, the PAR aspect of PPB leads into a study of the recent and future contribution of analysis in all forms to management.

ANALYSIS

The Nature of Analysis

I have mentioned that in the U.S.A. the word analysis, which is now in constant use, is often preceded by the word 'systems' to mean what in Britain is described as operational research. The word 'analysis' has not been much used here in management in the public service, although one major operational research unit incorporated it in its title—the Defence Operations Analysis Unit. But I believe it is a useful concept for it brings out the essential element in a much larger number of developments which have occurred in the British public service under so many different titles, employing staff with so many varieties of specialized skill, that the scale and pace of the change in total has been obscured.

The first essential element in analysis is that those engaged on it have the time to concentrate on a single issue, with the support needed in staff, and on occasions computer access. It may be a problem or an opportunity; a choice between strategies or the best method of implementing a plan; a structure or a process. It is this element of time to concentrate that is so lacking at almost all operational levels from the highest to the lowest of the public service in Britain and affects equally divisions which in business would be 'staff', rather than 'line', like establishments and finance.

I must emphasize that time is no more than the first pre-requisite of analysis. Stafford Beer deals severely[16] with those who claim more. 'This decisively disposes of a view often expressed in management circles that an operational research team is best regarded as a group made up of men who have the time to undertake some detailed thinking about a problem which the manager would undertake himself if he were not too busy.' This is a fair comment but the converse is also true; in a line or staff management post in the public service—and, I suspect, in business— neither the operational research expert nor, say, the economist, could bring to bear his analytical abilities because of lack of time to concentrate on the study in depth of a particular issue.

Besides time, analytical units bring to bear experience, which may be highly or slightly, directly or indirectly, relevant to the particular task. They should bring uncommitted attitudes, particularly a lack of commitment to what exists at present. And a wide variety of skill ranging from that so generalized that it is hardly to be distinguished from common sense to that so specialized and near the frontier of applied mathematics that perhaps those possessing it in Britain may be counted on the fingers of one hand—a situation less alarming than it may seem since the number of real-life situations to which the esoteric knowledge can be applied may be inadequate to keep even such a small group fully occupied.

In the public service it has been characteristic of the development of analysis to build up teams on a single skill or closely related skills basis, for example, O. & M. work study, economic analysis, operational research units. In management consultancy, multi-skill organizations are more typical deploying teams with the required mix of skills, of which the composition is decided *after* the initial analysis of the problem. The latter approach has advantages, as the former rests on the proposition that the nature of the task can be defined accurately in advance and assigned to the appropriate single skill, or related skills, analytical unit. And that the scope of most problems is no wider than the range of skill of any one specialized unit. I am not aware that evidence has established the validity of all or any of these assumptions: they seem inherently implausible.

From what I have written it will be clear that the nature of analysis places it in the same family as research. At times the distinction between them is not sharp—analysis will often result in the commissioning of research—but in so far as a difference exists, it may lie in the practical nature of the goals of analysis and in the greater probability of time constraints. It is thus more closely comparable with development or applied research than with pure or basic research and, as we have seen, some of the earliest analytical units were called development groups.

The Development of Analytical Capacity

It may be difficult for those joining the British public service today to appreciate the relative novelty of analysis. Traditionally the service had depended not on analysis but advice. Advice might be obtained from a committee ranging in formality or size from a royal commission to a small group called to an *ad hoc* discussion. Or, less frequently, an adviser might be appointed. At times, and in places, it was seen as a significant step forward to appoint 'an economic adviser' or 'an operational research specialist', rather in the manner in which those who had gardens designed by Capability Brown in the eighteenth century might take on to their payroll a hermit to inhabit the grotto and contribute to the aesthetic, or even intellectual, pleasure of guests walking in the garden. Such advisers would be invited to many meetings, sent copies of innumerable papers. Having no, or few, supporting staff they had no chance to obtain better information or to analyse what was available: they earned or lost a reputation by the Delphic quality of their off-the-cuff comments. For rather different reasons, the advice of committees was likely to be superficial even if, as was often the case, it was sensible. It was not until the sixties that committees began to refuse to give advice until relevant information was available and resources to analyse it provided. Thus in the past decade with the individual adviser now becoming rare, and the analytical teams normal, the dichotomy between advice and analysis has become much less pronounced.

Analysis as I have defined it embraces in the public service a wide variety of activities including organization and methods (O. & M.), work study, operational research, economic analysis, statistical analysis, cost–benefit studies, systems analysis for computer projects. And the work of those in the Exchequer and Audit Department devoted not to the preparation of the Appropriation Accounts but to detailed *ex post* enquiry into individual programmes or projects is also an important form of analysis relevant to management.

One of the first and most successful forms of analysis was set up soon after the war. In 1949 an Architects and Building Branch was established in, as it then was, the Ministry of Education. This branch incorporated a new form of organization in a 'development group' or inter-disciplinary team, which analysed the needs met by school and other educational buildings, considered alternative designs and forms of construction to meet needs with fewer resources, and implemented the selected strategies through the control of building programmes, building regulations and cost limits per school place. It was an important development from a management point of view. Plans were directly related to ends and alternatives analysed thoroughly by devoting the time of a group to concentrate on a single, although broad, subject free from day-to-day operational commitments. The organization was designed for the task and not for convention. Administrators, professional staff (including architects and engineers) and Inspectors of Schools (representing the user interest) worked as a team, not in the traditional separate hierarchies. The group was under the joint leadership of an administrator and an architect—a device which flouts much business, as well as official, conventional wisdom. And it not only succeeded, but could be seen to succeed. By 1962 it was claimed that in real terms a saving of 50 per cent over 1949 costs had been achieved: in money terms of over £250m. From a management point of view one might now prefer more emphasis on cost in use—under which discounted future costs of maintenance, heating, etc., would have been incorporated with initial capital costs into the analysis. But it was by any standards a successful innovation. It illustrates how less favourable an environment for change were the fifties, as contrasted with the sixties, that this success was so little exploited elsewhere. Some experiments with development groups were conducted in other parts of the public service but in less sympathetic environments they achieved little and did not become permanent parts of the system at that time. It was not until 1958, nearly ten years after the experiment had started in Education, that a new Directorate of Works, organized on somewhat similar lines, was set up in the War Office. The Ministry of Education's Architects and Building Branch initiated two changes—the importance of analysis by full-time specialists from several professions, and the need to experiment in organization form to break down barriers between 'classes' and professions. Both were to emerge as strong trends in the sixties. But the example of developing an analytical unit to deal with a strategy, rather than taking strategy problems to existing analytical units, has only occasionally been followed.

In the civil service there was by 1960 no more than a small O. & M. and work study capacity, operational research virtually confined to the Ministry of Defence, the small group I have described in the Ministry of Education, a dozen or so economists mainly in the Treasury and often working more as individual advisers rather than as analysts and some *ex post* accounting capacity in Exchequer and Audit. Statisticians were still employed mainly on the production of statistics rather than on analysis. By 1970 the total analytical capacity had expanded greatly. Since the distinction at the margin between analysis and advice, research or even in some areas line management is not clear, over-precise statistical measurement of the growth could be misleading. But 12 economists in central government in 1961 increased to 25 in 1964 and 150 in 1969. By 1969 there were 500 O. & M. and about 730 work study staff in central government. Several departments had what were in effect operational research units although not always described as such.[17]

In these and elsewhere statisticians were being increasingly used for analysis rather than for collecting and evaluating data, for example the work on a model of the power industries started by, as it was then, the Ministry of Power and the input–output work in the Department of Education and Science.

Over the whole of this field my own approximate assessment is that analytical capacity measured in numbers employed was at least ten times greater in central government in 1970 than in 1960, and since it was supported by far greater computer capacity the real increase in the power to analyse was much higher than that. In local government and in other parts of the public service like the health service the trends were similar. O. & M. developed in local government after 1953 when the Coventry City Council invited the Treasury O. & M. to examine and report on their administration. Both in this field and in work study the larger authorities set up their own units, the smaller tended to rely on consultants or help from other bodies. By 1963 there were over 250 work study officers in local government. But operational research teams could be supported only by the largest local authorities like the Greater London Council and to provide such a service for others a central agency seemed essential. The Royal Institute of Public Administration began experimental studies in O.R. for local government in 1959. By 1964 it had five O.R. specialists; in 1965 it set up a special unit which by 1969 had a total staff of sixty including nearly forty graduates. In the health service developments were similar; in an area of resource use where decision criteria and objectives are often many and complex, a surprisingly large range of problems suitable for operational research analysis emerged.

This growth within the public service of analytical capacity has been supplemented by a very rapid growth in commissions of independent consultants who, like internal units, provide essentially time, relevant if indirect experience, and specialized techniques. The use of consultants by the public service was hardly known before 1960. In 1969 central government alone commissioned fifty consultancy assignments. Other parts of the public service were also using consultants: a single organization had in the decade ending in 1969 reported on three such diverse public bodies as the Post Office, the British Broadcasting Corporation and the Bank of England.

Prospects for Analysis

I have mentioned that both cost–benefit and operational research were among forms of analysis which developed in the British public service in the sixties. But neither made the impact that some expected of them. Reasons supporting the expectation of a widespread development for both in government remain strong. A rational use of resources in the public service is concerned in whole or at least in part with the relationship of social benefits to social costs: so is cost–benefit analysis. Operational research is a way of thinking logically and scientifically about complicated problems: the public service has more than its fair share of complicated problems and presumably would prefer to think about them logically rather than illogically. But, despite this basic relevance, problems of capacity, practicability and organization had not been overcome by 1970.

The contribution of cost–benefit within a growing use of analysis may depend on it being regarded as a contribution to information rather than as a decision making or even advisory process. The information provided will allow some possible decisions to be ruled out. The choice between the remaining alternatives may not be made easier—it may be made harder. But it will be better informed and, on the proposition that better information is significantly and positively correlated with better decisions, should lead to an improved use of resources provided that risks of distortions and debasement can be avoided.[18]

Distortions arise through the occasional but not random use of cost–benefit analysis. If the decision on initiating analysis rests with those who advocate schemes, it can be expected that it will be used when prima facie social benefits seem likely to exceed social costs even if projected receipts seem likely to be less than projected payments. When opponents of schemes can demand cost–benefit analysis, bias in the opposite direction is probable. To avoid bias, 'comprehensive' cost benefit would be desirable but the resources, which are both large and scarce in skilled specialists, are inadequate. To overcome this problem it seems desirable to use two approaches.

The first is to introduce some basic cost–benefit factors into *all* decisions on resource use of a kind which, after economists have been involved in the initial analysis and advice on the values to the factors, could be incorporated by line managers without further need to call on the service of specialist analysts. Variables which might lend themselves to this approach include:

1 in a country in which there is at the time a severe balance of payments problem, which constrains economic objectives like growth, there could be for all public authorities using foreign exchange directly or indirectly (i.e. by purchasing imported goods) a shadow exchange rate which reflected the true opportunity cost of the transactions;

2 shadow wage costs of employment by public authority could reflect the social costs of such employment, e.g. below market rates in areas of high unemployment and above market rates where the skill concerned was producing a bottleneck situation not fully reflected in the current wage rate. Such wage rates could also reflect the wide differential between wage rates and the social costs of employing certain handicapped people—a most important but somewhat neglected contribution which cost–benefit analysis can make to the public use of resources;

3 uniform figures could be assigned to, say, the value of reducing wasted or waiting times, e.g. drivers of cars and their passengers in traffic jams or patients waiting for examination or treatment in hospital;

4 and, most commonly proposed, a standard rate of discount although I shall argue later this is open to question.

It should be kept in mind that while such standard cost–benefit values avoid one form of distortion it cannot be guaranteed or proved that the new situation is better than the old in which inconsistent values were in use.

The second approach is to avoid distortion by concentrating cost–benefit on analysing fully the alternatives in no more than one or two major systems such as transport. This will limit distortion provided that the claim is rejected that even low ranked projects show such an excess of social benefits over social costs that resources should be switched to the system using cost–benefit from other systems not similarly blessed.

Time and the Rate of Discount

Many forms of analysis require a value to be attached to time unless we are to proceed on the assumption that a cost or a benefit today has the same value as a certainty of the same cost or benefit arising in ten years time and unless we regard the latter as the equivalent to the same amount becoming due to be paid or received in twenty years time. Few would accept this assumption as rational although this measure of consensus vanishes as soon as we try to agree on a rate of discount which will express these figures over time in a common denominator such as an expected present value. The methodology is well-established— that of discounted cash flow. We need not debate whether present value or the internal rate of return contributes more to rational decision making. Both will often make a contribution. With the aid of computer time, which is almost essential in this work, both calculations can be obtained quickly and cheaply as no more than one part of a wide range of sensitivity analysis which is likely to be needed. Nor are we concerned here with the treatment of risk and uncertainty. This is a major problem but it needs other techniques than adjusting the rate of discount to aid the decision maker. The concern over the appropriate rate of discount can concentrate on a series of risk-free (or risk-compensated) flows of receipts and payments over time. In most countries, where the public service is using discounted cash flow, the problem of the appropriate discount rate has not been resolved so much as overridden by a decision from some central authority that the figure is x per cent; or it has been ignored with each public authority using the rate which appeals most to their own understanding of the dilemma or which is most expedient in furthering their own activities.

This lack of agreement is not surprising, for in one of the clearest expositions of the problem, William Baumol commented[19] 'Few topics in our discipline [economics] rival the social rate of discount as a subject exhibiting simultaneously a very considerable degree of knowledge and a very substantial level of ignorance.' And as different economists have at some time argued the case for a rate ranging from 3 per cent to 16 per cent the dispute here is not merely an academic search for absolute proof but has great practical significance.

In Britain discounted cash flow developed in the sixties on the basis of a decision, rather than of an agreement, on the discount rate. It was one of the earliest 'economic' techniques taken up in the public service, perhaps as a result of the support of some influential members of the Economic Section of the Treasury in the early sixties. It was given some emphasis in the training of civil servants at the Treasury Centre for Administrative Studies from 1963. DCF originally developed for use, at a rate of discount determined by the Treasury, in investment decisions in the nationalized industries. It spread slowly to other parts of central government and to local authority investment. But by 1970 the approach was neither universal nor had a completely standard rate of discount been achieved, although there were by then relatively few exceptions. The rate selected is an approximation to the social opportunity cost rate, i.e., intended to avoid distortion between public sector and private business investment—although not everyone would agree that the rates chosen (the rate was varied during the period) accurately reflected the social opportunity cost. But no conceptual or theoretical agreement underpins this most important variable in management decisions in government.

Irrespective of the lack of theoretical proof of a correct rate, some find the existence of more than one rate at any time within the area of any government's responsibility an indication of illogicality and inefficiency. I have myself only recently expressed a preference for attaching standard values to various social costs and benefits arising in several different areas of resource use. But there is a respectable case for dual rates of discount in government. A higher (social opportunity cost rate) would be applied in economic decisions, i.e. those which are primarily concerned to increase the future real income of society, in forms in which the increase would, say, be measurable in GNP statistics, while a lower rate were applied in certain predominantly social decisions—particularly those which involved irreversible changes in the environment. Baumol raises the issue in these terms:

> 'There are important externalities and investments of the public goods variety which cry for special attention. Irreversibilities constitute a prime example. If we poison our soil so that never again will it be the same, if we destroy the Grand Canyon and turn it into a hydro-electric plant, we give up assets which like Goldsmith's bold peasantry " . . . their country's pride, when once destroyed can never be supplied". All the wealth and resources of future generations will not suffice to restore them.'

But the same argument could be applied not merely to irreversible damage to the natural environment but also to the planting or destruction of slow-growing species of trees which, although not in one sense irreversible, may be beyond the capacity of any single future generation to create, however great their wealth. And to the preservation of historic buildings and even to bequeathing to these future generations at least a few examples of the best contemporary architecture and urban development freed from the constraints on, say, the use of materials likely to survive and weather well in the long-term, which may be 'uneconomic' at a high social opportunity rate of discount. Baumol, while recognizing the dilemma himself, prefers the solution of 'a set of selective subsidies', rather than a lower general discount rate that 'encourages indiscriminately all sorts of investment programmes whether or not they are relevant'. However both subsidies and a lower rate used discriminately might have a role to play if the need for special treatment is admitted. These alternative methods of support may not produce identical effects in the evaluation of projects.

In another interesting comment[20] on this issue H. G. Walsh and Alan Williams also suggest that a special discount rate might apply in some areas of investment. They mention as examples the preservation of historic buildings and of 'areas suitable for peaceful outdoor recreation' but advance a different argument that 'we might reasonably expect future generations to value these more highly (relative to other goods and services) than we do'. This too seems persuasive but involves a value judgement about the attitude of future generation which 'irreversibility' avoids. As against this, irreversibility would seem in logic to be relevant to a wide range of economic decisions including all uses of fossil fuel even where these leave no overt adverse effect on the environment. Debates of this kind, even when inconclusive, are important to the development of management in government. If too superficial a view is taken on what is a better use of resources, posterity may not commend us for our efforts or recognize the era of management in the public service as one in which resources were used better than in previous periods of history. Indeed it might be instructive, for once, to job backwards and to explore what proportion of the decisions on resources, for which we now commend decision makers over the past five hundred years, would seem likely to have complied at the time with some of the cruder criteria of acceptability now offered from some quarters as representing the highest level of rational analysis which mankind has yet attained.

Another significant consequence of the use of DCF at discount rates of 10 per cent or higher is to encourage 'phasing', i.e. construction in two or more separate schemes over time of projects where the benefits are expected to build up over time—since the 'present value' of benefits accruing five or more years ahead is insufficient to justify the immediate capital costs of a project or sufficient size to meet these future needs. But construction in separate stages uses more resources in total to achieve a given output, i.e. to build a two-lane road and to extend it in ten years time to three lanes costs more in resources than to build a three-lane road initially. Looking back over a twenty year period, the result of DCF in the public service at a significant discount rate is that in physical units less capital goods in, say, miles of roads are available than could have been provided with the same resources if DCF had not been used with the phasing of schemes which this causes. But the outputs which have been provided within the period will have met better the needs of the community as they developed in that period. So that this is no more than a special case of the proposition that DCF allows today's citizens to benefit at the expense of their successors.

In operational research, distortion of the kind described is a less serious problem. Here the problem is of an applied science tending to disintegrate into a series of specialized techniques where, once the limited but not unimportant applications of, say, stock control or queue-ing theory have been worked through, it may be found that the public service yields too few problems matching any single technique. The problems might be simplified and distorted to fit the techniques whereas what is needed is the application of the basic approaches, of the concept of the model, from which operational research developed originally. All experienced operational research specialists realize this: the public service should be in no danger if it keeps out of the hands of the single-technique specialist.

The organization and complexity of analytical teams is likely to be increasingly important in the seventies. Resources of the highest level of skill and experience will continue to be scarce. It seems desirable to minimize this problem in several ways:

1 Give line managers training in simpler approaches and techniques, e.g. network analysis which lend themselves to do-it-yourself activity—and incorporate some standard cost–benefit practices in all decision making on resources.

2 Develop the scope of O. & M. units to relieve operational research specialists of the least complex problems.

3 Develop large central analysis units with economies of scale in common service, e.g. computing support and the capacity to deploy a team of the size and with the mix of skills relevant to the problem after it has been given a preliminary analysis. Such units would normally include some members seconded from line management posts. Without this, there will always be a risk that, however thorough the preliminary briefing, however much dialogue there seems to be between analyst and decision makers, some totally unrealistic assumption will be built into the analysis. And of course units should include specialists in organization and from the be-havioural sciences even if they do not need to form part of every team.

The need to pool scarce analytical resources seems particularly important. It seems improbable for example that in an issue of the use of resources in rail transport which involves amenities the best use of ten analysts would be for four to be employed by British Railways, three by the Ministry of Transport, two by amenity societies, and one, part time, by the Treasury. Creative conflict if introduced in this way will produce much the effect to be observed in medical evidence in legal cases. If all ten analysts worked as a team—and preferably independently, that is, not paid directly or indirectly by any single party to the decision, conflict might be creative. If agreement cannot be reached on assumptions and imputed values the analysis should be reworked in several ways to show decision makers the sensitivity of the conclusions to different assumptions and imputed values.

I believe that some of the problems which have limited the use of analysis in the British public service in the past decade will be overcome in the next. Skilled analysts will be somewhat less scarce although demand from industry will also grow. And within the public service increases in appreciation of what analysis can contribute (and of its limits) and in the ability to hold a meaningful dialogue between decision makers and analysts will develop—partly through training.

INTEGRATION, INFORMATION AND THE SCALE AND SEQUENCE OF CHANGE

To complete this review of prospects for management in government in Britain in the seventies, I should like to emphasize some general points. The first is the extent to which a number of approaches which have developed independently have at least a chance to converge and reinforce one another. I have argued that management needs to be developed in terms of systems and models. Accountable management will help to identify systems. So, to a greater extent, would PPB or Programme Analysis Review. PAR will help make analysis in depth a normal and respectable process of management in government rather than a rare and inquisitional activity. Analysis of this kind will often be based on models and will certainly emphasize systems rather than organizations. Each of these processes will require better information than has existed in the past. More computer access will be available in future to support analysis and to provide information to line managers—perhaps the spare capacity of computers taking over programmed tasks. Better flows of information will compel thought to be given to the complex subject of the extent and nature of the costs relevant to particular decisions on the use of resources. No single set of costs can meet all needs: the problem will be to use the building-block technique of coding to allow the same data to be re-processed in several different ways. Even so there will be relevant costs such as some imputed social costs and benefits, or some costs falling on the public by way of calls on their income or time, which will have to be assessed *ad hoc* and are unlikely to be incorporated in flows of information.

All this may happen. But no great feat of the imagination and no extreme of pessimism is needed to note the possibility of the reverse situation arising with all these strands in change conflicting and off-setting rather than reinforcing each other. The outcome will be determined by the sequence and scale of decisions. On sequence I have commented earlier that there seem to be forces which operate towards producing change in the reverse order to the optimal. And there will be persuasive voices who will argue for scale to a degree which may prejudice any progress, granted the constraints which operate in a democracy with elections at intervals not greater than five years. Stafford Beer has, for example, suggested that operational research should be directed to the whole health service before being applied to any part of it. Others have called—or, if not, certainly soon will call—for a total information system. The logic behind such demands is irrefutable. That is how life should permit us to proceed. But it does not seem to me to be consistent with any life the manager or the analyst in government is likely to experience in the seventies or even for some time beyond this decade. I fear that the effective choice is between change of a far more sub-optimal kind or no change at all. At this time, I would doubt whether there are many areas of government where a series of integrated changes can be planned and introduced in systems much larger than say the Prison Department of the Home Office for which such studies were in hand as the seventies opened.[21]

The prospects may seem to some to predict a technological, mathematical or impersonal approach to the use of resources in government which offers little to the official or to the public. I do not myself believe that this is a real issue. In systems seeking to use resources better to achieve objectives, success or failure will be highly dependent on how those working in the system view their role, regard the form of organization in which they find themselves, respond to the reward system prevailing. The approaches I have mentioned may do nothing in themselves to solve these human and organizational problems at the working-level. But they would have to be introduced with a degree of insensitivity to these aspects of management, which I hope I shall not later be regarded as over-optimistic if I say that I would find incredible, in order to make the solution of the problems impossible or even more difficult. What solutions may emerge is not at this stage clear. But since by definition they will be closely related to the nature and task of the system concerned, I would expect them to be as varied and numerous as the many kinds of system found in government. In this area I would expect to find uniformity and centralization wither away as the seventies pass.

In the whole area of progress in management, the public service needs external centres of research, bases of informed study and criticism, and organizations providing consultancy and analytical service with the breadth of view and the inter-disciplinary approach that rational discussion of the use of resources in government surely requires. Alas, in the past the service has too often been confronted with a host of rival technique-mongers most of whom are narrowly interested and seem often as concerned to knock their rival's product as to advance their own. If there are charlatans, I have not met them. Most of these techniques have something to offer to somebody somewhere in government. As so many derive from common sense, logic or mathematics, their validity in some circumstances is hardly surprising. But few are substitutes for others: most are complements. The public service is left to work out this fact for itself but may grow impatient in the process and dismiss the lot as no more than a set of gimmicks. In the academic world, matters are no more favourable to government—academic life does not after all exist with the primary purpose or even the secondary aim of being favourable to government. But, while the need in government is increasingly for inter-disciplinary studies, of far greater breadth than is academically fashionable, to debate the theoretical basis for the development of management in government,[22] the trend remains for academic reputations to be founded increasingly on the division of even single disciplines into separate sub-disciplines. The business schools may point the way to a solution, but although integrated courses have been developed, which incorporate a broad and coherent view of management in business, it is difficult to detect any similar trend in the main weight of research effort. At least some major consultancy firms provide a breadth of advice and skill greater than that yet developed in more narrowly specialized units within government. But the interface between pragmatism and theory remains in many areas obscure— operational research being an exception where the academics and the practitioners are either the same people or can at least still communicate. It is of course, a very new discipline. . . .

NOTES ON CHAPTER 9

1. *Bulletin de l'institut international d'administration publique: revue d'administration publique*, July–September 1970.
2. For an account of the development in Britain of central planning and control of public expenditure see 'The Presentation of Public Expenditure Proposals to Parliament' by Sir Samuel Goldman, *Public Administration*, Autumn 1970. The development of the PESC procedure can be followed in detail through a series of White (or Green) Papers: Cmnd. 2432, July 1961; 2235, December 1963; 2915, February 1966; 3515, January 1968; 3936, February 1969; 4017, April 1969; 4234, December 1969; 4578, January 1971.
3. For those not familiar with the British system of control, it should be explained that a transfer of funds between two votes during a financial year needs the formal approval of Parliament to a Supplementary Estimate even if there is no net increase, i.e. savings offset increases. The same is true if both gross expenditure and gross receipts are higher—even if the amount of the increase is identical or if receipts grow more than payments. Between sub-heads of the same vote, the Treasury may authorize a transfer of funds provided the total is not exceeded. Any connection between votes and sub-heads and systems and sub-systems or, in PPB terms, programmes and elements, is purely coincidental.
4. In a series of six lectures organized by the Civil Service College in London early in 1971.
5. One or more of the works on Management by Objectives by John Humble is recommended for the reader unfamiliar with this approach. And for the relevance of the technique in government; *Management by Objectives in the Civil Service* by John Garrett and S. D. Walker, CAS Occasional Paper No. 10, HMSO, 1969.
6. Fulton Report, op. cit. (Notes to Chapter 1).
7. Published in Second Special Report from Select Committee on Procedure 1968–69, H.C. 410, HMSO.
8. In a statement on August 23, 1967.
9. For descriptions of PPB see: Alan Williams, *Output Budgeting and the Contribution of Micro-economics to Efficiency in Government*, CAS Occasional Paper No. 4; J. M. Bridgeman, 'Planning, Programming Budgeting Systems', in two parts in *O & M Bulletin*, November 1969 and February 1970. There is also an interesting exchange, on whether PPB should start at the level of the major system and work down or at the level of the operational sub-system and work up, in *The Times* on November 9 and 16, 1970. 'PPB: dangers of the wrong approach' by Dick Taverne and 'PPB: top-down or bottom-up' by Professor Alan Williams.
10. On this point and on some other references to American experience,

I rely on information given by Professor Robert Anthony at a seminar on PPB in London in 1969.

11. Professor Aaron Wildavsky's views on this question are most readily available to British readers in the *Political Economy of Efficiency* reprinted in CAS Reprint Paper No. 2 (HMSO), originally published in *Public Administration Review* in December 1966.

12. For an account of the British attitude at the time see the Treasury memorandum and oral evidence to the Select Committee on Procedure Session 1968–69, op. cit.

13. Herbert R. Balls, 'Planning Programming and Budgeting in Canada', *Public Administration*, Autumn 1970.

14. Huet, op. cit. (Notes to Chapter 5).

15. On this implication of PPB and similar approaches, there are some interesting comments in the address by J. C. Swaffield to the Annual General meeting of the RIPA in London in 1970 (printed in *Public Administration*, Autumn 1970).

16. Stafford Beer, op. cit. (Notes to Chapter 4).

17. Particularly noteworthy was the unit of the Ministry of Transport which sought to achieve the insight of both operational research and cost–benefit analysis. Both should be used as complementary in this way: in some areas such as linear programming and marginal analysis of optimal production the two approaches coincide precisely. An interesting, if unrecorded, landmark of the period, involving this unit, was the publication of a White Paper on a scheme of port development (at Portbury) in which the mathematical analysis based on the model used was published in an appendix. (HMSO, 1966.)

18. This is perhaps a more encouraging impression of the future and importance of cost–benefit than the reader might infer from an article like that by Professor Peter Self 'Nonsense on Stilts: The Futility of Roskill' (*New Society*: July 2, 1970). I would not disagree with many of Professor Self's comments on the limitations of cost–benefit. But I can find nothing in his arguments to lead me to the conclusion that the decision on the site of the third London airport would have been likely to have been better without cost–benefit or, even if I believed this to be so, that cost–benefit could contribute nothing to other decisions. Whether this particular study pre-empted for too long too large a proportion of the limited national capacity for analysis is a more interesting question.

19. Professor William Baumol, 'On the Social Rate of Discount', *The American Economic Review*, Vol. LVIII, 1968.

20. H. G. Walsh and Professor Alan Williams, *Current Issues in Cost–Benefit Analysis*, CAS Occasional Paper No. 11, HMSO, 1969.

21. 'Management Review: A Case Study from Prison Department of the Home Office' by John Garrett and S. D. Walker, *O & M Bulletin*, August 1970.

22. On the need for integrated studies, there is an excellent discussion in *Public Policymaking Re-examined* by Professor Yehezkel Dror (Chandler Publishing Company 1968), Chapter 17, 'Changes Needed in Knowledge'.

CHAPTER 10

CONCLUSIONS

The initial demands made by any society of its public service are modest. It is required to be incorrupt and effective. A lower standard of achievement is expected in the latter quality than in the former where nothing short of perfection is acceptable. This is right for, in the words of a distinguished citizen of a country which has yet to approach this ideal standard, 'nothing is so corrupting as a suspicion of corruption'. Underlying this demand by society is a hope or an expectation that public servants generally should be men of high ethical standards. This requirement would be accepted as just by most officials. If outside observers suspect that civil servants, as flexible in responding to external pressure as described by Charles Sisson, might find difficulty in maintaining ethical values, they will have been at least partly reassured by Sisson's hope that 'officials are men who might in the last desperation exhibit a scruple'. Certainly in Britain most officials would defend their ethics more vigorously than their achievements in management and would assert that they were seen as exhibiting scruples, even at the risk of seeming priggish, well in advance of the last desperation. But every widely held and important assumption can usefully be explored from time to time. The ethical assumption was the subject of some profound thought by Mr D. Morrell in an address to his colleagues in the civil service shortly before his death. Certainly any wholehearted search for better management in government will need to rest on assumptions about ethics. The same statement could be made of management in business: it is encouraging to find British business schools raising the subject for discussion.

On effectiveness, the standards required by a community are relatively modest in general although in one or two respects they may be demanding. In Britain we have noted that the norm, the generally acceptable level of quality at any time, is set extremely high for accuracy. This fact of life pre-empts a substantial quantity of resources, although they are seldom identified and never brought together for the total to be quantified. And the search for infallibility over matters of accuracy leads to such other endearing traits of the public service as the 'Dear Sir or Madam' letter, which displays a commendable willingness to hedge in an area of uncertainty which, as I have argued earlier, could with advantage to management be adopted in other decisions where far more resources are at stake. In other respects, the accepted norms of effectiveness are set far lower than for accuracy. For example the accommodation provided by most public bodies for the reception of visitors and as waiting-rooms varies from place to place, without even at the higher end of the range creating the impression that perfectionism has been sought. And while in such places, or awaiting replies to letters, the public normally contributes a fair measure of patience to lower the level of effectiveness expected to that of the level provided.

But, even if the public service has no reason to complain that the two main demands made on it by the community are unreasonable or unattainable, it is in fact in no more than a minority of countries that they have yet been achieved or closely approached. Until they are, management, or the search for efficiency in the use of resources, is unlikely to find ground where it can take root and flourish. I make this assertion in the knowledge that there are countries today where corruption and ineffectiveness co-exist with the effort to introduce sophisticated computer-based models of decision making with the aid of highly skilled operational research experts. Those responsible for government in these countries will at the end of the experiment echo the words:

> Je suis comme le roi d'un pays pluvieux,
> Riche, mais impuissant . . .

and the management consultant may not earn his fee

> Le savant qui lui fait de l'or n'a jamais
> De son être extirpér l'élément corrompu

But Britain has not been a 'rainy country', in this sense, for seventy years or more and the search for efficiency and the development of an important role for management should by now have made evident progress. In some respects it can be shown to have done so. Certainly we should not assume that the relatively late arrival of the word management in the vocabulary of the public servant indicates that practices founded in the search for a better use of resources were not well-established at a much earlier date. But much of the progress was, as I have argued, in the first level of improvement in management where effort is concentrated on fulfilling a given plan with fewer resources. Later, in the sixties, a series of progressive improvements in the control of public expenditure created an environment more sympathetic to an intensive search for the better use of resources, itself led directly to some saving in resources by minimizing short-term changes in the levels and distribution of resources and may have improved the allocation of resources between a small number of major functions.

It is in the second level of improvement in management that most remains to be done. Here too there are important achievements on record such as, for example, the substantial saving of resources on school building which resulted in the fifties from the establishment of a development group prepared to think about objectives, alternative strategies and detailed plans and carry out controlled experiments. But, both within and outside government, the going assumption is that there must be scope for far more change and improvement at this second level than we have yet seen. It would seem a hypothesis that should be tested although, as I have remarked earlier, there are no absolute or even relative measures of performance in the use of resources that allow us to know at any time how far achievement falls short of the highest level attainable in practice (which itself will always fall far short of some theoretical optimum or ideal level) or even to assert without risk of contradiction that the general level of management is improving over time or in relation to that in other countries.

When government is considered as an environment for management a number of features are evident which explain both why the problems and opportunities are substantially different from those in business and why some of the developments on which the main hopes of improvement have rested in Britain in the past decade—or which have at least absorbed a high proportion of the effort and of the capacity of the structure for change—have yet to produce any widespread and dramatic results by way of a better use of resources. The main thrust of effort to improve management in recent years has been directed towards such propositions as that resources would be used better if public bodies were reorganized at the top or if there were fewer of them; that public servants could almost all be brought to think and act as managers if they had had experience in business or had businessmen to advise them or were trained in management in business schools or in training establishments set up within the public service; and that exhortation from the centre and the exposure of public servants to as many management 'techniques' as possible would contribute to efficiency. Now each of these efforts may have improved management and produced changes of which the value represents a good return on the resources invested in the efforts. Since the resources include several years of my own career I must declare a personal interest in the conclusion that they have been useful. But they have probably contributed less than some hoped—if more than others expected—and it is evident that they are not in themselves sufficient.

The features of government which have acted as constraints in Britain on the improvement of management include:

1 The many different species and varieties of systems which are found in public organizations and the fact that but one of these— and that not necessarily the most numerous or influential—has the attainment of the best use of resources as a primary task

and can therefore be regarded as a management system like a business company. Many probably most of those employed in the public service are not, therefore, 'managers'.

2 All these kinds of system in government use resources, but procedures for allocating, and accounting for, these resources has taken a form, for historical reasons, which conceals from those in any system the range or volume of the resources used and even more effectively conceals their value particularly in any form valid for management such as opportunity cost. The inadequacy of data on costs has been matched historically by a lack of current flows of information to the system on output and by a lack of incentive to speculate about and, even more, to carry out research or to establish monitoring procedures to measure the relationship of output to outcome and to the objective.

3 If the on-going use of resources suffers from the absence of relevant information, change to alternative strategies was inhibited by the absence of generally acceptable criteria of analysis or process to assess whether a change in the use of resources was in fact 'better'. At times systems adopted criteria *ex ante* in the hope that they would escape challenge or would find support *ex post*. Even when this succeeded, there remains in many multi-objective uses of resources insuperable difficulty in defining in any authoritative way (either theoretically or in the sense of being generally acceptable) the rate of trade-off between these objectives or in attaching values to many of the variables.

4 Although the public service has considerable capacity for change, and far more inclination to apply it than is often assumed, change to achieve a better use of resources by making a major change in strategy could often be foreseen as certain to cause controversy— and to overcome this often involves a further cost in resources— while the certainty that the preferred strategy could be proved superior did not exist. In the use of resources the *status quo* enjoys a privileged position.

5 These formidable constraints on management change beyond the first level of improvement might be more readily overcome if management were regarded within the service as the most valuable attribute to be displayed by those seeking to advance their careers and if the environment in which the public service operated, provided a process, in parallel with the effort devoted to bringing to light errors or mistakes, for the recognition of success in management. But neither internally nor externally has the environment been as concerned with success as with failure. And at the interface between government and the public there is little mutual comprehension of the significance of risk and uncertainty, of prob-

ability and of hedges, of a kind which is a necessary condition of any improvement in certain important management decisions.

Thus the public service faces real problems over management. Some are inherent in the concept of a public service with regulatory tasks which give the administration system its characteristic features and attitudes contrasting with those appropriate to the management system. And the different style and values of the diplomatic system has its origin partly in the demands of a democratic society and partly in those of scale of organization. Many of the problems of criteria, of trade-offs between objectives and of attaching values to variables have no absolute solutions. There is therefore no easy path, nor even a difficult path, to a golden age of management. But I remain an optimistic pessimist. I accept that the achievement, in terms of a better use of resources, of organization change, new approaches to decision making, management techniques and training and rigorous forms of analysis supported by far better flows of information may all fail in some measure, and at times in full measure, to fulfil the claims of those who advocate them. Nevertheless it is still possible to believe that all these strategies for change will, if selected by those who understand both their strengths and limitations, and used as complements rather than as substitutes, produce a valuable return on the investment involved in their cost. In the last resort we must keep in mind that life goes on and vast quantities of resources are being used. Even a tiny proportionate improvement in this use of resources represents a most substantial amount in absolute terms and even if we could say no more than that the use of resources in any area is less bad, this would still be significant.

Forms of analysis associated with management will often allow us to eliminate the bad or distinguish the worse even in areas of choice when they will not reveal unequivocally which of several of the preferable strategies is 'best'. And if absolute proof of the correctness of some choice will often be lacking the greater part of human life proceeds on the basis of balance of probability rather than proof. The manager in the public service should keep always in mind the advice offered by Dr Relling in *The Wild Duck* '. . . Do not allow yourself to be dunned by the claims of the ideal'.

I have yet to meet an official from any part of the public service so complacent as to believe that there were no gains in efficiency to be obtained, so unimaginative that he had no ideas of his own on how to achieve them or so unreceptive to new concepts that he did not consider that at least one of the approaches, which I have mentioned in this book, might be of potential value in some part of government. So if public servants are not all managers, they can at least all be, and to an increasing extent are, concerned with management.

It is said that the British civil servant never calls a meeting without having prepared in advance the draft of the conclusions and an outline of the minutes. If this myth is not spread by officials, it is not refuted by them with any indignation. Some may find in their experience a recollection of at least an occasional event of the kind. Others may not feel unhappy to have attributed to them an ability to pre-plan and to influence events which they may doubt whether, in reality, they possess. If I refer here to this myth, it is only because it is at this stage that I realize that it was an error of judgement to have written the preface before starting the main part of the book and to be writing the conclusions as my final task. This sequence of events could with advantage have been reversed. I could then have refrained from suggesting in my opening comments that the book would explain the rules of the management game in government, how goals are scored and referees provided. As with so many management decisions, the outcome has fallen far short of the aim. I have perhaps left the reader with no more than an impression that government is a great playing field in which many different games are in progress at any time. The lines marking out the pitches are far from clear: when goals are claimed, dispute is the rule rather than the exception. Nevertheless there is at times a consensus that one team is winning or another losing. One point at least is clear. The public does not provide the spectators. The public is both joining in the game and acting as referee.

I started the book with a quotation from the Brownlow Committee's report of 1937 in the U.S.A. Another is appropriate at this stage: 'The efficiency of government rests upon two factors: the consent of the governed and good management.'

There still seems much that is true and relevant in this statement but 'consent' may suggest an attitude that is more passive and acquiescent than management in government in a democracy is likely to experience —or indeed needs if there is to be any hope of achieving efficiency in a broad sense.

Thirty years later Stafford Beer's comment on the same point was '. . . the task of a government is to define structures so that their entropies move towards a more probable state desired—*also made explicit*—by the government. One might think that in invoking the principles of self-organizing systems, it would be unnecessary to make explicit what the aim of the system was supposed to be. But this reckons without the psychological factor which is in fact the major variable with which the government must deal.'

I have tried in this book to indicate that the prospects for better management are promising despite the complexity of the task. There are more entrophies and they are moving towards aims more explicitly stated. The opposition will be from those who see all choices as between the *status quo* and the ideal and, in the absence of proof that any alternatives can be proved to guarantee the latter, will always opt for the former. If the reader has not reached this conclusion, I can only express my regret in the terms used by Clausewitz in his introduction to *Vom Kriege*: 'System in this treatise is not to be found on the surface, and instead of a finished building of theory there are only the materials. . . . Perhaps soon a greater brain may give the whole work a coating of pure metal instead of these single grains.'

BIBLIOGRAPHICAL ADDENDA

The notes which follow each chapter list the published works which proved most relevant to those aspects of management in government with which this book is concerned. There is one exception to this statement: a work which was helpful to the analysis in Chapter 3 but to which no reference was made at that point is *Welfare Economics and the Theory of the State* by W. J. Baumol (Longmans, 1952). But when this book was almost completed, and while it has been printing, a number of further works have appeared which should, by way of this postscript, be brought to notice.

Four important general works, which throw light on the role of management in government and in nationalized industries are:

R. G. S. Brown, *The Administrative Process in Britain* (Methuen, 1970).
James Robertson, *Reform of British Central Government* (Chatto and Windus and Charles Knight, 1971).
Richard Pryke, *Public Enterprise in Practice* (MacGibbon and Kee, 1971).
David Coombes, *State Enterprise: Business or Politics* (Allen and Unwin, 1971 for PEP).

Also the final report of the Roskill Commission has appeared: Commission on the Third London Airport, *Report* (HMSO, 1971). Because of, or despite, this event there was a valuable increase in the literature on cost–benefit analysis which included: Roskill, *A Debate on Values* (BBC, 1971); the best theoretical introduction to the subject which has yet been published—E. J. Mishan, *Cost–Benefit Analysis* (Allen and Unwin, 1971); there is an interesting account of the application of cost–benefit in various countries, and a short but valuable introduction by Ralph Turvey in *Cost–Benefit Analysis* edited by M. G. Kendall (English Universities Press, 1971), while a commentary on British experience comes from the RIPA, namely Trevor Newton, *Cost–Benefit Analysis in Administration* (Allen and Unwin, 1972).

Finally the reader of the section on the National Interest in Chapter 3 will profit by reading the case made by a distinguished economist for a particular allocation of resources in the article by Lord Robbins, 'Unsettled Questions in the Political Economy of the Arts' (*The Three Banks Review*, September 1971).

INDEX OF SUBJECTS

INDEX OF NAMES